GW00838519

"The Space of Words"

Studies in German Literature, Linguistics, and Culture

"The Space of Words"

Exile and Diaspora in the Works of Nelly Sachs

Jennifer M. Hoyer

CAMDEN HOUSE
Rochester, New York

First published 2014
by Camden House

Camden House is an imprint of Boydell & Brewer Inc.
668 Mt. Hope Avenue, Rochester, NY 14620, USA
www.camden-house.com
and of Boydell & Brewer Limited
PO Box 9, Woodbridge, Suffolk IP12 3DF, UK
www.boydellandbrewer.com

ISBN-13: 978-1-57113-551-3
ISBN-10: 1-57113-551-0

Library of Congress Cataloging-in-Publication Data

Hoyer, Jennifer Miller.
  The space of words : exile and diaspora in the works of Nelly Sachs /
Jennifer M. Hoyer.
      pages cm. — (Studies in German literature, linguistics, and culture)
  Includes bibliographical references and index.
  ISBN 978-1-57113-551-3 (hardcover : acid-free paper) —
  ISBN 1-57113-551-0 (hardcover : acid-free paper)
  1. Sachs, Nelly—Criticism and interpretation. I. Title.

PT2637.A4184Z666 2014
831'.914—dc23
                                                                          2014034035

This publication is printed on acid-free paper.
Printed and bound by CPI Group (UK) Ltd, Croydon, CR0 4YY.

Contents

Acknowledgments

I WOULD LIKE TO ACKNOWLEDGE the following individuals and groups for their editorial and moral support in the preparation of this manuscript: Leslie Morris (University of Minnesota); Jeffrey L. High (California State University, Long Beach); Friederike von Schwerin-High (Pomona College); Joseph C. High; Judith Ricker (University of Arkansas); Kathleen Condray (University of Arkansas); Gerhard Weiss (University of Minnesota); the students and faculty of the German Summer School at Taos, New Mexico, especially Katja Schröter (University of New Mexico, Albuquerque) and Peter Pabisch (University of New Mexico, Albuquerque); Corinna McLeod (Grand Valley State University); Ehrhard Bahr (UCLA); Ariane Huml (Uni-Freiburg); Juliana Perez (University of Sao Paolo); Meagan Tripp; Florian Strob; Daniel Pedersen; the staff at the Deutsches Literatur-Archiv in Marbach am Neckar, Germany, especially Katharina von Willucki; the staff at the kungliga bibliotek in Stockholm, Sweden; Carolyn and Michael Hoyer; and a special thank you to my editor, Jim Walker. The deepest thanks of all go to Ruth Dinesen.

I would also like to acknowledge the following permissions.

Reprinted by permission of Farrar, Straus and Giroux, LLC:
"O the chimneys," "To you that build the new house," "O the night of the weeping children," "But who emptied your shoes of sand," "Even the old men's last breath," "A dead child speaks," "Already embraced by the arm of heavenly solace," "What secret cravings of the blood," "You onlookers," and "Peoples of the earth" from O THE CHIMNEYS by Nelly Sachs. Translation copyright © 1967, renewed 1995 by Farrar, Straus & Giroux, Inc. "Someone blew the Shofar," "Hands," "How long have we forgotten how to listen!," "The shadows fell long ago," "When in early summer," "Hasidim Dancing," "Israel is not only land!," "Late firstborn!," "This land," "Still midnight on this star," "Daniel with the mark of stars," and "Maternal water" from THE SEEKER AND OTHER POEMS by Nelly Sachs, translated by Ruth and Matthew Mead and Michael Hamburger. Translation copyright © 1970 by Farrar, Straus & Giroux, Inc.

"An Stelle von Heimat": An Introduction

Nelly Sachs and the Limits of Iconic Status

THE 1966 NOBEL PRIZE FOR LITERATURE was split between two writers cast as voices for Israel: Israeli S. Y. Agnon for the geographical and political State of Israel, and German Jewish refugee Leonie "Nelly" Sachs for her poetic treatment of the current "state"—the psychological, historical, diasporic or exilic state—of the abstract Israel, that is, of the Jews. She is, along with Paul Celan, the quintessential German-language Holocaust poet. Such a significant position in German literature has proven to be paradoxically limiting and limited, however. Although she was also active as a translator and playwright, and indeed had written and published poems and prose long before she fled to Sweden in 1940, reading of and scholarship on her work has only rarely moved beyond the foundational psychoanalytical approach to her mystical poetic imagery that revolves around the Shoah. But there is much more to discuss in Sachs's work. Recent scholarship has begun to explore new avenues in Sachs's oeuvre, for example her later poetry or her theater pieces; but her prewar work remains largely unexamined. This book undertakes an examination of her early writing and poetics, in order to help situate them in the larger history of twentieth-century German Jewish literature, but also to show what critical insights they provide for a more nuanced reading of her iconic Holocaust poetry.

Nelly Sachs herself sought to put distance between her postwar poetry and her earlier works; indeed, it seems that Sachs feared her early work would distract from the significance of her postwar poetry. Scholars and critics adopted the position that her early work is negligible, either based on Sachs's own views or because they found her early texts merely conventional. Ehrhard Bahr, for example, refers to her postwar work as "Nelly Sachs' gültiges Werk" (the work that counts), because Sachs herself, as evidenced by her correspondence especially with exile scholar Walter Berendsohn, "wollte nur gelten lassen, was sie seit dem Durchbruch von 1943/44 verfaßt hatte" (only wanted the work that she composed after the breakthrough of 1943/44 to receive attention).[1] At that time, she began writing her play *Eli*, and also a series of epitaphs that later became "Grabschriften in die Luft geschrieben" (Gravescripts Written into the Air), published in her first postwar poetry volume *In den Wohnungen des Todes* (1947). On the other hand, Bahr also noted that Sachs's prewar texts are not without influence on her postwar work, which suggests, too, that they are also relevant for reading it.[2] Since 1980, however, only a handful of scholars have taken up this thread, most notably Ruth Dinesen, who is to date alone in the book-length pursuit of Nelly Sachs's prewar work in its own right. Dinesen's *"Und Leben hat immer wie Abschied geschmeckt": Frühe Gedichte und Prosa der Nelly Sachs* (1987) is a thorough overview of the published and many unpublished manuscripts in the archives, with supplemental critical commentary; but the commentary is by no means exhaustive. Gabriele Fritsch-Vivié's and Aris Fioretos's monographs provide more precise descriptions of earlier texts, but little more has been done to explore Sachs's early texts beyond cursory overviews or summaries that are punctuated by conclusions like this most recent one from Fioretos's 2012 Sachs biography: "Extant [prewar] works show a growing technical skill, particularly in terms of rhymes and meter, but few instances of stylistic individuality and even fewer of thematic originality."[3] That is, they lack the weight, seriousness of purpose, and stylistic innovation of her later work, or indeed of more avant-garde work of the early twentieth century. On closer examination, and emphasizing Sachs's own postwar admonition that her texts speak for themselves, we find that the early texts are important, both in their own right and as springboards for the later work, which was recognized by the Swedish Academy as "outstanding lyrical and dramatic writing, which interprets Israel's destiny with touching strength"[4] and which made her, for Walter Berendsohn, the "Dichterin jüdischen Schicksals" (poet of Jewish fate), that is, of the Holocaust.

Between 1947 and 1970, Sachs came to be both celebrated and condemned as the Jewish German woman who forgave, who memorialized, who helped heal.[5] These are descriptions she never agreed to, but also never refuted. Sachs routinely directed inquiries about meaning or interpretation back to the work itself; her texts, however, like her national identity and indeed her personality, defy easy categorization. Bahr writes: "Der Ton, mit dem ihre Lyrik nach dem zweiten Weltkrieg einsetzte, erschien archaisch und avantgardistisch zugleich." (The tone of her lyric poetry after the Second World War appeared at once archaic and avant-garde.)[6] Descriptions of her work in the reviews and scholarship range from conventional[7] to prohibitively complicated,[8] a testament to the surprising (and often overlooked) complexity resulting from this untimely, unorthodox mix of "archaic and avant-garde." Audiences who sought the comfort of traditional poetry refused to buy her work, while younger writers saw in her and her poetry the reflection of a past from which they aimed to break. The hybrid "archaic and avant-garde" nature of her work shows, in fact, that she was neither forgiving nor healing, and that she was thoroughly skeptical of memorialization. Sachs wrote poems that are open wounds of the twentieth century that can never heal, sobs and sighs that mark inarticulable moments; especially the immediate postwar poems are essentially broken poems, poems that show how literary convention can no longer function as it once did, in effect a similar sentiment to Adorno's widely misread comment that poetry after Auschwitz would be barbaric—that is, it is no longer traditional, it no longer "speaks Greek." Already in the mid- to late 1940s, she writes that "der Äon der Schmerzen darf nicht mehr gesagt, gedacht, er muß durchlitten werden" (the aeon of pain may no longer be said, or thought; it must be suffered through), that is, it cannot be fixed in words, it must be suffered through and experienced.[9] Since her medium is nonetheless the written word, this would mean the words are neither absolute nor conventional, nor stable; they are rather a fragmented and unresolved, eternally current experience. She maintains this position, expressed in different images of gulf and rending, throughout the 1940s and '50s: in her work she approaches an "Abgrund" (abyss, 1946); postwar poets live in a time "aufgerissen . . . wie eine Wunde" (ripped open like a wound, 1948) that makes traditional literature impossible; between yesterday and tomorrow "liegt die Wunde, die offen ist" (lies the wound that is open, 1950); and she herself "wurde aufgerissen" (was ripped open, 1958).[10]

These insights find clear reflection in her poetry. This book takes up the fundamental topos of *space* (in all its meanings) in Sachs's work—prewar and postwar—in order to help throw this more theoretical and critical layer of her work into relief, to encourage further rethinking of the significance and relevance of her early work, and to reconsider in the poetry for which she is most known those gestures most often associated with her—healing, memorial, forgiving—in light of what we learn from close reading of her early texts. To expand the context of her work in one more way, I undertake to read her poems in their entire cycles wherever possible, rather than individually, which also helps make clear how the landscape of the texts does not do what it may seem to do on the surface.

As Aris Fioretos recently pointed out, Sachs was adept at sleight-of-hand self-presentation. She frequently described herself in terms that present her as a vessel for the poetic act, rather than as an active, intentional poet. In 1944, she writes, for example: "Ich habe nichts an den Elegien getan, ich habe sie niedergeschrieben, wie die Nacht sie mir gereicht hat. Das ist alles." (I did nothing to the elegies, I wrote them down just as the night gave them to me. That's all.)[11] Fioretos notes that this

fits in with the vision of a poet with an Orphic mission. It is furthermore easy to identify traits which are traditionally perceived as feminine. Sachs is less active than passive. She does not compose poems, but rather is overwhelmed by them. She is more receiver than sender. Sachs's literary estate shows that she rarely rewrote or edited her texts. Many of them were printed in versions nearly identical—bar the odd word or comma—to the original. Yet must that mean she was a mere medium without intent—a handful of strings moved by the divine wind? At the same time as the circumstances following her escape from Nazi Germany were far from comfortable, she conscientiously worked in the service of poetry.[12]

I would go so far as to argue that Sachs was no more or less passive than any poet who becomes inspired to write; and not only is she intentionally, meaningfully engaged in the act of writing, her texts show that she was thinking consciously about the agency and power of the poet and the reader. Sachs often presented herself as simpler than her insights suggest she was; her work can likewise appear quite a bit simpler than it is. Deceptively simple appearances, moreover, are often part of the theme at stake in a text. The idea that Sachs is a vessel, for example, is fairly antithetical to the treatment of poets and poetry in her work. The agency of the writer and of the reader is a consistent theme in her prose and poetry, and this theme is cast, from the early 1920s well into the 1960s, in terms of space and wandering.

Sachs's texts show that she thought about text and language in spatial terms, that is, the text or even the word is a space in which we can exist. In this she is very much a product of the twentieth century and the Modernism that surrounded her earliest writing—simplistic and unoriginal as that writing may seem. In the introduction to his 1958 *Poetics of Space*, an analysis of the poetics of space in architecture and literature, philosopher Gaston Bachelard, though not primarily a literature scholar himself, succinctly describes the plane of existence in poetry generally that I evoke when I talk about Nelly Sachs's space of words: "the reader of poems is asked to consider an image not as an object and even less as the substitute for an object, but to seize its specific reality."[13] The signifier may be something recognizable or familiar, but the reader is asked to suspend that conventional knowledge and experience the image or the word as signifying something in this new, specific reality of the specific text. We might read the word "nightingale" in a poem, but as we read the poem, and experience how each word works with the others, we realize that "nightingale" signifies something different in this text than we expect, or something more in addition to what we expect. It changes in this specific reality; and each time we read, it changes again, since each reading discovers new associations, new levels of meaning, new and novel possibilities for the sign, metaphor, or symbol. In this poetic act we find again that hybrid of the archaic and the avant-garde: lyric poetry's "characteristic extravagance [to engage] in speech acts without a real-world counterpart" is already the property of antiquity.[14] The sense of language as space and landscape tended to find more resonance in the twentieth century, as poets shifted ever further from strictly mimetic representation. The "specific reality" of the text in Sachs's oeuvre is conceived as an ever-shifting space or landscape, that is, the poet herself conceives of language and text in spatial terms. Lines like "Weltall der Worte" (space of words), "Landschaft aus Schreien" (landscape of screams), or "So rann ich aus dem Wort" (thus I ran out of the word) are clear examples of the poet describing text or word as space, one created by poets but ultimately also navigated by (and hence also created by) the reader.[15] In the following I want to consider the relationship to space in texts where the link is less explicitly stated.

For Sachs, the text is a space of linguistic experience; even the word itself can be a space in which the reader and writer co-exist: they experience one another and language, and must navigate to find some meeting point in meaning across time and borders. Because a text changes with each reading, this space is forever being shaped and created. It is not sovereign, it is not complete, and it is not the domain of an authoritarian author or poet prophet. It may have recognizable traits, objects, or contours, but they often appear in unfamiliar contexts or are written in such a way that refuses to allow them to be what they have conventionally been. The poet is asking us to consider recognizable elements in an unfamiliar and constantly changing context, making us aware that we are in both familiar and unfamiliar territory and thus making us more cognizant of our thoughts, assumptions, and expectations. We become wandering sojourners in the space of the text, a space where we are subsumed if we do not actively participate. The space of the text presents an opportunity to gain awareness of ourselves and our agency within the text, and perhaps then in the empirical reality we occupy beyond the page. Experiencing the "specific reality" of the poem, and becoming aware of our active role in shaping that reality as well as our empirical reality, is the urgent postwar task poet Ilse Aichinger proposes in her 1946 essay "Aufruf zum Mißtrauen" (Call to Mistrust):

> Sich selbst müssen Sie mißtrauen! Ja? Haben Sie richtig verstanden? Uns selbst müssen wir mißtrauen. Der Klarheit unserer Absichten, der Tiefe unserer Gedanken, der Güte unserer Taten! Unserer eigenen Wahrhaftigkeit müssen wir mißtrauen! Schwingt nicht schon wieder Lüge darin? Unserer eigenen Stimme! Ist sie nicht gläsern vor Lieblosigkeit? Unserer eigenen Liebe! Ist sie nicht angefault von Selbstsucht? Unserer eigenen Ehre! Ist sie nicht brüchig vor Hochmut?

> [You must mistrust you yourself! Did you understand that? We must mistrust ourselves. The clarity of our intentions, the depth of our thoughts, the goodness of our deeds! We must mistrust our own earnestness. Doesn't "lie" swing within it? Our own voice! Is it not

glassy for lovelessness? Our own love! Is it not touched with the rot of selfishness? Our own honor! Is it not brittle before pride?][16]

Aichinger insists that the reading public be inoculated against complacency and self-righteousness, "damit Sie das nächste Mal um so widerstandsfähiger sind!" (so that next time you will be all the more capable of resistance!)[17] The poetic text is a call to reexamine all that we take for granted. The opportunity afforded to experience the specific, destabilizing reality of the text can translate into self-awareness—the mistrust of which Aichinger speaks—in the empirical reality beyond the text. We must be thrown into a situation where we are compelled to see as an outsider what is otherwise our privilege to overlook; the poetic text can achieve this through its specific reality. This is Sachs's postwar space of words. And lest the reader be tempted to isolate a complacent sense of certainty in the years from 1933 to 1945, Aichinger goes on to assert that anyone who would wish to have lived in the previous century is overlooking that the reason, goodness, elegance, and humanity we perceive there is a façade. This resonates with Sachs's prewar texts. They often subtly challenge their own conventionality by exposing the absurdities, contradictions, and even dangers within idyllic, conventional narrative or poetry. Made self-aware by the new reality of the text, we cannot be fooled into thinking we are safe, or at home, in a place where we know the rules, the contours, the meanings, or the cartography. Sachs's prose and poetry leave the reader out in the open, wandering in an undefined and constantly changing landscape. Let us consider our (and her) relationship to that space in which we wander.

Space: *Heimat*, Exile, and Diaspora

In many analyses of Sachs's poems, the space of the text is regarded as a space of asylum or exile, a space of refuge. German poetic language was all that was left of the homeland she fled, and so she found, according to a number of scholars, a "Heimat in der Sprache."[18] But that relationship to the space of words presumes several things that her early texts prove to undo. First, it presumes that Sachs only began to think about language as a space after she fled Berlin in 1940; second, it presumes that Sachs considered this space innocent, safe, sovereign, or even sacred before the Nazi propaganda machine.[19] The early texts prove both of these presumptions untrue. As Fioretos surmises: "neither the private correspondence nor the poems written before the flight [to Sweden in 1940] conjure up an intact world in which the clocks are frozen in the non-time of legends."[20] Indeed, those texts expose the time of legends as something far from "intact" or "frozen." Already in Sachs's prose of the 1920s, language is linked to spaces of conflict and engagement (for example the royal court or the city, as opposed to places of sanctuary or solitude like the forest or the monastery, where semantic expression is hindered and often useless), and the space of words is consistently malleable, fluid, treacherous, and unstable. This is not a refuge or an asylum, it is a space one must dynamically interact with and shape if one wants to survive and keep individual subjectivity intact. In the early texts we see how the poet may drown in the word he or she allows to engulf him or her; how the person who cannot negotiate figurative language may suffer even fatal consequences; how the person who gives in to a linguistically dominant power loses all sense and even memory of him- or herself. In the postwar era, the poet who gives him- or herself up to a collective calcifies or becomes irrelevant; the nation that is subsumed in land forgets itself; memorials obscure what they attempt to fix in place. Stasis in space is closure, and closure puts an end to interaction and discussion, to wandering—and to production. Wandering is lack of closure, and that lack of closure means that interaction and discussion continue, awareness of self continues, and production continues. That is what is ultimately at stake in Sachs's space of words: the preservation of the thinking, active, engaged self. The surviving self does not succumb to anything; it remains flexible, marginal, and mobile. Language is a space of constant wandering, of constant uncertainty, of constantly being neither at home nor completely estranged.

Germanist and writer Ruth Klüger wrote in 2007 that Sachs is "der ganz ungewöhnliche Fall einer Dichterin, der das Exil nicht die Rede verschlagen hatte" (the completely unusual case of a poet whom exile did not rob of language).[21] Indeed, true to and reflective of the poetics of her earliest work, displacement made her more prolific. Wandering in Sachs's work is always a condition for more, and more sophisticated, language; it is stasis that robs people of speech. This difference relates to spatial categories we can use to discuss her work. Because images of flight and wandering in her poetry have been linked to her flight from Germany, she is regarded as an exile poet. But such images predate her flight by a good twenty years. Exile, additionally, represents a particular relationship to a lost homeland, to time, and to memory that, on closer examination, is more the object of critique in Sachs's texts. Exile longs for home, for closure, seeks to fix memories and objects in timespace that cannot be recovered, and mourns a lost wholeness. Sachs clearly does write in spatial terms of wandering, and her poems of the very late 1950s and early 1960s do gravitate more toward longing for a return to a wordless beyond; but for her works dating between 1920 and 1957, I propose diaspora, rather than exile, as a useful category for discussing Sachs's prose and poetry. In distinguishing these terms and describing her poetics as diasporic, I aim to recast Sachs's work within a framework of German Jewish writing, not only related to the Holocaust but to the larger context of Jewish writing in German in the twentieth century.

In the context of Jewish writing and experience, diaspora and exile are central; they place the text, and interpretation and reinterpretation of text, at the center of community, while describing a condition of always being a wandering sojourner, never belonging entirely to the place where one lives. The words "exile" and "diaspora" are both used to translate the Hebrew word "galut," the term for the historical phenomena of the dispersal of the Jews from their homeland and their existence in other countries; but each word emphasizes a different way of looking at life away from Israel and Jerusalem. The fundamental difference between diaspora and exile is summarized by Howard Wettstein:

> the term *exile*, as opposed to *diaspora*, suggests anguish, forced homelessness, and the sense of things being not as they should be. *Diaspora*, on the other hand, although it suggests absence from some center—political or religious or cultural—does not connote anything so hauntingly negative. Indeed, it is possible to view diaspora in a positive light.[22]

Diaspora connotes as strength the same absence that exile connotes as anguish. Diaspora is a condition of always being marginal, but regards the marginal position as, among other things, a productive challenge to a dominant power—like the valuable distance afforded by the poetic text. Diaspora also represents a very different relationship to space, land, time, and memory, which proves productive in reading Sachs's early and later work. Diaspora, according to Erich S. Gruen,

> seeks refuge in a comforting concept: that Jews require no territorial sanctuary or legitimation. They are "the people of the Book." Their homeland resides in the text—not just the canonical Scriptures but an array of Jewish writings that help to define the nation and give voice to its sense of identity. [. . .] A geographical restoration is therefore superfluous, even subversive. To aspire to it deflects focus from what really counts, the embrace of the text, its ongoing commentary, and its continuous reinterpretation.[23]

Gruen would also find a "Heimat" in the text in place of a geographical space or place; Sachs transposes the condition of geographical wandering described by diaspora onto the text as well. Geographical restoration is problematic for Sachs, as her letters and poems attest.[24] Her poetry reflects this preference for wandering by way of its structure while also thematizing it. She does view text and language as a space of community, but of diasporic community, a space in which we all wander, a space in which commentary and reinterpretation are always continuing. The space of words is always changing, always interactive. It is not a fixed or sovereign space, the authority of the author is never absolute, and there is never closure, nor even the goal of closure.

These aspects of diaspora that Sachs weaves into the theme and the structure of a text constitute a diasporic poetics. Her texts might deal with life in the diaspora as a theme, or structurally articulate diasporic conscious-ness, an ongoing diasporic commentary, or a way of looking at space, time, and memory that reflects the diaspora. Theme and structure might reflect absence from Israel or Jerusalem, a "political or religious or cultural" cen-ter, they may represent or constitute a convergence of place of residence and a distant homeland or cultural tradition, or they may contain dialogue and cultural tradition from many times and places that all exist concurrently.

Bluma Goldstein, for example, maps out the diasporic poetics in Heinrich Heine's "Hebräische Melodien," looking for

> the poetic articulation of the connection between a new understand-ing of diasporic life and the construction of Jewish identity by sit-uating the text within two different, yet interrelated, frameworks: on the one hand, the "Orientalization" of Eastern European Jewry and glorification of medieval Sephardi culture by early nineteenth-century European Jews, especially German Jews; and on the other, a more nuanced account of diaspora and exile that explores the via-bility of a truly integrative relationship between subdominant and dominant cultures.[25]

Goldstein demonstrates how in each poem, different articulations of Jewish life from medieval Spain are represented and reinterpreted for and by the modern European, so that "the 'Hebräische Melodien' seems to be uniquely directed toward both articulating a critique of the disabilities of Jewish exilic life and reconstructing a historically grounded diasporic alternative."[26] She argues, finally, that Heine's "Hebräische Melodien," understood in the context that differentiates exile (forced homeless-ness and "anguished longing to return") from diaspora ("an integration of dominant and subdominant cultures"), "seems invested in establish-ing the importance of an integrative diaspora that promotes interactive dialogue across borders—cultural and social, temporal and geographi-cal—and in developing a poetics that communicates that possibility."[27] Primacy of geographical place would effectively put an end to this con-stant cyclical dialogue. The awareness of living in the diaspora thus means an awareness of presence in a place one does not completely belong, and at the same time an awareness of an absence from a place that cannot, and in fact need not, be reclaimed or returned to. Diasporic poetics aim to accomplish a task like Aichinger's "Aufruf zum Mißtrauen," very much a part of Sachs's longstanding poetic interest in wandering and marginal existence. Sachs's diasporic poetics revolve primarily around the power of the wanderer to challenge reified notions of dominant power, ranging from masculine dominance, calcified tropes, and literary convention to the nation-state and conventional modes of memorialization.

Sachs's sense of text or word as space in which we wander, more-over, has relevance for her position as a writer in a politically and socially charged climate where literature and nation are deeply intertwined. Her texts often place countries and nations in question, destabilizing some-times their lyrical or legendary heroes, sometimes their literary conven-tions, and sometimes their borders or claim to place at all. Gruen suggests that the continuous reinterpretation mentioned above helps "to define the nation"; Jonathan Boyarin unpacks this paradox further, and in a way that finds reflection in Sachs's prose and poetry:

> Whatever we ["Israel"] are is founded on an acknowledgement of absence, or lack. [. . .] We remind ourselves of what we are by reminding ourselves of what we miss, of the "without anything" [beli-ma, not-what] on which the earth depends. Whenever this wis-dom threatens to blind us, we are in danger of losing it. We simulta-neously tell the stories of our specialness and remind ourselves how risky those stories are. We sustain the wisdom by embodying and reiterating the question, "*nahnu ma*," we are—what is? This is the paradoxical power of diaspora. On the one hand, everything that defines us is compounded of all the questions of our ancestors. On the other hand, everything is permanently at risk.[28]

The awareness of being in the diaspora is an awareness of absence of fixed answers, identity, or location, or, as Gruen states and Goldstein demon-strates, an awareness of ongoing commentary and reinterpretation, both of text and of the place one lives. In place of a projection in space with sovereign boundaries (that is, a nation-state) are ongoing questions, ongoing commentary, a constantly present dialogue that crosses cultural, geographical, and indeed temporal boundaries—or as Sachs poetically put it: "An Stelle von Heimat / halte ich die Verwandlungen der Welt—" (In place of homeland / I hold the metamorphoses of the world—).[29] This is the final stanza of the poem "In der Flucht" (In Flight), punctuated with Sachs's characteristic unresolving long dash, refusing closure thematically and structurally. It is as significant for postwar Germany as it is for the State of Israel. Gruen argues that "[t]he whole idea of privileging home-land over diaspora, or diaspora over homeland, derives from a modern, rather than an ancient, obsession."[30] That obsession revolves around the establishment of the nation-state model, as Boyarin explains:

> For the modern understanding, the Jewish question had to do with understanding Israel's place among the nations. What was to be done with this diaspora that threatened, that constantly questioned the very attempt to organize the world polity as a neatly bounded set of so many defined, autonomous centers—the attempt to realize what was called the nation-state system?[31]

As we shall see, in turn-of-the-century Germany, precisely this threat was at the heart of a discussion of what makes a "Jewish" or a "German" literature, or what the advantage or disadvantage to the nation might be of a hyphenated—neither German, nor Jewish, but both German and Jewish at the same time—existence and a hyphenated writing. That writer or literary figure who does not entirely belong to one category or another, who is a wanderer, stands as a challenge to a singularity or wholeness that cultural critics since the seventeenth century have sought in and prescribed for German literature in hopes of defining the nation, and then the country. The diaspora places this drive fundamentally in question by asserting that one can be both Jewish and German (or American or Swedish, etc.), with no need, desire, or even ability to belong only to one or the other. Such plurality is a threat to a "neatly bounded" nation-state and its insistence on a whole identity rooted in common cultural and linguistic roots. The wanderer forces that awareness and mistrust that Aichinger insists is so important for a modern, thinking subject. Sachs's texts afford this awareness, first in conventional legends that unravel themselves and then in poems that resist German memorialization of the Holocaust and at the same time stand as a diasporic commentary for the State of Israel. In both scenarios she is writing as an outsider: in the prewar years as Jewish German woman writing conventional *Heimatkunst*-style stories often more associated with nationalist Christian male writers, and in the postwar era as a Jewish German refugee who became a Swedish citizen and rejected the idea of moving to Israel. Diaspora, as opposed to exile, challenges the nation-state's insistence on stable presence by maintaining absence, loss, and lack. What defines "Israel" is resistance of a closed definition. "Israel" is an ongoing discussion, ongoing questions, ongoing awareness of wandering.[32] This depends on a kind of memory in which, through that constant commentary and reinterpretation suggested by Gruen, and also Goldstein, absence and lack represented in events from all epochs are always present. The Sabbath is regarded as a sanctuary in time where all observant Jews come together; during the High Holidays the dead and the living are judged simultaneously (and interrelatedly!); during Passover the Exodus is reexperienced through the Seder. Diaspora carries within it a concept of space and time that collapses into a textual space where past and present are always present (as in "present tense," but also as in "present in space"). Sachs's oeuvre from 1920 to 1957 reflects these varied aspects of diaspora. The space of words is a space where writer and reader wander, never at home, never completely estranged, always reinterpreting, always in dialogue, always in opposition to closure.

The Landscape of This Text

In order to make a sustained consideration of her poetics possible, the reader must conceive of Sachs first and foremost as a poet with a vested interest in writing for an audience and consciously working with the structure of language. To that end, the next chapter traces Sachs's career from its inception rather than from 1945, focusing less on her biography, which has traditionally been the basis for interpreting her work, and more on her publications and reception in order to make clear that Sachs was a prolific and theoretically engaged poet long before the Nazi genocide. The chapters then proceed in sets: two chapters deal with Sachs's prewar work, and three deal with her postwar work, first surveying several texts for general patterns, and then providing a close reading of one longer text and two entire cycles, respectively. Chapter 2 makes a case for Sachs's early conceptual link between words and spatial metaphors, moreover with attention to a diasporic conception of that landscape. Close readings of the prose texts "Eine Legende vom Fra Angelico" (A Legend of Fra Angelico, from *Legenden und Erzählungen*, published 1921), "Die stumme Nachtigall oder der Umweg zu Gott" (The Silent Nightingale or the Detour to God, unpublished, 1930s), and "Chelion: Eine Kindheitsgeschichte" (Chelion: A Story of Childhood, unpublished, 1930s), and the poem "Abschied, du Nachtigallenwort" (Parting, you Nightingaleword, published 1938), show that Sachs linked words with particular spaces and places, and regarded language and texts as landscapes in and of themselves. These spaces of words are routinely characterized by power struggles and the use of poetic language as a tool of deception, agency, and colonization. The characters or figures who inhabit these works, the writer, and the reader all must negotiate this landscape; those who can adapt and work fluidly are generally more productive. Often Sachs's texts include a very clear self-referentiality, suggesting that she includes herself in her critique, and encourages the reader to question her work as well.

This self-referentiality is a pivotal attribute of Sachs's most well-known early prose text, "Wie der Zauberer Merlin erlöset ward" (How Merlin the Sorcerer Was Saved) from *Legenden und Erzählungen* (1921), the subject of chapter 3. In her Merlin narrative, Sachs takes advantage of the tensions inherent to the Merlin tradition, in particular Merlin's dual heritage and the blurred line between myth and history, in order to lay bare choices involved in shaping what becomes a definitive narrative. Here, the wandering versus stasis dynamic, in addition to making the consistent point that wanderers control expression and dominate static characters, touches on the rhetoric of race and nation. Already in her earliest prose, we can see that Sachs is considering the problems of a symbiosis between literary production and national identity.

Having established that Sachs enacted an early spatial, diasporic poetics that undertook both aesthetic and political commentary, we can turn with a fresh outlook to Sachs's postwar poems. Chapter 4 positions two of her most well-known isolated postwar poems against discussions of immediate postwar aesthetic theory and literary movements. Read in this context, the poems "Völker der Erde" (Peoples of the Earth) and "Wenn im Vorsommer" (When in Early Summer) (appended in the 1961 collected works volume *Fahrt ins Staublose* to the volume *Sternverdunkelung* as "belonging to *Sternverdunkelung*," 1949) throw into relief Sachs's continued wariness of literary innocence, and her more urgent warning against submitting to literary or political authority. If Sachs was a critic of false security before, the abyss of Auschwitz intensified her dedication to self-referential, embattled poetry that demands intellectual engagement of the reader, now even more urgent as an antifascist assertion of individuality as it traverses the deceptive landscape of language.

Sachs conceived of her poems in cycles, conceptual spirals of text in which words, phrases, and ideas change, reform, and inform one another in an ever-reverberating, potentially endless engagement of reader and text. Often the structure of a given cycle informs or reinforces the topics treated in the poems. A Sachs poem regarded in connection with the other poems in its cycle and within the structure of the cycle as a whole functions as an extended and dynamic landscape in which the reader and the writer travel and wander. It is a treacherous landscape that requires constant vigilance and engagement from the reader, who finds him- or herself displaced from his or her conventional *Heimat* and put into a space of text he or she not only must negotiate, but also to an extent write him- or herself as he or she reads.

The diasporic poetics came into intense focus as the State of Israel was formed and Germany sought to literally and literarily rewrite itself as a new nation. Chapter 5 undertakes a close reading of the 1957 cycle "Flügel der Prophetie," which has as its primary topic the value of the diasporic history of Israel. The cycle is based on a mystical prescription to experience the events recounted in a text as if they are happening now. Wandering and uncertainty are inscribed into the form of the poetic cycle itself, while structural and stylistic choices in each of the poems reinforce the power of the wanderer and of the continually evolving multicultural discourse of the diaspora.

This same power is brought to bear on issues of memory, mourning, and memorialization of the Shoah. Sachs's immediate postwar poems maintain open wounds of the Shoah and its legacy rather than serve as a memorial. As I have argued elsewhere, for example, the disaggregation and fragmentation in the cycle "Grabschriften in die Luft geschrieben" indicates that the poems are the equivalent of the initials that mark a missing grave hanging forever in the air. Likewise the central shofar poem of the cycle "Dein Leib im Rauch durch die Luft" (Your Body in Smoke Through the Air) from *In den Wohnungen des Todes* (1947), the focus of chapter 6, suggests the creation of the cycle, a call to the reader (or in the lexicon of the poem, the hearer) to hear and experience moments of loss from the most ancient to the most recent tragedy. Because Sachs's reception is constructed primarily around an ethos of mourning and memorial, it is especially important to underscore her diasporic conception of memory (time is not linear, but cyclical and spiraled, which allows past and present to coexist in a textual present), and then to compare how her diasporic poetics dismantles space and time with her reception as a poet of memorial (which solidly fixes memorial in space and time, i.e., a projection in space). The cycle defies "remembering" by keeping all things in the present tense, and demanding each reader to examine his or her own deeds. Her own poetic position on memory is very much at odds with what has become her reception as a quintessential Holocaust poet of memorial. Ironically, her work has taken up a position in Holocaust discourse it actually seems to reject and even seeks to negate.

What we find fairly consistently is that Sachs conceives of language in spatial terms, as a space or landscape that readers, characters, and writers traverse, and that anyone's ability to survive is proportionate to his or her ability to navigate figurative language. Wanderers of all kinds represent a fluidity and control of figurative language; he or she who wanders on the earth or in the text is also more able to navigate the space of words as a participant (as a reader and as a creator), rather than being condemned to be a victim. Prowess and power come from nuanced ability to control, shift, be flexible and fluid with meaning in a ceaseless dialogue; since the nation is as much tied to figurative narration as the poetic text is, this is as true in empirical reality as it is on the page. Our resistance to stasis, our resistance to absolutism, our resistance to hegemony is rooted in our active ability to resist static, fossilized linguistic experience. For a writer, this means a text is always being reshaped, and never insists on its sovereignty. It is plastic and mutable and resists location. As readers, this means we do not relinquish our power to the authority of the author, but rather recognize and actively pursue our own agency in shaping the space of words, resisting location, resisting stasis, insisting on our subjectivity and our subjective experience of words. We can recognize that we shape the space we occupy; it is not and should not be shaped for us. If we allow it to be shaped for us, we relinquish our selves. Doing so would be antithetical to the red thread running through Sachs's work, touching on creative agency, nation narration, and indeed, especially, finally, Holocaust memorialization. In the 1920s and early 1930s, Sachs cleverly emulates conventional style to undermine conventional social roles and even national narrative, not unlike her role model Selma Lagerlöf. In the postwar era, Sachs's poetry is akin to what James E. Young came to describe as a "countermonument." The countermonument is largely the purview of the generation following Sachs, but in this, as in other things, Sachs was ahead of her time. Countermonument artists, like Art Spiegelman and Shimon Attie, reject "art's traditional redemptory function in the face of catastrophe," something Sachs's first postwar volume *In den Wohnungen des Todes* does consistently.[33] As I have written elsewhere, the cycle "Grabschriften in die Luft geschrieben" is a categorical rejection of art's—specifically the memorial verses's—redemptory function; at its most fundamental level, from the title of the cycle to the structure of the poems, the "Grabschriften" are counterepitaphs. They ultimately refuse the closure and redemption that epitaphs are meant to provide. Other cycles in the same volume, as I will demonstrate in this book, resist similar overtures of redemption and fixity.[34]

Most of the aims in Young's description of countermonuments apply to Sachs's poetry: her poems aim to provoke, they demand interaction, they invite their own violation, they do not accept graciously the burden of memory, and they painfully underscore a presence of absence. The presence of absence is indicated in these poems through initials Sachs refuses to complete with names, thus leaving the uncomfortable awareness that something is missing; or through images such as ghostly eyes that stare out from behind hedges; or blood, ash, and sweat of the dead that are the remnants of destroyed, anonymous, eradicated human beings whose absence is painfully felt, though their remnants are present everywhere. These poems do not attempt to lay it all to rest; they maintain the wound. They do lay a claim to everlastingness—but while they do so, they also place in question their own longevity, continually warning of the inherent forgetting that is the consequence of accepting the burden of memory. Even Sachs's earliest texts refuse that kind of stasis, always preferring wandering and questioning "an Stelle von Heimat."

1: Biography of the Poet: "a frail woman must do it"

It would take a Dante, a Shakespeare to capture this abyss . . . but so it is that a frail woman must do it.

—Nelly Sachs

THE UNORTHODOX MIX of avant-garde and archaic that we find in Sachs's prose and poetry, often taking the form of a simplistic façade masking more complex observations, reflects the person and the poet that her letters and secondhand accounts suggest she was. She famously claimed that she was never a poet,[1] that she was merely a frail woman,[2] that she wrote to combat melancholia or trauma,[3] that her person was unimportant, and that she wanted to disappear behind her work.[4] Her depiction bears every hallmark of conventional prescriptions for feminine behavior of her era and milieu, and as is the case with so many women who are described this way, there was a great deal more going on under the surface. The artist Sivar Arnér, who was her neighbor, observed that Sachs had many masks to suit the occasion and could take part in serious aesthetic discussions or play the role of the unengaged housewife if the situation called for it.[5] While Sachs's public persona tended to assert, just as she did in the letter to Elisabeth Borchers referenced above, that she was never a poet and ill-suited to academic discussions of aesthetics, the poet Ilse Blumenthal-Weiss noted that Sachs often played host to spirited discussions on literature, among other topics, at her apartment in Stockholm.[6] The variation in style in even her earliest writings indicates that she exercised careful control over every text she wrote, was familiar with a broad range of writers, movements, and schools, and made good use of her bourgeois private education. Though she was very much in control of her work, she usually retreated behind it whenever anyone attempted to initiate a more critical dialogue about her writing (as in some of the exchanges in her correspondence with exile scholar Walter Berendsohn),[7] though she was quick enough to assert her own critical voice if she felt her work was being manipulated (again, with Berendsohn, but also with the composer Moses Pergament, for example). She does conceal herself behind her work; but she is nonetheless actively constructing its reception, and her own. The public persona she created trickled into the way we read her work. As a child, she was shy, unassuming, and delicate, therefore her early legends and poetic efforts must also be unoriginal flights of girlhood fantasy. Yet she was not completely unaware of where she stood (or did not stand, but rather hovered or wandered) in the world at any given moment. By the time she began seriously devoting herself to writing it seems unlikely that she could have been completely naïve about what it meant to be an assimilated Jew in Berlin—she was by that time in her mid-twenties, and by the time her first book was published in 1921 Nelly Sachs was thirty years old. The characteristics of "Germanness" and "Jewishness" were a major topic in the public sphere in early twentieth-century Germany, just as they had been since Moses Mendelssohn's grandchildren participated in the creation of the intellectual culture of the nineteenth century and Heinrich Heine sought his ticket into German culture by converting to Christianity. Stripped of her German citizenship like all Jews under the Nazi regime, she was technically "stateless" for a period of about seventeen years; after fleeing in 1940, she was ultimately unwilling to return to Germany, unwilling to move to Israel, and unable to attain Swedish citizenship until 1952. She was a wanderer in many respects, well traveled in aesthetics and world literature, most adept in German but not at home in German or in Germany, or anywhere else. The questions and problems related to the stasis inherent in any kind of "belonging" occupy her writing, though not necessarily as a reflection of her own trauma. Here I want to sketch out her biography, to help orient the newcomer to Sachs, contextualized within her work as an active writer and poet, rather than as a victim-vessel.[8]

Leonie "Nelly" Sachs was born on December 10, 1891, in Berlin to William Sachs, a businessman and inventor, and his young wife, Margarete Sachs, née Karger. She remained an only child and enjoyed the doting but distant bourgeois upbringing of the wealthy Tiergarten section of Berlin. Because of her frail health and nervous disposition, Nelly Sachs attended different schools in the city and in the country, had private tutors, and ultimately also visited a therapist. The Sachs's were an assimilated family, and it is unclear how important a role Jewishness played in the household. Sachs's friend Bengt Holmqvist presumes that they were part of the Jewish community because that was a traditional formality, but were not observant. The biographers all suggest that Nelly Sachs was aware that she belonged to a Jewish family, and that at least once during her childhood someone outside the family mentioned this fact, but all maintain that anti-Semitism was alien to her.[9] Sachs's mother was by all accounts a typical upper-class turn-of-the-century woman: in charge of the household, nervous, neurotic, fragile, and demanding. Sachs's father was by all accounts a typical upper-middle-class turn-of-the-century man: factory owner, distant, demanding, doting, and materialistic. Both parents inspired her interest in creative expression: her father was an amateur musician who played piano while his daughter danced, which she credits as the root of her interest in expression beyond the word, while her mother is credited with inspiring Nelly Sachs's interest in the written word. As a seventeen-year-old girl in 1908, Sachs experienced a heartbreak that is often cited as an impulse to write;[10] she never divulged exactly what happened, though the experience haunted her for decades. Several biographical portraits assert that it was a young man who went on to be involved in political turmoil that resulted in his death; this is widely credited as the root of her postwar cycle "Gebete für den toten Bräutigam" (Prayers for the Dead Bridegroom, 1947), among other cycles.[11] While the failed love affair has become the legendary impetus for her career as a writer, her childhood and adolescence are characterized by interest in and attempts at different kinds of creative expression. Whatever the root of her writing was, what we do know for certain is that in 1915, at the age of twenty-three, Nelly Sachs offered both prose and poetry to the prestigious Cotta press. There is no record of their response, but Sachs's intent to publish, and therefore to write for an audience, is clear.[12]

Sachs's first publication, a collection of fairy tales and legends called *Legenden und Erzählungen*, appeared in 1921 through what is presumed to be a private publishing contract[13] with the publisher F. W. Mayer in Berlin-Wilmersdorf. The book is divided into two sections, "Legenden" and "Erzählungen"; the legends are "Eine Legende vom Fra Angelico" (A Legend of Fra Angelico, discussed in the next chapter), "Die Närrin von Siena" (The Fool of Sienna), "Vom Manne, der am Tage der unschuldigen Kindlein starb" (Of the Man Who Died on the Day of the Innocent Child), "Das Christusbild" (The Image of Christ); and the tales are "Wie der Zauberer Merlin erlöset ward" (How Merlin the Sorcerer Was Saved), "San Marcos Taube" (San Marco's Dove), "Der Tod im Pfarrhof" (Death at the Pastor's Home), and "Der gefesselte Silen" (Silenus Bound). The majority of the titles suggest a focus on folktales revolving around Christian iconography, but the inclusion of Merlin and the Greek myth of Silenus suggest something more is at stake.[14] While most of the stories do tell of loving self-sacrifice (which the biographers link to both Christian values and gender norms),[15] they also, intriguingly, revolve specifically around politics of iconography: a person or a thing becomes imbued with a significance that is somehow at odds with the story it represents. Under the guise of simple folktales, the stories pose questions about who controls narrative and who controls interpretation. Most of the stories thematize parting in death, most of them have protagonists who wander, and all of them are about figures who exist on the margins of society: monks, mystics, fools, social outcasts, a wizard, and a Dionysian man-horse. Several of the stories, that of Merlin in particular, exist in multiple variations in Sachs's body of work. Although he does not appear in her postwar publications, Sachs continued to write Merlin texts throughout her life; it is the one example of her early work to which the biographers dedicate close attention. Dinesen relates it to good, evil, and the failed love affair of 1908, while Fritsch-Vivié relates it to sexual aggression; Fioretos undertakes a brief but thorough examination of the evolution of Merlin in Sachs's writing from the 1910s to the early 1960s, from salvation to sexual aggression to powerlessness. In chapter 3 I will highlight another level of Sachs's Merlin fascination through an artistic-political reading of the Merlin legend.

Legenden und Erzählungen is the only known prewar narrative prose publication by Nelly Sachs; the archives in Stockholm and Dortmund, however, contain large catalogues of unpublished work. Among them are prose, poetry, and marionette play scripts, many of which treat the common themes of parting, injustice, or wandering. Her texts often thematize or mix different art forms: she sometimes included her own watercolor paintings, she sometimes began prose works or plays with a musical staff, and she wrote poems about pieces of music and dance. The prose collection "Apfeltraumallee" (1930s)[16] contains fourteen stories that deal with different kinds of outsiders and silence, including the short piece "Die stumme Nachtigall oder der Umweg zu Gott" (The Silent Nightingale or the Detour to God) discussed in the next chapter. The titles of the stories all include birds or flowers; some begin with a musical phrase, and some are variations of material she treated in other forms. "Vom Bauer der durch die unschuldigen Kindlein in den Himmel kam" (The Tale of the Farmer who Got in to Heaven through the Innocent Child) is the title of one of Sachs's marionette plays, but it also turns up in a shortened version in "Apfeltraumallee," and is the story of the man who died on the day of the innocent child in *Legenden und Erzählungen*. Other frequent storylines, for example "Der Jahrmarkt der Träume" (The Market of Dreams), "Galaswinte" (Galaswinte, which is the name of the main character) and various other legends and tales become cameo anecdotes within Sachs's unpublished longer prose narrative "Chelion: Eine Kindheitsgeschichte" (Chelion: A Childhood Story, early 1930s), and turn up many years later in her postwar work. Although her early texts appear largely conventional, they demonstrate familiarity with a wide array of styles, including more avant-garde attempts at form and content.[17] She wrote sonnets and occasional poetry for friends, family, and people she admired, notably Nobel Prize–winning Swedish writer Selma Lagerlöf, to whom Sachs also sent a copy of *Legenden und Erzählungen*. Lagerlöf wrote her a thank-you card in return that said she could not have done it better herself. Lagerlöf also wrote, as Jennifer Watson has argued, texts that appear conventional, but that are more than meets the eye.[18]

Although Sachs's next publication after *Legenden und Erzählungen*, her first published poem "Zur Ruh" (To Rest), did not appear until October 1929 when it was printed in the *Voßische Zeitung*,[19] her work and ambition had already come to the attention of writers Heinrich Böll and Stefan Zweig. It is unclear how Zweig became aware of her work, but in approximately 1925 he referred to Sachs's work either in a recommendation or review obtained by Leo Hirsch, the feuilleton editor at the *Berliner Tageblatt*[20] who became her sponsor and promoter, positioning Sachs's writing in direct contrast to the majority of women's poetry as demonstrating "eine ekstatisch aufsteigende Linie, die sonst in der Frauenlyrik ungewöhnlich ist" (an ecstatic rising line that is otherwise unusual in women's poetry). According to Zweig, Sachs's work contains "außerordentliche innere Vehemenz" (extraordinary inner vehemence) and is "jeder Stelle zur Ehre gereichend, die heute noch Lyrik druckt" (deserving of honor from any place that still publishes poetry today).[21]

Aside from the qualitative assessment, Zweig's observation touches on another topic that is curiously present and yet difficult to consistently describe in Sachs's work, namely gender. Her early works do differ from those of other, well-known women of the early twentieth century in style and topic; they lack the materiality of Gertrud Kolmar's verse, and the sensuality of Else Lasker-Schüler's, for example. Sachs's writing does emulate texts usually associated with men, specifically those writing idyllic *Heimatliteratur*, and yet it also does not entirely follow their paradigm. The bucolic legends and tales of conventional, popular turn-of-the-century literature celebrate the simplicity and authenticity of German peasant life, a wholesome counterweight to the urban, degenerate literature of Realism, Naturalism, New Objectivity, and Expressionism (all, according to the nationalists, the purview of "Jewish" writers). Sachs did not write much in the way of urban literature; "Chelion" is the only narrative that takes place in a contemporary urban setting, though it draws heavily on the tropes of more idyllic literature. But in "Chelion" those tropes help expose the unconventional process woven into the more conventional legends and tales: these stories actively undermine the wholesome appearance of idyllic literature by exposing the rifts, exploitations, and injustices pervasive even in fairy-tale settings. There is no embrace of Germanic national essence, no tidy storyline where a strapping man upholds moral truth or a dainty yet strong woman dies to preserve her or others' purity; instead, what is conventionally held to be moral truth is often exposed as chauvinism, and the women and girls die engaged in very personal undertakings that are ultimately futile. These diverse narratives are a complex demonstration of power in the hands of the person who wields control over figurative language: the more pleasing such language appears, the more dangerous it often is. Many of Sachs's early texts look curiously similar to idyllic, conventional texts that celebrate the poet-prophet or the idyll of a fatherland; but the variety of texts she mimics suggests this is more than mere epigonism. Indeed, Sachs creates poetry, or the written word in general, as a space that problematizes "truth" or "fatherland." Zweig sees something essentially masculine in her writing, yet biographers link her values and pathos to femininity; she clearly held some interest in probing female typologies in literature, as both her early and later work show, though it is difficult to establish a consistent pattern of analysis—except to say that both genders can hold power, yet both are also subject to being marginalized. No character, image, or concept ever remains static.

While Sachs apparently avoided the various literary groups of Weimar-era Berlin, she was part of her own sort of salon. Aris Fioretos and Ruth Dinesen describe Sachs and a group of her friends in the 1920s and '30s in terms that suggest something of a counterexample to the group of writers attending Stefan George, known as the "George Circle": "Arguably the demonic aspects exhibited by the George circle were missing. Nor is there any honoring of the fatherland, of either the inner or the outer kind, in which poetry would be the vessel of truth."[22] Sachs's circle of friends was an intimate group of similarly artistic women who engaged in writing, music, dance, and painting. Dora Jablonski (later Horwitz, 1891–1942), who painted still lifes and landscapes, Gudrun Harlan (later Dähnert, 1907–76) a physical therapist who evidently studied movement and dance, and Annaliese Neff (1910–92), who had studied Classical Greek and German, all made up a sort of salon. They read and discussed the Romantics, and philosopher Martin Buber and the legendary Hassidic rabbi known as the Baal Shem Tov. Neff and Sachs both attended a well-known series of open university lectures on Romanticism held by theater scholar Max Herrmann. Neff apparently also had ties to the George Circle. Sachs divided her time between her friends and her ailing father. William Sachs died on November 26, 1930. One of the poems among the unpublished work is called "Inschrift auf die Urne meines Vaters" (Inscription on the Urn of My Father). Years later, she had his urn sent to Stockholm, so that she could have it buried alongside her mother, who died in 1950.

Nelly Sachs's reception began in the 1930s, when reviews of her work began to appear in the *C.-V.-Zeitung* and the *Jüdische Rundschau*. With Hitler's rise to power, Sachs became involved in the Central-Verein deutscher Staatsbürger jüdischen Glaubens, where she and others performed her work in a public forum that included such notable performers and writers as Erna Feld-Leonhard, Gertrud Kolmar, Kurt Pinthus, and Ilse Blumenthal-Weiss. Ruth Dinesen's book *"Und das Leben hat immer wie Abschied geschmeckt": frühe Gedichte und Prosa der Nelly Sachs* provides the most exhaustive survey to date of Sachs's works performed in the context of the Jüdische Frauenbund and the Central-Verein, and the reviews of them that were published in the *C.-V.-Zeitung* and the *Jüdische Rundschau*.[23] Among the works performed were selections from "Chelion: Eine Kindheitsgeschichte," the marionette play *Jahrmarkt der Träume*, and a selection of poems. Reviewers criticized the "sweetness" of her word choices and the "heterogeneity" of her figures; nonetheless, she was consistently considered among the significant woman poets within the Jewish community, along with Else Lasker-Schüler and Gertrud Kolmar. Sachs's prose and lyrical dramas were regarded as escapism, especially under the lens of the politically engaged Zionist critics of the *Rundschau* and often the *C.-V.-Zeitung*. Despite the accusation of thematic weakness in Sachs's work, critics recognized her technical ability and desire for innovation in poetry.

Between 1933 and 1937, Sachs published a number of poems in newspapers for the Jewish community, though none in literary or artistic journals. In 1933 she published "Die Rehe" (Deer), "Das Vogelnest" (The Birds' Nest), and "Schlummer-Reise" (Slumber Journey) in the *Berliner Tageblatt*. In 1935, "Sternschnuppe" (Shooting Star), "Rehe" (Deer), and "Herbstlied" (Autumn Song) appeared in *Jugend*; "Rehe" then appeared again, in the *C.-V.-Zeitung* in April 1936. Also appearing in the *C.-V.-Zeitung* in 1936 was the poem "Dörfer im Spätsommer" (Villages in Late Summer), and "Gebet" (Prayer), "Lichter zum Trost" (Lights for Comfort), and "Grabinschrift" (Epitaph) were published in the *Israelitischen Familienblatt*. 1937 was a particularly successful year for Sachs, in quality and quantity, with seven publications (individual poems as well as cycles): five in *Der Morgen*, a Jewish community journal that focused on the arts and humanities, one in the *C.-V.-Zeitung*, and one in the *Israelitische Familienblatt*. The poems in *Der Morgen* are particularly notable, in part because of the quality of the journal, and in part because of the poems themselves. Based on the subject matter, namely musical compositions, these poems have been dated very early. In later poems, Sachs began to take up biblical themes or more complex depictions of melancholia, whereas poems based on objects or music appear to be much earlier efforts. If this is true, Sachs's choice of the music and dance poems for submission to *Der Morgen* indicates continued work with earlier texts, and also demonstrates continuous engagement with combinations of form and genre.

Sachs continued to be very active in 1938. She published "Das Mädchen am Brunnen" (The Girl at the Well), "Mailied" (May Song), "Abschied, du Nachtigallenwort" (Parting, you Nightingaleword), and "Schlaflied" (Lullaby) in *Der Morgen* in May. Her work was mentioned in September of 1938 in the *Jüdische Rundschau*, in the context of women's poetry publicly performed by Erna Feld-Leonhard under the title "Ungehörte Stimmen" (Unheard Voices).[24] According to the October 27, 1938 issue of the *C.-V.-Zeitung* she published a poem in the 1938 *Jüdisches Blindenjahrbuch*, published by the Jüdischer Buchverlag Leo Alterthum,[25] and "Lieder vom Abschied" (Songs of Parting) appeared in what proved to be the final edition of the *C.-V.-Zeitung* on November 3, 1938. In 1939 her poem "Nachtlied"

(Nocturn) was published in the *Monatsblätter* of the Jüdischer Kulturbund in Deutschland. This marked the end of Sachs's publishing career in Germany until after the Second World War.

After her father died, Nelly Sachs eventually took over the administration of certain aspects of his factory and of their household, and became her mother's caretaker. In 1935, she and her mother, like all Jews in Germany, lost their citizenship, and their rights were increasingly restricted. Sachs was also interrogated, which yielded a stroke of luck: the police official is said to have comforted the frightened Sachs, given her his phone number, and to have told her to contact him for advice if she was in danger. This later proved vital. By 1939, Sachs and her mother had moved into a small room in a pension in Charlottenburg, stripped of many of their possessions. For several years, Sachs had been trying to appeal to Selma Lagerlöf to act as a sponsor for her and her mother's application for Swedish asylum, to no avail. Early in 1939, Gudrun Dähnert undertook the journey to Lagerlöf's estate at Mårbacka to personally ask for her support; she also managed to gain an audience with Prince Eugen, the "Painter Prince," who, in the end, also sponsored Sachs's application. Dähnert then appealed to various Jewish community members and refugees to help secure the required 200 kronor per month to support Sachs and her mother. American affidavits were eventually secured, and by early 1940 most preparations were in place. When long-awaited paperwork was finally in order, Sachs made arrangements for train travel to Sweden. Then the order arrived for her to report for forced labor. In a desperate moment, Sachs contacted the police official who told her to call if she ever needed assistance. She told him of the order and that she had gotten train tickets. He told her to tear up the order, change the train tickets to plane tickets and get out of the country immediately; they would never make it out by train. This she did. Nelly Sachs and her mother made it out of Germany on May 16, 1940.

Almost immediately upon arrival in Stockholm, Sachs began looking both for translation work and for a venue for her poems. A single woman supporting an ailing mother, Sachs's official occupation now became writer. Her first poems appeared in the Swedish publication *Vi* (We) already in 1941. In that same year, Nelly Sachs and her mother moved into a tiny apartment at Bergsundsstrand 23 in Stockholm. In 1948 they moved into the apartment at Bergsundsstrand where they spent the rest of their lives. It consisted of a bedroom, a living room, and a kitchen. Sachs spent her nights writing at the kitchen table, storing her manuscripts in a drawer. The apartment has been reconstructed in the Royal National Swedish Library in Stockholm, down to details such as a to-scale photograph of the view from their window overlooking the bay. This installation houses Sachs's private library, including the books she took with her when she fled.

Nelly Sachs essentially ceased to write prose after her flight from Germany, with the exception of autobiographical reflections or notes, most significantly "Leben unter Bedrohung" (Life under Threat, published in 1956) and "Briefe aus der Nacht" (Letters of the Night, 1950/1953, long unpublished, but now available in *Werke IV*).[26] Sachs concentrated instead primarily on poems and what she called "Szenische Dichtungen" or "Versuche," experimental compositions for the stage. Between 1940 and 1945, Sachs composed most of the work for which she is known today—astonishingly, this represents a small sliver of her entire oeuvre. Once she was in a position to contact German publishers again after the war, Sachs began trying to find a venue for her poems. As they unabashedly confront war crimes, and everyone's complicity, and describe a world in which the murdered observe the living from every tree and bush, indeed from within the very air we breathe, Western allied publishers, beholden to an occupation mandate that eschewed confronting the past, were likely not in a position to publish Sachs's poetry; the Soviet sector, however, which advocated an active antifascist confrontation of the past, was home to publishers who were in such a position. Sachs's first postwar volume, *In den Wohnungen des Todes* (In the Dwellings of Death, 1947), was published by Aufbau Verlag, a Soviet-sector publisher that eventually became the primary literary publisher in the German Democratic Republic. She also published her first volume of translations of Swedish poetry, *Von Welle und Granit* (Of Wave and Granite) with Aufbau, which includes poems by notable Swedish poets Pär Lagerkvist, Edith Södergran, Johannes Edfelt, and Gunnar Ekelöf.

Von Welle und Granit attracted the attention of Munich-based publisher Willi Weismann, who wrote to Sachs asking if she might not create such a volume for his press, too, presumably as part of a reeducation effort to acquaint German audiences with literature they had no access to during National Socialist rule. Sachs agreed, and suggested he also try to acquire the rights to *In den Wohnungen des Todes*. She also offered to send another of her translations that might interest him, of the antifascist novel *Kallocain* by the Swedish writer Karin Boye (1900–1941). Unfortunately, her work with Weismann never came to fruition, but her proposed work for his press helps us contextualize her postwar mentality. The content of *Kallocain* (and a number of the poems in *Von Welle und Granit*) resonates with the themes and ethos of *In den Wohnungen des Todes*, in particular in its multifaceted critique of totalitarianism: it is not only a dystopic allegory for the regimes of the 1930s and '40s; it makes clear each individual's complicity in the maintenance of totalitarianism and warns that one form of totalitarianism can easily supplant another.

In den Wohnungen des Todes takes up similar issues and adds to them problems of memory and memorial in the wake of genocide. The volume also exemplifies the state of postwar literature, while confronting the role of literature in memory, memorial, and in national consciousness and conscience. It consists of four cycles: "Dein Leib im Rauch durch die Luft" (Your Body in Smoke through the Air), to which the last chapter of this book is dedicated, is a comparative examination of mourning and complicity; "Gebete für den toten Bräutigam" (Prayers for the Dead Bridegroom) probes the different states of memory and mourning, and was presumably inspired by the fate of the person involved in her failed romance of 1908; "Grabschriften in die Luft geschrieben" (Gravescripts Written into the Air) deconstructs the role of art in memorial; and "Chöre nach der Mitternacht" (Choirs after Midnight) presents a series of choirs singing commentary on complicity, forgiveness, mourning, and nationality from different perspectives, including the dead, the living, nature, inanimate objects, and finally the Holy Land.

After *In den Wohnungen des Todes*, a critical but not a popular success, her poetry found a home in 1949 with Bermann-Fischer Amsterdam, a publisher specializing in exile and refugee work. *Sternverdunkelung* (Eclipse of the Stars, 1949) continued in the vein of *In den Wohnungen des Todes*, but then expanded into more theoretical and at the same time more directly political territory. It consists of four cycles and, in its later incarnations, an addendum called "Zur *Sternverdunkelung* gehörig" (Belonging to *Sternverdunkelung*). The four cycles explore different kinds of boundaries: between nations (involving especially Israel, as a concept and as a country), between life and death (in particular regarding the illness of her mother), between increments of time, components of music, forgetting and remembering, silence and speech, and different epochs. According to Sachs, *Sternverdunkelung* represented a more experimental style compared to *In den Wohnungen des Todes*. She wrote to her friend Gudrun Dähnert: "Vielleicht gibt Dir *Sternverdunkelung* stilistisch einige Rätsel auf, darum finde ich grade die aufklärende Rezension [von Bruno Balscheit] wichtig. Wir können einfach nicht mehr die alten verbrauchten Stilmittel anwenden" (Perhaps *Sternverdunkelung* will give you some stylistic riddles, that's why I find this enlightening review [by Bruno Balscheit] important. We simply can no longer apply the old, used styles).[27]

The public and critical receptions of Sachs's first two postwar poetry volumes reflect the complicated state of literature in the immediate postwar era in Germany. Literary critics of the mid- to late 1940s puzzled over the role literature was to have in a life and landscape destroyed by National Socialism, war, and mass murder.[28] Poetry in particular presented a problem, because it is historically linked to beauty, order, and abstraction; its conventions no longer seemed appropriate in the physical and moral upheaval of postwar Germany. Writers of the era harbored this same unease, but fell into three categories in their view of the problem. Older writers, like Ricarda Huch, tended to advocate for a return to the literature that existed before 1933; younger writers took issue with this point of view, asserting that such literature, for all its truth and beauty, had done nothing to prevent or confront National Socialism and was no longer valid, therefore German literature had to be completely reinvented. A third group, sometimes identified with the term "Trümmerliteratur," rubble literature or literature of the ruins, occupied a middle position. Here we find writers like Nelly Sachs, or Thomas Mann, or Günter Eich, writers who felt they could no longer write in the styles and conventions of prewar literature, but also acknowledged that they could not entirely leave the conventions behind, not only because they had been a large part of their lives, but also because they felt literature and art had an obligation to expose what Nazi policies and the German war machine had done to Germany's rich humanistic heritage. German art and letters lay in ruins, just as the cities and landscapes lay in ruins. *In den Wohnungen des Todes* exposes the invalidated conventions of literature: the forms, the intentions, even the established semantics that had been appropriated by the Nazis and degraded by association with their policy and crimes. This was not what the public or the government wanted, however. The public was not yet ready for Sachs's poetry, and it did not want to be confronted with the Jewish experience of the war. The Western allied occupiers, moreover, and their reeducation/denazification program actively discouraged any confrontation with the past, promoting instead the forward-looking Americanization and practical consumer reconstruction of land and economy. Sachs wrote in several letters between the late 1940s and late 1950s that the public was not yet ready for her work, for example in a letter to poet and translator Johannes Edfelt in 1953: "In Deutschland lehnt man bei fast allen Verlegern Dichtung ab, die noch über Rilke hinaus eine Form für diese unsere zerbrochene Welt sucht. Es soll alles glatt und harmonisch im früheren Sinne sein. Wie ist das möglich, fragt man sich, aber das Publikum gibt die Antwort und kauft neue Dichtung nicht" (In Germany nearly every publisher rejects poetry that seeks a form beyond Rilke for this, our broken world. Everything is to be smooth and harmonious like it once was. How is this possible, one asks oneself. But the public gives the answer and does not buy new poetry).[29] *In den Wohnungen des Todes* and *Sternverdunkelung* confronted audiences with a number of themes they were not yet ready to face, in structures that were at once archaic and avant-garde; it took until the late 1950s and early 1960s for the public to embrace Sachs's poetry.

Between 1949 and 1960, Sachs slowly worked on her third postwar volume, *Und niemand weiss weiter* (And No One Knows What to Do Anymore), published in 1957 by the Heinrich Ellermann Press, and her next translation volume, *Aber auch diese Sonne ist heimatlos* (But This Sun, Too, Is Homeless), published in 1956 by the Georg Büchner Press, but the 1950s were more directly dedicated to the composition of theater pieces. On February 7, 1950, her mother, Margarete Sachs, died, and Nelly Sachs suffered her first of several nervous breakdowns. Her letters of 1950 show Sachs working intensively on the play *Abram im Salz, Ein Spiel für Wort-Mimus-Musik* (Abraham in Salt, A Play for Word-Mime-Music, begun in 1944), a piece drawing on ancient cult theater with elements of Japanese Nô theater: "Das Wort ist hier nur Haltestelle für Mimus und Musik, die weiter führen sollen" (the word here is a stop [waiting] for mime and music, which shall carry us further).[30] Her theater pieces all actively employ a mix of genres and art forms, attempting (as the subtitles indicate) to explode the conventions and constraints of both theater and spoken word. The dramatic texts of the mid-1950s, *Simson fällt durch Jahrtausende, Ein dramatisches Geschehen in vierzehn Bildern* (Samson Falls through Millennia, A Dramatic Occurrence in Fourteen Images), *Nachtwache, Ein Albtraum in neun Bildern* (Nightwatch, A Nightmare in Nine Images), *Der magische Tänzer, Versuch eines Ausbruchs* (The Magic Dancer, Attempt at an Escape), and the very short *Versteckspiel mit Emanuel, Ein Delirium aus Einsamkeit* (Hide-and-Seek with Emanuel, a Delirium of Loneliness) continued to push these boundaries. She went on to write eight more theatrical works by 1962, including *Vergebens an einem Scheiterhaufen* (Uselessly at the Stake), *Was ist ein Opfer?* (What Is a Victim?), and *Beryll sieht in der Nacht* (Beryll Sees in the Night).[31] Each of them approaches fundamental questions of the human condition, many raised anew by the genocide against the Jews, with increasing abstraction through a return to puppets (playing alongside people), stylized performance, and unique use of visual and sound cues.

While Sachs worked on her newer, more abstract and experimental plays, *Eli, ein Mysterienspiel vom Leiden Israels* (Eli, a Mystery Play of the Suffering of Israel), which she had finished in 1945 though it did not appear in print until 1951, was in the process of becoming her most well-known theater piece. *Eli* is perhaps slightly more conventional than the plays Sachs wrote in the 1950s, if nothing else in its adaptation of the mystery-play genre (as opposed to the other plays' forms—described by Sachs variously as "attempt," "occurrence," "nightmare," or "delirium"). It is longer than the later plays, it has three major characters, and a large supporting cast that includes a number of villagers and ghosts, and has little in the way of music. The set and staging are minimalist but challenging: rubble, grass made of grasping fingers, smoking chimneys, twisted ghost trees, chattering teeth, disembodied voices, and perhaps most complicated: one dissolving body and one transforming body. Although it was finished already in 1945, *Eli* was first printed in a limited edition in Malmö, Sweden, in 1951, and was first performed on stage in 1962; in the late 1950s, following the publication of *Und niemand weiss weiter* (1957), *Eli* also became a radio play and an opera. Sachs's letters surrounding the collaboration and broadcast of the opera provide some insight into the limits of her patience. Generally, she appreciated any attention afforded her work—though she rarely clearly validated anyone's interpretation of it; her work with composer Moses Pergament, however, shows the poet trying to steer both her reception and the presentation of her work. The correspondence between Sachs and Pergament, and *Eli*'s reception history, also exemplify the complications of Holocaust-related theater.[32]

Eli is a Jewish mystery play. It is set in two villages, one Jewish and one gentile, on either side of the German-Polish border "after the martyrdom." In the Jewish village, where the majority of the play takes place, the survivors mourn and work to rebuild their village as the High Holidays approach. The act that drives the plot has been committed before the play begins: as the Jews were being marched out of their village, the little shepherd boy Eli raised his head and played his shepherd's pipe. A soldier, fearing this to be a secret signal, hit the boy in the head with the butt of his rifle, killing him. The play then follows the village shoemaker Michael—whom the villagers suspect of being one of the Thirty-Six Zaddikim, or Hidden Just Men, of mystical Jewish legend[33]—who is inexplicably compelled to find Eli's murderer. As he walks through the countryside, he encounters ghosts and ruins, remnants of war; the villagers, meanwhile, engage in complex discussions (in varied verse) of guilt, complicity, forgiveness, justice, and coincidence. When Michael finds the perpetrator, who is haunted by the sound of chattering teeth and has lost his own child in the meantime to a mysterious illness, they turn to face one another. As the perpetrator cries out for justice and fairness, he crumbles to dust, and Michael disappears in a primeval light. The play simply ends there, without commentary or clear resolution. Audiences (and actors and composers) are left to draw their own conclusions. In its tangle of impossible and unresolved questions, the play magnifies the state of postwar Germany. This is both the play's greatest strength and its most profound danger: audiences, actors, directors, and composers read into it what they needed to. When Pergament, interpreting Michael as an avenger, sought to make him a heroic tenor, Sachs was compelled to intervene—in letters and even in the Swedish press—and argue that he was not.[34] At the conclusion of the 1962 premiere in Dortmund, the audience left the theater in silence; reviews lauded the poet, but found that the Dortmund theater company was simply not capable of doing justice to the material. The theater company found the text alienating and overwhelming, which apparently transferred to the audience, and despite critical acclaim, *Eli* failed to become a part of German stage repertoire.[35] Uwe Naumann suggests that "es müssen wohl die ästhetischen Mittel sein . . . die Nelly Sachs zu einer viel gelobten, ungespielten Dramatikerin machen" (It must be the aesthetic means [she uses] that make Nelly Sachs a much praised, unperformed playwright).[36] Ehrhard Bahr, however, argues that "die Gründe für die mangelnde Rezeption ihres szenischen Werkes sind dieselben wie im Falle der Lyrik. Nelly Sachs's dramatische Dichtung wurde in der Bundesrepublik als "Wiedergutmachungstheater" stigmatisiert. Der Hinweis auf die bühnentechnischen Schwierigkeiten . . . erweist sich als leicht widerlegbarer Vorwand" (the reasons for the lack of reception for her theatrical work are the same as for her poetry. Nelly Sachs's dramatic work was stigmatized in West Germany as "Theater of Reconciliation." The assertion of technical difficulties proves to be an easily refuted pretense.)[37]

There is no entirely satisfactory interpretation of the play, which is in keeping with the tone of Sachs's immediate postwar work: there are no simple answers in the wake of Auschwitz. The in-between nature of the play is also captured in its setting, straddling a border between two villages. The sense of renewal linked to Rosh Hashanah may give the impression of healing, but the villagers' celebration of Rosh Hashanah also signals the approach of the other High Holiday, Yom Kippur, the day of atonement, a divine but also profoundly earthbound day of judgment. The extensive conversations of the supporting cast never resolve the matter of justice or forgiveness, in part because everyone is simply too shell-shocked, and in part because their experiences have destroyed any belief they may have had in causality or logic. What can justice even look like "after the martyrdom"? The play suggests that the past offers no vocabulary for the problems of the postwar era, let alone solutions. Sachs's letters show her fighting Pergament's manipulation of her work; she emphasizes that Michael is not to be fixed in a traditional theatrical role—which is perhaps also already clear from the paradoxical genre of a Jewish mystery play. *Eli* remains a rarely performed play, but it is nonetheless a striking work that has generated decades of discussion, which was doubtless part of Sachs's intent. It has remained the most well known of her scenic compositions.

In 1957, Nelly Sachs finally achieved a major breakthrough. In the run-up to the publication of *Und niemand weiss weiter*, she was featured as a translator of Swedish verse in an issue of Alfred Andersch's journal *Texte und Zeichen*,[38] dedicated to contemporary Swedish literature and the history of Swedish-German literary relations. In addition to the poems she translated, four of her own poems, "Ein schwarzer Jochanaan" (A Black Jochanaan), "Nicht nur Land ist Israel" (Not Only Land is Israel), "Daniel mit der Sternenzeichnung" (Daniel with the Constellation), and "Landschaft aus Schreien" (Landscape of Screams), were also featured. These four belonged to the forthcoming *Und niemand weiss weiter*, and won a very surprised Sachs sudden international renown. In an unpublished letter to Käte Hamburger from March 1, 1957, Sachs wrote:

Meine eigenen Gedichte werden im Herbst bei Dr. Heinrich Ellermann München erscheinen unter dem Titel: Und Niemand weiß weiter. Es sind 10 Zyklen. Auch die 4 Gedichte in "Texte und Zeichen" gehen ein darin im Zyklus: Flügel d[er] Prophetie. Diese 4 Gedichte haben mir aus der Schweiz, Italien, Holland und Deutschland viele Briefe eingebracht mit Übersetzungen und Verleger Angeboten. Wie merkwürdig meine beiden anderen Gedichtbücher mit allen schönen Recensionen [sic] sind lange in Vergessenheit geraten und so finden nun 4 Gedichte das Ohr der Menschen.]

[My own poems will appear in the fall with Dr. Heinrich Ellermann's press in Munich under the title: And No One Knows What to Do Anymore. It is ten cycles. The four poems in "Texte und Zeichen" are also in it, in the cycle: Wings of Prophecy. These four poems have brought me offers of translation and publication from Switzerland, Italy, Holland, and Germany. How curious that both my other poetry books with all their beautiful reviews have long since been forgotten, and now four poems find the ear of the people.]³⁹

Und niemand weiss weiter does continue to explore themes of memory, time, and Jewish experience, but its array of referents is markedly broader than the preceding volumes. Sachs contextualizes her themes within eight associative cycles drawing from current events, fairy tales, Shakespeare, the Torah, Hassidic mysticism, music, and anesthesia. The mosaic of references highlights a sense of brokenness and uncertainty, though it also at times reconstructs a sense that fragementation is all that can be certain. After *Und niemand weiss weiter*, audiences began to discover *In den Wohnungen des Todes* and *Sternverdunkelung*. In 1958 and 1959, they were introduced to *Eli*. Between 1957 and 1961, respect for and recognition of Sachs's work grew, and her reputation as a Holocaust poet was established. In 1957, she was voted a corresponding member of the German Academy for Language and Letters; in January of 1958, she was awarded the Lyric Poetry Prize of the Swedish Writers Union; in 1959, she won the Literature Prize of the Cultural Circle of the Federal Union of German Industry; in 1960, she was honored with the Meersburg Droste Prize for Women Poets, and in 1961 she was elected a corresponding member of the Free Academy of the Arts of Hamburg. That same year the city of Dortmund established the Nelly Sachs Prize. Gabriele Fritsch-Vivié reminds us, as we consider the growing list of honors, that

der Grund dieser Ehrung liegt in der künstlerischen Wertschätzung der Dichterin Nelly Sachs. Gleichzeitig aber muß man auch auf die allgemeine Euphorie hinweisen, mit der sie in den sechziger Jahren gefeiert wird. Sie gilt nur in zweiter Linie dem Werk der Dichterin, vor allem gilt sie ihr als der deutschen Jüdin, der gegenüber eine große Wiedergutmachungsschuld offensteht.

Ohne Eingeständnisse glaubt man, diese Schuld mit Preisen und Ehrungen einlösen zu können."

[the reason for these honors lies in artistic appreciation for the poet Nelly Sachs. At the same time, one must point to the general euphoria with which she was celebrated in the 1960s. It only secondarily applies to her work; primarily it applies to her as the German Jewish woman to whom a great debt of reconciliation can be paid. The debt can be paid, without any admissions of guilt or atonement, through honors and prizes.][40]

The various summaries of scholarship on Sachs make the same point. The summaries also point out that the majority of reviews and descriptions of her work up through the 1980s focus mostly on her biography and explain the roots of her mystical Jewish imagery, and say little about her poetics, except the pronouncement that her work captures the fate of the Jewish people.[41]

In honor of Sachs's seventieth birthday in 1961, literary personalities from Germany and Sweden came together in Stockholm; Suhrkamp published *Nelly Sachs zu Ehren*, a collection of poems and essays honoring her life and work. 1961 also saw Hans Magnus Enzensberger's first edition of Sachs's collected poems, *Fahrt ins Staublose* (Journey into Dustlessness), published by Suhrkamp, which included the volumes *In den Wohnungen des Todes*, *Sternverdunkelung* (with the appended poems "Belonging to *Sternverdunkelung*"), *Und niemand weiss weiter*, and 1959's *Flucht und Verwandlung*, itself one long cycle composed of thirty-five poems on the dialectic of flight and metamorphosis (originally published by the Deutsche Verlagsanstalt). *Flucht und Verwandlung* represents a very clear shift in Sachs's poetry. There is a much more pronounced sense of mystical rumination and clear, sustained longing for transformation and return to a long-lost place or condition. Her view of life and the world changed rather drastically around 1959, owing perhaps to her increasingly serious health problems and the deteriorating political conditions she saw around the world.

Since the mid-1950s, Sachs had made the acquaintance of a number of important writers, among them poets Hans Magnus Enzensberger (1929–), Ingeborg Bachmann (1926–73), and, crucially, Paul Celan (1920–70), with whom she had an intense correspondence.[42] She met Bachmann and Celan for the first time at the award ceremony for the Meersburg Droste Prize in 1960—the first time she had returned to Germany since her flight in 1940. (Sachs refused to stay overnight on German soil, instead staying at a hotel in Switzerland and crossing the border during the day.) As a result of this encounter, both Bachmann and Celan wrote poems for Sachs, "Ihr Worte" (You Words) and "Zürich Zum Storchen" (Zürich, To The Stork [the hotel at which both Celan and

Sachs resided]), respectively. Enzensberger became a close friend and the primary editor of her work, and is today the executor of her literary estate. Since 1961, Suhrkamp has published Sachs's work. In the 1960s, Sachs continued to compose cycles, though she did not publish another full volume of poetry like the four reprinted in *Fahrt ins Staublose* (which also included the new cycles "Fahrt ins Staublose" (Journey into Dustlessness) and "Noch feiert Tod das Leben" (Death Still Celebrates Life). As of 1961, many of Sachs's individual poems, older and newer, were published in journals. The new cycles *Glühende Rätsel I–IV* (Glowing Enigmas; I and II published 1963/1964; III published in 1965; IV published in 1966), and *Die Suchende* (She Who Seeks, 1966) carry the ethos of *Flucht und Verwandlung* further, employing a vocabulary that is at once dense and sparse, focused on signs and signifiers, desperation in stasis, and darkness.

Writing became difficult for Sachs as her health deteriorated. After her travels following the Meersburg award, she was admitted to the psychiatric hospital at Beckomberga. Throughout the 1960s, she experienced different forms of therapy, including electric shock therapy, to combat her worsening paranoia. She experienced several heart attacks, and finally cancer, in addition to her paranoia, and spent much of the 1960s alternating between living alone in the small apartment in Bergsundsstrand and care at psychiatric clinics and hospitals. The psychosis appears to have laid bare that Sachs's calm, hard-to-read outward countenance concealed an unusual mix of anxiety and strength. As Fritsch-Vivié pointed out, Sachs even exhibited two very different handwriting styles—the ramrod-straight, slightly right-tilting script that is familiar to those who have read her letters and manuscripts, and very occasionally a much rounder, softer, more haphazard script.[43] In both states of clarity and states of desperation, Sachs continued to write poetry, and her papers at the Royal National Swedish library from this time contain a number of handwritten sketches and snippets of dramatic dialogue. Many of the poems she wrote during her time in psychiatric care explore the perspectives of her fellow patients or different states of awareness. Here again, then, she found beings on the margins of society or the borders of reality whose voices help us see through the illusions of normativity that govern everyday life.[44]

Sachs went on to receive prestigious literary awards and honors: she became a corresponding member of the Bavarian Academy of the Arts in 1963; she was honored with the Peace Prize of the German Book Industry in 1965, for which she made her second and final postwar trip to Germany, visiting Frankfurt for the prize ceremony and then Berlin; and on December 10, 1966, her seventy-fifth birthday, she was awarded—along with Israeli writer S. Y. Agnon—the Nobel Prize in Literature. Sachs and Agnon were awarded the prize for their work representing "Israel's message,"[45] Agnon for the actual State of Israel, and Sachs for the more abstract "Israel." The three-line autobiographical statement she submitted to the Academy reads:

> Leonie Nelly Sachs, born in Berlin on December 10, 1891. As refugee, arrived in Sweden with my mother on May 16, 1940. Since then living in Stockholm and active as writer and translator.

This statement, and her likewise very brief banquet speech in which she thanked Sweden and then read her poem "In der Flucht" (In Flight, from *Flucht und Verwandlung*) exemplify her contention that her work speaks for itself and that little attention should be paid to her biography.[46] At the same time, the identity conferred upon her by the Nobel honor was and is fundamentally at odds with both her poetics and the identity she constructed for herself. Ruth Dinesen writes that Sachs was constantly engaged in a balancing act between fixed identities: the German one she was born into while at the same time denied; the complex Jewish identity she was born into culturally, had foisted on her by the Nazis, and ultimately constructed for herself; the identity of writer; and the identity of outsider and exile. She belonged nowhere, and her work consistently probes both the pain and the benefit of that balance. Dinesen has pointed out that Sachs's later work contains poetic images of concepts like "Meridian, Äquator, Längen- und Breitengrade, Exil als Asyl, Flucht als Heimat" (meridian, equator, longitudes, and latitudes, exile as asylum, flight as homeland), commenting that they are "Bilder für ein neues Identitätsganzes" (images for a new composite identity). She goes on to say that this identity "wird in Frage gestellt, angegriffen und zerschlagen, will man sie einseitig auf eine jüdische Identität fixieren" (is placed in question, attacked, and obliterated if one wants to fix her one-sidedly in a Jewish identity), like the Nobel committee, among others, did.[47]

In a final act of reconciliation, Sachs was made, in 1967, an honorary citizen of her former hometown of Berlin. Health concerns prevented her from attending the ceremony. From 1967 to 1970, Sachs contended with her health problems and continued to write as best she could. Fioretos's descriptions of her work after *Flucht und Verwandlung* give the sense that she had moved beyond the need to write poetry that grappled with literary politics, concerns of form or formalism, or cross-genre play. It reads like lyric poetry in its purest form:

> Around 1960 Sachs' poetry took a new turn. From now on she would not just delineate and conjure silence, but try to transform it into a structural element of the texts themselves. The two principles she had named in the title *Flucht und Verwandlung* radicalized her poetry and freed it from the last remnants of the so-called "poetry of ruins" (*Trümmerlyrik*). The rhetorical pathos disappeared, the over-burdened vocabulary was abandoned. The poems were given a

steeper syntax and a metaphorical terseness which moved them ever closer to the "silence" that the last book of the 1950s declared "a new land."[48]

Many of the poems composed during the 1960s were published posthumously by her friends Bengt and Margarethe Holmqvist, who also oversaw the collection of her library and papers into the Nelly Sachs Archive at the Royal National Swedish Library in Stockholm. Nelly Sachs died on May 12, 1970, at St. Göran's Hospital in Stockholm. Finally, in 2010, her collected works, including unpublished texts—but unfortunately, still not her prewar texts, which she expressly forbade republishing—were published, in four volumes.[49]

2: Wandering and Words, Wandering in Words

T HE AESTHETIC AND POETIC ROOTS of images such as "So rann ich aus
dem Wort" (Thus I Ran out of The Word, 1959) or "Landschaft aus
Schreien" (Landscape of Screams, 1957), which clearly conceive of the
word and the poetic text as a "Raum" (space) and a "Weltall" (cosmos),
are located in Sachs's earliest compositions. In order to conceive of the
text as a landscape of screams or a space out of which one can run, one
must first regard it as a space in which one can move, a landscape that one
can traverse. Sachs's early texts show a consistent link between space and
words, and ultimately an association of words with space, such that the
text is a landscape, and the word itself a space that characters, the writer,
and readers attempt to navigate.

Sachs's prose texts of the 1910s to the 1930s lay a clear foundation
linking speech with landscape or space through a consistent pattern of
wanderers adept in speech juxtaposed with static characters who either
struggle with expression or are mute. "Eine Legende vom Fra Angelico"
(A Legend of Fra Angelico, 1921) and "Die stumme Nachtigall oder
Der Umweg zu Gott" (The Silent Nightingale Or The Detour to God,
unpublished, 1930s), for example, feature interactions between wandering speakers and static figures who possess some ability of expression
through means other than speech. The power dynamic that plays out
between them reads as an allegory of aesthetic conflicts encompassing
modes of expression, artistic agency, and the role of the audience in deter-
mining meaning. Static characters in Sachs's narratives succumb to the
wanderer's power, represented most often in the static character's inability
to distinguish literal from figurative language. Sachs makes the struggle
with figurative language in the empirical world and the aesthetic world
(that is, plays and stories) a main theme in the unpublished prose work
"Chelion: Eine Kindheitsgeschichte" (Chelion: A Story of Childhood,
1930s). "Chelion" is the story of a child who is learning to navigate a
landscape between the aesthetic world of plays and stories and the everyday world of her house and family, and is vexed by the conflict between
literal versus figurative language. Ultimately, the child learns that even her
own writing has consequences.

Because the narratives thematize wanderers skilled with words,
Sachs's prose contains a metanarrative where she as the writer is skilled

with words, and therefore a wanderer, which then places us as the readers within this metanarrative space and includes us in the dynamic of wandering versus stasis. The reader's task is to remain aware of the tools and skill of the writer; Sachs encourages the reader not to lose him- or herself in the text or take it at face value. The more critical distance we as readers maintain from the language of the wanderer, the more we ourselves become wanderers in the space of words, and thus we maintain our subjectivity and agency. This critical distance and agency is all the more important in the lyric poetic text, which as a genre demands more active engagement of the reader. By the mid to late 1930s, Sachs had generally abandoned prose for lyric poetry. In her prose, wandering or static characters interact in the main narrative, while the metanarrative involves the reader as a participant in a more general examination of modes of expression and interpretation; in the poetic text, there is no narrative. The text or the word itself is the space that the lyrical "I," the poet, and the reader must all navigate. The poem in question here, "Abschied, du Nachtigallenwort" (Parting, you Nightingaleword, 1938) examines a word as a space, and as such is a prototype for the later poems that clearly depict the text and the word as landscape and space.

Ultimately, it is important to recognize that Sachs does not view language, and especially not figurative language, as a safe space or refuge. These are the roots of the diasporic poetics that Sachs increasingly employs, a poetics that emphasizes the power of the wanderer to act as a challenge to hegemony. In the following examination of three early prose texts and one early poem, we will examine the ways Sachs has consistently linked the state of wandering with both the power to skillfully create with words and the power to remain at a critical distance from them.

Wandering and Stasis in Sachs's Early Prose

The earliest verifiable example of the dynamic of wanderer versus static character is the encounter of a wandering mother ("die Fremde," in this case both "the foreigner" and "the stranger," and notably female) and the painter-monk Fra Giovanni in the story "Eine Legende vom Fra Angelico." As the first story in her only published prose collection, *Legenden und Erzählungen* (Legends and Tales, 1921), this is Sachs's earliest known published text.[1] The story revolves around Fra Angelico, who was an actual painter and Dominican monk from Fiesole who lived from about 1395/1400 to 1455. He was known among his contemporaries as "Fra Giovanni" (his name in the body of Sachs's text) and was later known as "Fra Angelico" (his name only in the title of the story). Her choice to distinguish the two suggests that she was writing with the idea in mind that the artist one becomes is not identical with the private person one is. There is an art to creating the artist. Ruth Dinesen suggests that "eine Künstlernovelle als Einleitung zur ersten Veröffentlichung ist eine Programmbeschreibung. Und in der Tat enthält diese frühe Arbeit eine Kunstauffassung, die Nelly Sachs lebenslänglich vertrat." (a novella about an artist as the introductory story of one's first publication is indicative of the author's own program. And indeed, this early work contains a conception of art that Nelly Sachs represented her entire life.)[2] What Dinesen means is that the artist finds himself "vor die Aufgabe gestellt, in den irdischen Dingen das Göttliche zu erkennen" (placed before the task of recognizing the divine in earthly things); this is also reflected in the story's epigraph, "Ich weiß Gotts Konterfei: er hat sich abgebild / In seinen Kreaturn, wo du's erkennen willt" (I know God's countenance: he depicted himself in his creatures, where you will recognize it), a couplet from "Cherubinischer Wandersmann" by the German Baroque poet Angelus Silesius (Johann Scheffler, 1624–77). I would add to Dinesen's interpretation that the story also reflects Sachs's lifelong interest in the process of creating art and the role of an interpreting public; the story is first about artistic creation, and the role of both mechanical ability and inspiration within it, and second about how an audience interprets what the artist has created. It would appear, too, that the choice of Fra Angelico for these aesthetic questions is not coincidental. Preeminent Victorian art historian John Ruskin, whose writings on art were made available to the German public in the early twentieth century, discusses Fra Angelico in terms that resonate with Sachs's text. Angelico was known less for his technical skill than for his sensibility, and Ruskin discusses in particular his determination to depict the presence of the divine: "[Angelico] invariably uses inferior types for the features of humanity, even glorified (excepting always the Madonna,) nor ever exerts his full power of beauty either in feature or expression, except in angels or in the Madonna or in Christ."[3] Because Ruskin was internationally known for his interest in refining public taste, it is not inconceivable that a bourgeois family like Sachs's would have been exposed to Ruskin in translation. If Sachs was not reading Ruskin, she appears to have been influenced by someone who was.

"Eine Legende vom Fra Angelico" follows Fra Giovanni as he leaves his monastery to seek artistic inspiration in the forest. Once there, he encounters a small boy and his mother ("die Fremde"), who ask him to paint their portrait. He is hesitant, since he does not wish to paint earthly things, but after some consideration, he agrees, and as he paints the woman regales him with four tales from her travels. Fra Giovanni loses himself in these stories, but keeps painting, and finds that the virtue described in each story is also depicted in the features of the subjects he paints. The final tale sends Fra Giovanni into a reverie from which he awakens when his Dominican brothers find him the next day. His subjects are nowhere to be found, but they have left the painting, which Fra Giovanni interprets as rejection. He attempts to explain to the other monks what happened. His abbot suggests the painting is a divine creation, and the monks carry the painting back to the monastery to make it an altarpiece, as Fra Giovanni trails behind them deep in contemplation.

In this story, wandering is the condition that allows for creative expression, both with words and with visual art. The stranger is the first in a long line of wanderers who possess power with language. Although she is not a threatening character, as other wanderers prove to be, her gift for storytelling makes her the dominant presence in the narrative and disempowers Fra Giovanni, who falls under the spell of her stories. Woven into the narrative of the forest encounter between the stranger and the painter is a conflict of artistic agency, which is set up in the opening lines of the story when the narrator describes the monk contemplating the mysteries of life and his own ability to reproduce them on a canvas:

> Die Jahre, welche an Fra Giovanni vorüberzogen, waren von einer stillen und erhabenen Schönheit. Wäre es ihm beschieden gewesen, sie auf seiner Tafel festzuhalten, er hätte sie darstellen müssen, angetan mit einem blassen, rauschenden Gewand und silbernen Schwingen daran, auf ihren geneigten Stirnen einen Stern, aus dem ein ewiges goldenes Feuer glühte; in ihren Händen aber, irdischen Blicken entzogen, die Geheimnisse der Erde und des Himmels haltend.
>
> Fra Giovanni indessen, vergönnte ihrer äußeren Gestalt alsbald keinen Blick mehr, hingegen suchte er mit wachsender Sehnsucht die Dinge zu enträtseln, welche sie in ihren Händen trugen.[4]

> [The years that passed over Fra Giovanni were of a still and sublime beauty. If it had fallen to him to hold them fast on his canvas, he would have had to represent them in a pale, rustling gown with silver clasps, upon their lowered foreheads a star from which an eternal golden fire glowed; in their hands, however, withdrawn from earthly gazes, holding the secrets of earth and heaven.
>
> Fra Giovanni soon turned his gaze away from their outward appearance, and rather sought with growing desire to unravel the things they carried in their hands.]

Here the artist is engaged in the traditional mimetic project of seeking the truth to represent in his artwork, a task linked to the expression of that which defies expression and which gives Giovanni pause to consider his own artistic capabilities. The narrator describes Giovanni's dissatisfaction as he thinks about his paintings:

> Des öfteren freilich ward der fromme Bruder von einem tiefen Kummer überfallen. Dergestalt, daß er der Bilder, welche er bisher gemalt, mit Mißvergnügen gedachte, ja sie ihm plötzlich fremd und unberührt erschienen von der heißen Inbrunst seines Herzens.

Gleichwohl deuchte es ihm, als ruhe tief verborgen in seinem Innern ein golden schimmerndes Gewebe, unsagbar fein gesponnen aus den Fäden der Liebe und des Glaubens. (FA, 7–8)

[Ever more often, admittedly, a deep worry descended over the pious monk, such that he thought with displeasure on the pictures he had so far painted; yes, they seemed to him suddenly foreign and untouched by the hot ardor of his heart. At the same time, he felt that there rested deeply hidden within him a gold and shimmering fabric, finely woven of the threads of love and faith.]

Giovanni feels that he has much to express, but he cannot entirely grasp it, nor does he possess the skill to express it on his canvas. He kneels and asks God "ihm jene Kraft zu verleihen, die ihn fürder dazu befähigen sollte, seinen Sinn gänzlich von der eitlen Luft der Erde abzuwenden, und ihm, den Ausblick in die Sphären zu verstatten, in welche einzukehren seine Seele heftigstes Verlangen trug"; to *grant him* the power, the ability to see into the abstract spheres, so that he might find a way to articulate the depths he senses but cannot locate (FA, 8). The subtle content of this request is reflected at the end of the story, where it seems Giovanni was not asking to be a vessel for the divine, but rather hoping to be granted the ability to develop his own skill, to be granted admittance to whatever spheres the great masters occupied. Finding, understanding, and representing a magnificent subject are his primary aims, and they propel him out into the forest.

To recount the story in more detail: in the forest Fra Giovanni encounters a woman and her child; he judges from the woman's clothing that she is a foreigner and, despite her regal carriage and manner, a peasant. She answers that she is in fact not from here, confirming his assessment (FA, 10). The child tells him that his mother wants nothing so much as to have her portrait painted, and although it is not his objective to paint that sort of picture, he agrees to paint the portrait (FA, 9). The stories she tells while he paints are based on experiences she has had on her travels; she proves to be a literally spellbinding storyteller (FA, 9). Her ability to represent in words far outstrips Fra Giovanni's ability to represent anything on a canvas, and transports Giovanni into each story. The excellence of her storytelling has very much to do with the fact that she has wandered far and wide, and has thus found many sublime stories to recount, a wisdom, she tells the monk, he will not have had, living sequestered as he does in a monastery. Giovanni had come close to the same conclusion himself at the outset of the story, thus setting out into the forest, and indeed, in leaving his monastery he has found this new subject (which he nonetheless regards as merely earthly). In their exchanges, the stranger has the upper hand, lulling Giovanni into a kind of trance as she talks and he paints. She is one of the few characters whose power remains more or less sovereign and intact, with the exception that representing her ultimately falls to both Giovanni (as her portraitist) and Sachs (as the author of Giovanni's story).

As Giovanni emerges from his trancelike state after each story, he becomes aware of his subject and his artistic task: "Da die Fremde also gesprochen hatte, wollte es Fra Giovanni bedünken, als spiegele sich in ihren Zügen der nämliche demütige Ausdruck wider, dessen sie soeben . . . Erwähnung getan. Und er beschloß denselben, soweit es ihm gelingen konnte, auf seinem Bilde festzuhalten." (FA, 11; As the foreigner had thus spoken, it seemed to Fra Giovanni that the very humble expression of which she had just made mention . . . was mirrored in the stranger's own features. He decided to capture the expression on his canvas as best he could.) In painting this earthy picture he curiously finds the opportunity to capture something abstract: each of the stranger's four stories highlights a virtue, and as she speaks, Giovanni perceives the virtue reflected in her countenance and attempts to capture what he sees—as far as he is able. Although he makes a conscious decision after each story to focus on the painting, the stranger pulls the painter—and the reader along with him—into each successive story and away from his painting. The trancelike state Giovanni repeatedly enters culminates in a mystical experience, the description of which resembles the actual Fra Angelico's representation of the coronation of the Virgin Mary, with a host of angels playing musical instruments.[5] Giovanni feels himself driven to attempt to capture these, too, on his canvas. All the while engaged in seeking, understanding, and capturing mimetically the sublime features he first hears in the stranger's narrative tales and then perceives reflected in her facial features as she tells each tale, Giovanni, when he is aware of anything, is aware of the gulf between what he sees and what he feels capable of producing—as indicated by the use of the phrase "soweit es ihm gelingen konnte"—and is correspondingly amazed as he is drawn deeper into his own work. The narrative of this encounter fades with an ellipsis, without resolution or comment (FA, 11).

Awakening in the forest to find his abbot and fellow monks admiring the painting, he cannot entirely remember what has happened, but notices that the painting is still there, while the subjects, who said they wanted nothing more than for him to paint their portrait for them, are gone. Giovanni's artistic production thus encounters the interpreting audience. He is deeply upset that his subjects "verschmähten" (rejected) his work, then flattered and yet disconcerted by the abbot's suggestion that the painting is so perfect it is hardly believable that the hand of a human could have produced it (FA, 16). Giovanni sets forth the argument between artist and interpreting audience, insisting that the painting is merely a picture of an earthly woman and child, and tells them the story of what happened, making special mention of the stranger's storytelling. The narrator relates the response of the abbot (called "der Greis," the old man):

> Fra Giovanni, entgegnete der Greis kopfschüttelnd, es mag wohl so sein, wie du berichtest, allein zweifelsohne hatte Er, Gott in der Höh', indessen du dieses Bildnis schufest, deinen Blick aufgetan, jene Wunder zu schauen, die uns anderen Sterblichen verschlossen bleiben. Wie auch hätte es dir sonst gelingen können, vier der höchsten Tugenden in das Antlitz dieser jungen Frau hineinzuzaubern. (FA, 16)

> [Fra Giovanni, replied the old man shaking his head, it may well be as you say; but it is doubtless He, God on High, who has opened your gaze to paint this picture, so that you might see this wonder that remains locked away from us other mortals. How else could you have managed to conjure four of the highest virtues into the countenance of this young woman.]

Fra Giovanni concedes finally that there is something unusually abstract captured on the canvas; it would appear his call to God at the beginning of the story has been fulfilled. And yet, Giovanni does not rejoice. His fellow monks lift the painting and carry it to San Domenico to make it an altarpiece, rejoicing all the way. They are followed by Fra Giovanni, "mit nachdenklich gesenktem Haupte" (FA, 17; with his head sunk in pensive thought). He feels that the stranger, who requested the portrait, rejected the work, which he painted as if in a trance, and the abbot cannot imagine that Giovanni's hand alone has produced this picture. Giovanni is left to contemplate his total lack of agency as an artist.

Fra Giovanni's story suggests a number of things about Sachs's aesthetic interests at the time. In writing about a painter who seeks the essence of an object and is concerned with expressing the inexpressible, she was aware of and pondering the rules of aesthetics; in writing about a painter who seeks divine inspiration, but then, having received it, does not rejoice in it, she was pondering the agency of artistic production. Sachs was aware of the power of a good storyteller to literally remove readers or listeners from their faculties, and links the masterful wielder of words with wandering (whether the stranger is divine or not, she has wandered and tells good stories); and she is aware of the power of the interpreting audience. Whether or not inspiration is divine seems secondary to the point that active searching and wandering beyond the confines of home are necessary conditions for aesthetic expression: the masterful storyteller travels; Giovanni, who has limited his vision by staying in one place, finally produces a sublime painting by venturing outside his monastery.

Interestingly, the idea that wandering creates a better storyteller while stasis impedes expression is also reflected in the structure of the narrative itself. The story begins with an epigraph from Angelus Silesius's "Cherubinischer Wandersmann" ("Ich weiß Gottes Konterfei: er hat sich abgebild / In seinen Kreaturn, wo du's erkennen willt"),[6] which is meaningful in several ways. First, Angelus Silesius is a pen name that reflects both the divine (Angelus) and the earthly (Silesius—for Silesia, now part of Poland); the poet chooses to represent a very precise location, identifying himself with a particular region. Second, Silesius's collection of epigrammatic couplets carries the title "Cherubinischer Wandersmann," or "Cherubic Wanderer," thus establishing from the beginning that wandering equals insight. Third, in writing epigrams about recognizing the divine in all things—including human beings—Silesius is essentially engaged in the same task as Sachs: the trace of the divine is found in all things, but it takes an artist or poet and the attendant technical skill to make that clear to an audience. This is the theme of the narrative, and is reflected in the form and structure of the text.

Sachs exemplifies this conception of wandering in an abstracted way. The stranger can transport her audience (Fra Giovanni, and also the reader), because as a wanderer, she tells with skill the tales of virtue she learned in her travels. Sachs is also a storyteller, but her "travels," from which she has learned her stories and how to tell them, are textual in nature: she is well read, within literature (here, clearly Silesius, and the style of her language suggests Kleist[7]) and, as the story of "Fra Angelico" shows, in art and art history, as well. She has taken what she has learned in her textual travels and incorporated it here, to transport us first into the space of the painter-monk's tale, and then into the space of the stranger's tales. What she does for Fra Giovanni, Sachs does for the reader. We are left pondering the questions Fra Giovanni ponders. Is art technical skill or inspiration, and what role does the audience play in establishing the interpretation or the meaning of the artist's work? The "well-traveled" writer made clever use of all she had learned, and imbued her narrative texts with the aesthetic questions of agency, expression, and interpretation that continue to constitute a thread throughout her work. These questions are addressed in the power dynamics between the stranger and Fra Giovanni, God and Fra Giovanni, and finally the abbot and Fra Giovanni. Giovanni is always at the mercy of someone else's authority; we have the task as readers to maintain our autonomy, that is, to remain aware and critical of the authority of the author. Submitting to the power of the character who controls language, especially figurative language, not only leaves one powerless, but it can even have fatal consequences, as is the case in the short story "Die stumme Nachtigall oder Der Umweg zu Gott" (The Silent Nightingale or The Detour to God).

"Die stumme Nachtigall," an unpublished six-page story from a collection Sachs titled "Die Apfeltraumallee" (The Appledream Avenue), contains another variation of the wandering-versus-static dynamic.[8] Many of the stories in "Apfeltraumallee" deal with transgression and boundary crossing, and many begin with bars of music written at the top of the page. "Die stumme Nachtigall oder Der Umweg zu Gott" should presumably also begin this way, as the blank space following the opening line "Die Nachtigall singt:" (The nightingale sings:) indicates. Whether the absence of musical notation here is intentional, since it does reflect the silenced nightingale of the title, or was meant to be filled in later, the text begins with the clear indication that the nightingale will represent the role of wordless expression. The choice of the nightingale for this role is significant. Since antiquity, the nightingale has been a frequent metaphor for the poet, because its song is said to be extremely beautiful, highly complex, and difficult to imitate. Also, originating from the tale of Philomela and Procne,[9] the nightingale stands for the voice of someone who has been silenced, or is meant to transmit information to those who have the insight to understand it. To silence a nightingale is a grave thing, indeed. Sachs composed several texts involving silenced nightingales; in this story it is ignorance that renders the nightingale silent (it is not understood and thus "silent," and then dead and literally silent). While the constellation of elements in this story differs from "Eine Legende vom Fra Angelico," it presents the same dynamic of wanderer-wordsmith and static figure struggling with expression.

"Die stumme Nachtigall" is the story of a little girl who lives in the woods with an adoptive mother who knows the secrets of herbs. The little girl cannot speak, but instead has as a companion a nightingale, whose song and gestures speak for her. One day, a young scholar comes to the woods in order to study the secrets of nature with the old woman. She sends him with the girl to collect flowers and stones, and he is astonished that the girl can communicate with animals but cannot speak with him. Over the course of his stay in the woods, he attempts to explain God and the wide world to her, encouraging her to speak and to see the world as he does; but she either cannot or will not. He also tells her that to find God, one must seek Him resolutely, and the more she resists his instruction, the more insistent he becomes. When it seems he will make no progress with her, he simply falls silent. At the onset of autumn, he decides to return home to his fiancée, whom he will marry at Christmas. As they make their goodbyes, the nightingale lands on the girl's shoulder and sings a song so sad that the young man tears up and says the song of the nightingale would be the loveliest wedding gift he could give his bride. That December, the little girl and the nightingale set off into the wider world to seek God like the young man told her, and to see if they can manage to attend the wedding, so that the nightingale can sing. The bride and bridegroom find them just as they freeze to death.

This text focuses on communication through language: the wanderer is a young scholar who has entered the woods to learn the mysteries of nature, and the static figure is a girl in the woods who is mute. The narrative enacts a struggle between them, a struggle concerning language. The young man speaks and thinks the girl should, too; the girl cannot and/or refuses to try. The resulting tension between them is mediated by the nightingale's song, which the young man interprets as mere decoration, but which for the girl has meaningful value. For the young scholar, the beauty of the nightingale's song is incomprehensible, except as an object to possess and bestow as a gift to his bride, and aesthetic in a purely decorative sense;[10] for the mute girl, the nightingale is a lifeline. It is her only recourse to vocal communication, and therefore carries deep meaning—for those who have the insight to understand and appreciate it. But as the nightingale's song lies outside of logos, and therefore reason, it is without meaning for the young scholar; for him, language is the absolute value, a system into which knowledge can be organized, which is the reason he comes to know this mute girl in the woods to begin with. Like Fra Angelico, who wanders into the woods to find inspiration, and the stranger, who has wandered far and wide and gained knowledge, the young scholar comes into the woods because "[e]r wollte die Kräuter erlernen, . . . und die Geheimnisse der Natur erforschen" (he wanted to become proficient in herbs and come to know the secrets of nature).[11] He intends to study with the old woman; but in order to find things in the forest, the old woman pairs him with the young girl, who "nur schwer wußte . . . sich in der Sprache der Menschen zu verständigen" (SN, 57; hardly knew how to make herself understood in the language of humans). He is perplexed by this girl, who apparently has nothing to fear from animals in the woods, and yet, Sachs's narrator tells us, it seemed to him "als hätte er niemals ein törichteres Wesen erblickt wie dieses Waldmädchen. Kaum ein Wort hatte er mit ihr auf Menschenweise wechseln können." (SN, 58; that he had never seen a more foolish creature than this forest girl. He could hardly exchange a single word with her in the manner of humans.) Logos is clearly his basis for wisdom and value, and, as Sachs repeatedly stresses, the girl has no faculty for it. He thus attempts to teach this system of value to the girl: "Er versuchte es wohl dem Kinde von der großen schönen Welt zu erzählen, aber als sie ihn gar so hilflos anblickte, schwieg er." (SN, 58; He tried to tell the child of the wide, beautiful world, but he fell silent as she but stared at him helplessly.) He stands in an estranged position to nature and wordless communication, the natural environment of the girl, which is further underscored by the passage where the young man first encounters the nightingale:

Der Jüngling aber wunderte sich sehr über das Kind. Mit schmeichelnder Hand wandte sie ihm die Angriffe der wilden Tiere ab. Des Abends aber, wenn er Abschied nahm flog eine Nachtigall vom Baum, setzte sich auf ihre Schulter und sang ihr Lied, so wehmütig schön, daß der Jüngling sich in eine ferne unerkannte Heimat versetzt glaubte. (SN, 58)

[The youth puzzled over the child. With flattering hand she stopped any animals attacking him. But in the evening, whenever he took his leave, a nightingale flew down from the tree and sat itself upon her shoulder, and sang a song so wistfully beautiful that the youth believed himself transported to a distant unknown homeland.]

In this moment, the young man has the opportunity to appreciate the significance of the nightingale and the power of expression beyond the word, represented in his feeling transported, displaced by the beautiful song. If this carries any comprehensible meaning for him, however, he does not show it. Frustrated by the girl and unable to appreciate her wordless manner of communication, but aware of her respect for nature, he relies on the power of words to explain to her metaphysics and the concept of God, of which she is unaware. He begins to speak "leise und immer eindringlicher" (SN, 58; quietly and with increasing urgency), praising the creator of the things she values most, describing nature as "Zier" (decoration) on the seam of the cloak of the eternal (i.e., nature is mere decoration; what he sees as the power behind it, God, is the important thing). The critical words of the story are spoken here, when the young man tells the girl, "Du mußt Gott nur recht suchen . . . damit er dir den Weg weiset, welcher zu Ihm führt" (SN, 59; You must but seek God resolutely . . . so that he shows the way that leads to Him), a figurative prescription she fatally misunderstands.

Come the autumn, when the young man decides that he has learned enough from nature, the nightingale sings its—and the girl's—final goodbye, to which the young man remarks, "wenn dieser Gesang . . . von meiner Braut vernommen werden könnte, so wäre dies wohl das schönste Hochzeitsgeschenk, welches ich ihr darbringen könnte" (SN, 59; if this song . . . could be heard by my bride, that would be the most beautiful wedding present I could bring her). He fails to comprehend that the song functions as the girl's voice, just as the nightingale itself is an extension of the girl's physical being, and departs none the wiser. He has not adapted to the ways of the forest, his attempt to colonize the girl's mind has failed, and he returns to his world.

The young man's turn of phrase "Gott nur recht suchen," however, propels the young girl to do just that: in December, she and the nightingale set out into the woods to literally seek God, who, she says in her wordless fashion that Sachs only describes as a language of the heart, apparently does not live with them in the woods, but perhaps out in the wide world (SN, 60). While they are out looking, they plan to stop at the young man's wedding, so that the bride and groom might hear the nightingale's song. The unprecedented singing of a nightingale in the dark winter night draws the attention of the wedding pair, who find the girl and the nightingale just as they freeze to death, the girl in the arms of the young man and the nightingale in the hands of his bride. In this way, it seems, the girl and the nightingale have indeed found the "detour to God" of the title.

Whereas in "Fra Angelico," the power of words gives rise to questions of artistic agency, in this story the power of words raises questions of interpretation, and finally proves fatal. What is more, words are clearly depicted as a tool for domination. The tone of the narrative establishes the girl as the innocent protagonist and the young man as the antagonist. Though he does not bear her ill will, he does believe she should think and communicate like he does, and words are the tool he uses to accomplish this task. Finding the girl foolish, he tries to enlighten her to his way of thinking; when she resists, he does not try to understand her way of thinking or communicating, but rather becomes increasingly adamant. When it is finally clear that he will not win, he gives up. He has, however, left an impression on the girl, and because she has no sense of the distinction between figurative and literal language, she understands "seek God" literally, and then sets out to do it. Wandering in an unknown landscape in winter, ill-equipped to think critically about the young man's words and therefore looking for a thing she does not understand, the girl perishes. The young man meant she should find God through study and contemplation, but she inadvertently finds a different, unexpected route to her uncertain destination.

In this story, negotiating the space of words uncritically by trusting in the innocence or authority of language (and by extension the author), that is, by assuming the benign authority of the author or the innocence of meaning, is dangerous. If we read the young man as the allegorical author, and the girl as the allegorical reader, then the aesthetic observation Sachs weaves into this text implores the reader to regard the author's words carefully. Language, and in particular figurative language (in this case "seeking God"), is not a place of refuge or asylum. It requires the reader to do critical work to avoid relinquishing subjectivity or losing the self. The story also tells us, in the figures of the forest girl and the nightingale, to be mindful that things that look very simple often are not; the girl could not express herself in words, but the nightingale marks her as something more than what she seems to be on the surface.

Additionally, since Sachs indicates that she is aware of and therefore critical of the power of a person who controls language, it seems unlikely that she does not also proceed carefully with her own writing. Her stories clue us in to consider the power an author has to make skilled use of language. Sachs carefully chose the words she wrote for a particular effect, and while that may seem obvious, it apparently has not always been, considering how many critics have written off especially her early work as simple, or merely sweet and nostalgic, as is the case with the next piece I will consider.

Sachs took care to make clear her vested interest in enacting her own aesthetic questions of agency and meaning in the unpublished prose text "Chelion: Eine Kindheitsgeschichte" (Chelion, A Story of Childhood), composed in the 1930s. "Chelion" is less a story than it is a series of vignettes told by a narrator from the perspective of a little girl. It is thought to be somewhat autobiographical, or at least reflective of Sachs's own childhood.[12] Chelion lives in an apartment in the city with her parents, several servants (most importantly her nanny Teresa, the kitchen maid Sophie, and a later nanny, Magda), and her dog "Flock" (Flake). The text is largely made up of her interactions with the people in her household and her experiences going to puppet plays, markets, visiting her grandparents, and dealing with school. Her mind is occupied throughout with words people use, and the concepts of parting and death. Most of the vignettes narrate how Chelion perceives the world around her and the words she hears. Quite often, she is amazed or perplexed by an adult's use of a word, sometimes within the everyday world of her home, and sometimes as part of a play or story. Examples under consideration here include interactions with Teresa the nanny, and Chelion's experience viewing the puppet play "Genofeva." Occasionally, Chelion shares her perception of the world, but the adults do not understand, and if they ask her to clarify, she finds that she cannot, for example in interaction with her father. And in two sections, Chelion discovers her own power with words, when she intervenes in a matter of the heart on behalf of the kitchen maid Sophie, and when she gets her nanny Magda to agree to her conception of heaven; both lead to bittersweet insights, the first about parting, the second about death. Throughout the series of vignettes, Chelion learns that there is a darker side to the words she hears, or that pleasant similes and metaphors mask something unpleasant, and in the instance of Sophie, she learns that sometimes adults use words that are usually used negatively to indicate something positive. All of this comprises the experience of a child who is learning to navigate language as if it were a landscape; Chelion is trying to navigate the space of words, a space that is always unstable and despite its often sweet sound, potentially threatening. The tone of the text is generally saccharine, though always with a threatening undercurrent, so that the content is reflected in aspects of the form.

It is not clear when in the 1930s Sachs began to write "Chelion," but a drastic change in tone towards the end suggests that it may have been completed after the rise of Hitler and the National Socialists. Although the text was never published, the research of Ruth Dinesen has revealed that Sachs read at least part of the text at an event sponsored by the Central-Verein deutscher Staatsbürger jüdischen Glaubens in 1937. A review in the April 6, 1937 edition of the Zionist newspaper *Jüdischer Rundschau* described

"Chelion" as a "Versüßlichung von Kindergefühlen" (schmaltzy children's emotions),[13] which evidently prevents it from having either social relevance or political appeal—which is true enough if one fails to perceive the resonance of Chelion's semantic troubles for the politicization of aesthetic production or aestheticization of politics, or indeed the general warnings any of Sachs's earlier prose texts carry regarding the power and authority of anyone skilled with language. "Chelion" is a lengthy engagement of metaphorical language in all its spaces, from the everyday to the theatrical, from the point of view of a kind of functional silence: Chelion's misunderstanding of and constant reflection on adults' use of everyday language, perceived finally as an extension of theatrical, poetic language.

"Chelion" shifts the confrontation with language from the forest to the twentieth-century metropolis, and concentrates on specific ways in which the urban landscape of language can confuse and disrupt. The reader experiences the mystification of language and its power through the eyes of Chelion, who is continually confronted with the instability of meaning and interpretation. She herself occupies both the roles of wanderer and static figure. She is not speechless; in fact, unlike her textual predecessors she persistently attempts to integrate herself into the landscape of words, but many of her experiences involve misunderstanding metaphors and figures of speech. In her interaction with the people in her life, she struggles to differentiate the empirical world from the world of stories or plays, or from her dream world. Words have the power to transport her, and she sometimes becomes trapped (i.e., when she cannot communicate, either because of a misunderstanding or because she is completely withdrawn into her dream), but twice she manages to bring the empirical world and the figurative world together in her own use of words.

The reason Chelion's difficulty with words is so important is that it reflects her intense difficulty negotiating the master narrative into which she is supposed to integrate. Chelion is trying to make sense of the world she must learn to navigate. She must learn to understand meaning, distinguish the literal from the figurative, and she must learn to communicate appropriately. If she does not, she will never integrate into society, leaving her always in someone else's power. Quite often when her attention is drawn to a word, the experience is linked to some kind of transgressive behavior. Already on the second page of the story, Chelion, instructed by her nanny, Teresa (Chelion's first guide into the space of words) to stop combing her doll Rosamunde's hair, is struck by a mystifying word:

> "Laß das Kämmen" sagt Teresa, das Kindermädchen, zu Chelin [sic], "du verdirbst Rosamundes Locken, sie sind nur künstlich Chelion." Und Chelion läßt ab von ihrem Vorhaben aber sie wundert sich das [sic] Rosamunde künstliche Locken hat.[14]

["Leave off the combing," says Teresa, the nanny, to Chelion, "you will ruin Rosamunde's curls, they are only artificial, Chelion." And Chelion leaves off her task but is puzzled that Rosamunde has artificial curls.]

Sachs never spells out what Chelion envisions "künstlich" to mean, but she is clearly puzzled by the notion that her doll's hair is artificial.

Throughout the text, individual words arrest Chelion's attention, often transporting her into another realm, and sometimes being transported themselves. As Teresa and Chelion read "Sleeping Beauty" in the "Oblatenalbum" (a scrapbook and storybook which Chelion regards as her favorite "Ort," or location, in which she spends time), the word "spindle" travels to her:

"Siehe hier, Chelion, Dornröschen sticht sich mit der Spindel in die Hand, und augenblicks wächst die Rosenhecke um das Turm-gemach.["] Spindel, denkt Chelion, und es ist ihr, als schwömme dieses Wort wie ein Kahn herbei aus fremden Lande, befrachtet mit einer Last von Feenschleiern. (C, 5)

["Look here, Chelion, Sleeping Beauty pricks herself on the spindle, and in a moment the thorn bush grows around the tower chamber.["] Spindle, thinks Chelion, and it seems to her as if this word floated like a vessel to her from a foreign land, loaded with a cargo of fairy veils.]

At once attractive and frustrating, the word "Spindel" is alienating and comes to Chelion from a foreign country; the word instantly becomes a visible object (though not the one it usually signifies), one that is like a veiled and misty boat.

The words that capture Chelion's attention, for example "Spindel" and "künstlich," are linked for her with unpleasant experiences: Sleeping Beauty pricks her finger on the spindle, and Chelion is told she is ruining her doll's artificial hair as she combs. Words that puzzle Chelion often are in some way associated with pain or transgression. Teresa takes Chelion to the theater one day to see a marionette production of the story of Genofeva and Siegfried, an experience that is profoundly confusing for Chelion. In the action of this children's play, Chelion is confronted not only with figurative language she misinterprets, but also the larger idea that beauty and metaphor can be used to obscure or even enact evil. At the beginning of the second act of the play, Chelion sees a character referred to as "der Veilchenfarbene" (the violet-colored man; presumably Siegfried's steward Golo, who plots to seduce Genofeva) kneel before the lady Genofeva and speak "viele Worte die Chelion nicht verstehen kann" (C, 19; many words that Chelion cannot understand).

Chelion then becomes aware of a discrepancy between what she sees and what she hears: the violet-colored man speaks of "umgarnen" (literally to wrap in yarn; here: to pull the wool over someone's eyes) whereupon Chelion whispers to Teresa that she has seen no "Garn" (yarn); Teresa tells her, "das wäre anders gemeint" (C, 19; that's meant in a different way). "That's meant in a different way" and "you won't have understood that" come to be refrains in the story; Chelion invents her own metaphors comfortably enough, but negotiating the landscape of conventional metaphor or figurative usage proves to be frustrating and disillusioning, as the conclusion of the Genofeva interlude demonstrates. Chelion leaves the theater confused by the fact that she is sad when the experience was so beautiful, and also concerned about the consistent discrepancy in the play between beautiful words and evil deeds. For Chelion there is no clear distinction between the world of fiction and the everyday world she occupies, and whereas she might sometimes be chastised for this childish inability to discern, the disillusionments she experiences, for example that beautiful words often conceal reprehensible acts, or that words rarely mean what they are "supposed" to mean, are all too relevant in the "real" world. If she cannot learn to distinguish and negotiate both worlds, she will not to able to communicate. This sometimes silences her, for example in a conversation with her father: "Chelion hat den Vater gefragt warum die Aepfel [sic] so traurig seien, da sie doch weinten. Aber wo siehst du denn ihre Träne fließen, hatte der Vater gefragt. Doch darauf hatte sie nichts zu erwidern gewußt." (C, 4; Chelion had asked her father why the apples should be so sad, since they were crying. But where do you see their tears flowing, her father asked. But Chelion did not know how to answer that.) Chelion is surprised to learn that others do not see the world as she does. She also comes to recognize that there can be a dark sense ("dunkler Sinn") even in her nanny Teresa's words, though it almost always remains the case that Chelion does not understand the meaning of that dark sense (C, 22). The dark sense of words is increasingly woven into the text itself. Toward the end, there is a section called "In der Dämmerung" (At Twilight), which begins with the ominous sentence "Es ist die Zeit der großen Dämmerung" (C, 77; It is the time of the great twilight). It seems that this may refer to Midsummer, for which Chelion, her friend Ännchen, and their teacher Fräulein Ulla are making flower wreaths. And yet, the entire section has a more uneasy feel; a forest of shadow grows in their room, a wild tree outside shakes water from its branches, the dog is doing something Sachs calls "Flammenlecken" (flame-licking), imitating the licking flames of the fire. Everything in the room is somehow agitated or tired. Ännchen has two stickers, one with a swallow, the other with an island in the sea depicted on it. Under each stands an English word, and Fräulein Ulla tells the girls that they will "diese Worte selber erlernen" (learn these words themselves): "Farewell" under the swallow, and "Nevermore" (C, 77–78) under the island. This literally means that they will learn these words, that is, in English, one day; but the ominous tone of the section and the consistent theme of a dark sense in words gives this remark the feel that Fräulein Ulla and the narrator are insinuating that Chelion will soon learn the depths of meaning in the words "Farewell" ("ein 'Abschiedswort,'" a word of parting) and "Nevermore" ("es bedeutet, was nimmer wiederkehren würde," it means something that will likely never return; C, 78).

As Chelion learns to navigate the space of words in the everyday, adult world, replete with double, increasingly sinister meaning, and becomes increasingly aware that words rarely mean what they literally "should" mean, Chelion also comes to realize that she has some control over language, and that her own acts of language can have repercussions. When Chelion finds Sophie the kitchen maid crying, Sophie explains: "Es ist wegen Herrn Mond, Chelion, und daß ich nicht soviel Taler habe, die er in seinen Strumpf stecken kann. Du wirst es noch nicht verstehen." (C, 27; It's because of Mr. Mond [literally, Moon], Chelion, and that I don't have much money for him to stick into in his sock. You wouldn't understand that yet.) With "You wouldn't understand that yet," Sophie simply means that Chelion is too young to understand love. What Chelion does not understand, however, is Sophie's turn of phrase regarding the moon, the money, and the sock. Chelion mulls over the literal meaning of these words she cannot understand for some time, staring out the window of her room looking for the sock that the moon has knitted for Sophie's money. When Chelion comes to find out that Herr Mond is their postman, Fritz Mond, who has been romantically involved with Sophie, and that he has threatened to leave Sophie because of her financial situation, she is moved to action—in the form of writing. Chelion personally hands Herrn Mond a note she has written, which he deciphers with great difficulty:

> liber Friz Mont
> bite pleip sofi gut. si kan nichs dafür si had keine taler imm Strumf si
> steigd sonnst in ein frües Grap.
> grus chelion. (C, 28)

> [deer Friz Mun
> stay gud to sofi. she cant help it shes got no mony in the sock
> or els she wil clim into a erly grav.
> greetings chelion.]

Sachs takes care to present the reader with Chelion's disruption of language that has to be "entziffert" (deciphered) by its intended audience. In her attempt to act, she disrupts linguistic order by using her best understanding of sound and signifier, both in terms of spelling and in her direct quoting

of Sophie. Rather than recasting the discussion in her own words, she rep-
licates words and symbols she clearly has not entirely understood. Through
this disruption, Sachs forces the postman in the story and the reader outside it to think through the layers of misunderstanding, demanding that we
recognize the process of the figurative constructions of not having enough
Taler for one's stocking and what is presumably Sophie's melodramatic
early grave[15] as we decipher Chelion's note. This part of the narrative goes
on to assert that every author has power. Chelion comes home from a trip
to her grandparents' house to find that "Auch Sophie ist nicht mehr da.
Aber die Mutter sagt, daran trüge nun Chelion selber die Schuld, denn
Herr Mond hätte Sophie geheiratet." (C, 55; Sophie isn't there anymore
either. But Mother says that Chelion herself is guilty, because Mr. Mond
married Sophie.) The conflict between figurative and literal language,
which up to this point in the story has revolved around pleasant words
masking unpleasant things, evidently flows in the other direction as well.
Chelion's mother uses the word "Schuld" (literally, guilt) in an approving,
doting manner, but as Chelion interprets words in a literal sense, she feels
guilty: Chelion was very close to Sophie, and as the author of the note that,
however unintentionally, led to Sophie's departure, she is also the author
of her own unhappiness. Chelion finds that writing (even her own simple
words) has consequences.

The other instance where Chelion is in control of language is in a
scene at a market where she is confronted with the fishmonger who is
killing fish. Chelion suggests to her nanny Magda that, logically, since the
adults have told her that birds and people go to heaven, fish must, too.
In applying the symbolic logic she has taken from the adults, she gets her
nanny Magda to agree to her conception of heaven and whether fish go
there. It is the only time in the story that someone says to Chelion, "es
ist wohl schon so, wie du sagst, Chelion" (C, 80; it must be just like you
say, Chelion).

"Chelion" thematizes a conflict between metaphor and literal meaning by having us see the struggle to differentiate the two through a child's
eyes. This strategy allows us to reconsider the words or turns of phrase we
use so often that we do not notice how figurative they are; at the same
time, we are privy to the child's perception of the world and her attempts
to describe it in language she sees as literal but that adults cannot follow.
Because several instances of misinterpretation involve plays and stories, we
see that the conflicts between metaphorical and literal meaning and literary and everyday language are parallel and overlapping. Metaphorical language is not only found in literature; everyday speech is filled with such
language, which is easy to overlook until we see it from the perspective of
someone who struggles to see the difference. Chelion's experience learning to navigate this landscape gives us a chance to reflect on how difficult
and powerful words are.

Perhaps "Chelion" is "Versüßlichung von Kindergefühlen," but—and the content of the story can certainly support this possibility—the tone may be strategically devised to underscore the point that style can be a sleight-of-hand gesture that obscures or distracts from the content. Whether in the world of stories or plays, where an author may try to make a subtle comment, or avoid censorship or conflict, or in the everyday world, whether we are trying to avoid telling children about death, or love, or in the realm of politics, where a politician may try to avoid conflict, or a dictator may try to avoid arousing suspicion, style can be used to obscure meaning. One of Sachs's greatest role models, Swedish Nobel Laureate Selma Lagerlöf, used in her prose a simplistic style in which she subtly embedded social commentary. Jennifer Watson has argued that Sachs appears to have modeled "Chelion" on Lagerlöf's childhood memoir "Mårbacka"; the styles are similar, using uncomplicated grammatical structures and simple vocabulary, and, Watson correctly notes, while this style is not unusual for Lagerlöf, "this simplicity was not typical of Nelly Sachs."[16] Indeed, even a cursory comparison of "Chelion" to the "Fra Angelico" excerpts in this chapter demonstrates that quite clearly. Sachs obviously cultivated this deceptively simple style for "Chelion." Watson also notes that Lagerlöf's "impression of artlessness is misleading," since closer examination reveals carefully constructed narrative structures, as well as social concerns embedded in a façade of conventional new Romanticism.[17] Both Lagerlöf and Sachs embedded social commentary in their conventional narrative styles, and because Sachs wrote stories about people constructing and interpreting stories, her texts invite us to be part of the reader/writer dynamic she examines or critiques.

Within the story "Chelion" itself, Sachs never broaches the topic of politics, but one wonders whether the audience who heard excerpts from "Chelion" read aloud in 1937—four years into Nazi rule, two years after the introduction of the Nuremberg Laws, and one year before the annexation of the Sudetenland—heard the resonance, or the "dunkler Sinn" in the words of "Chelion." The story sets Chelion as the protagonist, and so the reader must learn, as Chelion does, to think carefully about authorship and authority, the deeper meaning of metaphor, and the power of acts of language.

These three prose pieces composed and/or published between 1920 and 1940 present the basic issues to which Sachs returned repeatedly regarding the space of words: words and texts are spaces in which one can wander and create, but one cannot or should not feel secure in those spaces. The clever wanderer does not assimilate or impose his or her will on others (both lead to powerlessness in the texts we have studied so far), but does adapt to each situation. If Fra Giovanni could learn to see what he wants to paint without being placed in a trance, he would maintain artistic agency; if the young scholar or the forest girl were better prepared

to adapt to new environments, they might not have been rendered powerless, and the forest girl would not have died. Chelion is most successful
when she finds a way to balance figurative and literal language in her own
speech or writing. Fluidity in the space of words is powerful for authors,
characters, and readers. Stasis robs us of our agency.

Exploring the Space of Poetry

Sachs's 1938 poem "Abschied, du Nachtigallenwort" (Parting, you
Nightingaleword) also advocates engagement and movement over stasis,
but in a different way than her early prose. In moving from examining
Sachs's prose to examining her poetry, we must change what we expect
from the text, and in so doing, reorient ourselves in the space of the text.
We know, for example, that Chelion regards books as an "Ort," a location, a space in which she can wander. She is transported into this space,
in which the landscape is made up of words and images. She traverses, for
example, the story of "Sleeping Beauty." The words and images describe
people, places, and events in a progression, a "causal sequence,"[18] so that
Chelion traverses a landscape that is mimetic and narrative, and the reader
does also. As readers like Chelion, it is our task to carefully consider the
words that make up that landscape. Are they only what they appear to
be literally, or is there a different side, a darker side—in short, can this
landscape have more than one appearance? How and why does a landscape change, and how do its changes affect how we wander in it? If we
do not know how to proceed, we become static and trapped. In prose,
the possibility exists for concurrent narrative landscapes. Because lyric
poetry reflects on or analyzes an experience rather than telling a story, the
landscape of the lyric poem can go in many more directions, and because
there is no sequential plot progression, a lyric poem establishes its own
particular kind of time, which is essentially always "present."[19] This provides for a much more uncertain landscape, a space that can take on many
appearances and shift constantly. The wanderer in such a textual space has
a much more demanding task if he or she is to maintain his or her agency.

The philosopher Gaston Bachelard, although writing in the postwar
era about both text and architecture, describes lyric poetry in a way that
helps articulate it as a space: "the reader of poems is asked to consider an
image not as an object and even less as the substitute for an object, but to
seize its specific reality."[20] I would add that the poem itself is its own specific reality. The poem is a space like the story is a space, but it does not
necessarily describe people, places, and events, it rather asks us to consider
the words in and of themselves. Consider the way Chelion reacts to the
word "Spindel." That is a poetic moment in the text, where the word is
removed from its context and even from its representative function; the
word itself becomes an object that floats toward her from far away, like a

boat. If her reverie had continued, Chelion might well have climbed into the word "Spindel" and examined it as its own specific reality. The word itself becomes a space for us to explore. This is the shift that happens in Sachs's poetry from the 1930s onward.

Sachs was fascinated by wordless forms of expression, as we know from her letters as well as her poems; her earliest poems, which treat dance and music, probe the possibilities of capturing such wordless forms of expression in semantic form. Many of her poems seek a language beyond language, in keeping with the language crisis of the nineteenth and early twentieth centuries (most famously expressed in German literature in Hofmannsthal's Lord Chandos letter); yet she appears, from the treatment of language in the stories discussed above, to have no illusions about the power of language or the power of the writer. Perhaps the poem from the early texts with the most concentrated response to the space of the word, in which the writer pits herself against the word, is "Abschied, du Nachtigallenwort" (Parting, you Nightingaleword), published along with four other of Sachs's poems in the Jewish cultural journal *Der Morgen* in May of 1938.[21] While certainly no longer well known in its 1938 form, the notion of "Abschied" as a "Nachtigallenwort" may be familiar to readers from the 1949 poem "Abschied—" from Sachs's volume *Sternverdunkelung* (Eclipse of the Stars), for which the 1938 poem is the prototype,[22] and in which Sachs takes up much of the imagery from the earlier poem and develops it further, thus presenting a clear textual example of a significant link between themes and images in her pre- and postwar poetry. The basis of this poem is a word of space and dispersal, *Abschied,* but rather than writing a traditional poem of *Stimmungslyrik* (atmospheric poetry), as for instance Gertrud Kolmar does in "Nach Osten send ich mein Gesicht" (1932), or Rose Ausländer does in "Du gingst von mir, gefolgt von meiner Ruh" (1939), or Else Lasker-Schüler does in "Aber du kamst nie mit dem Abend—" (1914–43), Sachs addresses the word *Abschied* itself:

Abschied, du Nachtigallenwort,	Parting, you nightingaleword
Das sich zu Gott versang,	That sang itself off to God,
Du Tränenkrug, drin hier und dort	You tearjug, in which here and there
Ein Schluchzendes ertrank.	A sobber drowned.
Küßt sich in dir ein Schwalbenpaar,	Does a swallowpair kiss itself in you
Das auseinanderzieht?	that withdraws from one another?
Trennt dich der Tod, ein leises Haar,	Does death part you, a quiet hair
Das Lieb von Liebe schied?	That separated love from love?

Abschied, an act implying distancing, becomes itself a landscape explored and interrogated by the writer. As it is a spatial term, the taking of leave and distancing oneself from something, it is all the more interesting that Sachs then turns it into its own object, in that the poet asks what can part parting. The writer takes leave of the traditional representation of and confrontation with the experience and moves into the textual interrogation of the poetic word itself.

What should be stressed here is the understanding of the word as a space in which events occur. Here the power of the writer over and with words is both enacted and called into question. Sachs engages the power of conquering the inexpressible through expression, while pondering that the inexpressible ultimately thwarts the attempt to conquer it through expression. "Parting" is a word that objectively expresses a situation (it can be used in a poem, and the reader understands what is meant), and yet captured in the lines "Du Tränenkrug, drin hier und dort / Ein Schluchzendes ertrank" it is ultimately a container that overpowers the I who tries to put it into words. The person who sobs and chokes in it, drowns in it. The space of the word is deadly, and so the poet has taken the word as an object to examine, standing at an estranged distance, describing what she knows of it, asking what happens within it, and finally posing the question of what will finally break it apart, in the way it breaks things apart, and neutralize it. "Abschied" as a "Nachtigallenwort" marks two linked phenomena: the nightingale, a traditional metaphor for the poet, speaks for those who cannot speak;[23] it also represents an attempt to express what is inexpressible in words.

As the poet puts forth the word as an object to examine, writing it, describing it according to its attributes, Sachs ends the poem with what, grammatically speaking, would be the "parted" form of the word if it were separable (which it is not): schied. Cutting "Lieb" from "Liebe" leaves only an "e," which cannot stand alone (thus love is reduced to a meaningless fragment); although "ab" can be a separable prefix (one that signifies a thing that has been cut off or separated, in fact), as part of a noun it is no longer separable. The verb "scheiden" does mean "to separate" or "divorce"; it also yields in its past-tense form the fragment that would be left of "Abschied" if it were parted. The poet has in fact parted parting, and so she disrupts the space of the word, testing the deadly, deceptive hold it has in the poem, and in so doing in fact performs the word. Because the poem ends with a question, the dialogue remains unfinished, although the poetic act of destabilizing the authority of the word has been achieved. In line with the thought process of the prose works, language has not so much been overpowered or succumbed to as engaged: the act of the word has been performed, but in the process of critically approaching it, a paradox is exposed rather than a victory claimed.

The Spaces of Words,
Dominance, and Gender in Sachs

In the works examined here, speech and text are linked in various ways to "space": characters who wander (the stranger, the young scholar, and sometimes Chelion) control words, whereas characters who are static (Fra Giovanni, the forest girl, and sometimes Chelion) struggle with expression, so a character's relationship to and position in space is in direct correlation to his or her expressive capabilities. In "Chelion," texts are regarded as locations, and speech is regarded as a landscape that must be navigated; and in the poem, the word "Abschied" becomes a space that is explored. In Sachs's various treatments of the space of words, the emphasis on wandering and marginality (since so many of her characters exist on the margins of society) reflects elements of a diasporic rather than an exilic poetics. Whereas the exilic longs for return and redemption, the diasporic, based on dispersal and wandering, is more fluid and acts more frequently as an agent of challenge to hegemony. In the early texts the diasporic nature is reflected in the emphasis on the wanderer having a powerful position. The work of the wanderer to challenge the status quo is much more clearly represented in the "Merlin" text treated in the next chapter; in the four texts that have been treated in this chapter, the challenge exists in the dynamic between the wandering and the static, which yields the aesthetic observations that question artistic agency and the authority of the writer. As such, the texts themselves represent a challenge to the aesthetic tradition, a challenge with which Sachs's early texts have rarely been linked. These texts are but four examples of an aspect of Sachs's poetic and prose work that has never been analyzed, namely its literary-critical aspect. By creating her own new narratives that draw on, incorporate, and mimic texts and artists of the past, she creates meaningful patchworks of past and present, textual spaces that, as Bluma Goldstein writes of Heinrich Heine's "Hebräische Melodien," reflect a connection between "multiple cultures across vast areas of space and time."[24] Within the four works treated in this chapter, Sachs makes a concerted effort to demonstrate that language, especially figurative or poetic language, is not innocent or divine, but a creation that must be regarded from a critical distance, regardless of the author. Those who do not assimilate but instead challenge the spaces of words maintain their sovereignty; they do not dominate, nor are they dominated. For Sachs it is not a matter of finding the sacred, innocent origin of language; it is a matter of making thoughtful, active use of what one has. Ultimately, the space of the word itself is a space that must be wandered in, not settled.

Sachs consistently links the spaces of words with dominance, which on the one hand allows her marginal characters to expose the inherent violence of language, and on the other hand also submits them, and the author herself, to the same critiques: is language ever innocent? Should the readers/listeners subject themselves to the author? Sachs, by giving form to her artistic concerns, interrogates the uses of storytelling in terms of power differentials and domination. She subtly places the reader in a position to question as well. There is, moreover, a gender dynamic in the prose texts that indicates that Sachs was consciously grappling with women's then-standard symbolic role as that which must be protected and preserved by men. It cannot go unnoticed that the figures whose most significant attribute is speechlessness (here: the forest girl and Chelion) are almost always female, and that the two characters who are restrictively rooted in a system of thought (Fra Giovanni in his sphere of Greats, the young scholar in his Logos) are both male—in fact, both men are convinced that the empirical world is a frivolous distraction, whereas girls and women appear to value both empirical reality and abstraction (in music or in word) equally.

It is interesting to note that Sachs insists on making her speechless girls the heroines of the stories they inhabit—active heroes whose actions are firmly centered in their inability to communicate appropriately, which throughout their stories is perceived as a weakness, but in the end manages to accomplish what masculine feats of strength or rhetoric fail to do. The forest girl's sheer resistance to the young man finally silences him; when Chelion manages to write her error-ridden note, she effects real change. What Sachs's depictions advocate by way of allegory is still rooted in some sense of gender-specific roles; yet the relative value of these roles is destabilized, in that the men of action or words are not always the dominant force, and in that those traits that might be understood as weak and feminine are ultimately presented as valuable. The system Sachs constructs here, then, is not one that recognizes a specific set of male traits or roles that are always dominant and useful and an opposing female set that are submissive, but rather recognizes a more fluid conception where values change with the situation, so that speechlessness becomes an act, beauty is not merely admirable but also significant, and dominance through speech or scientific classification can ultimately be reductive and (self-)destructive.

In its subtle approach, this conception of gender mirrors Cheryl Walker's in her reading of the American educator and advocate Catherine Beecher (1800–1878), who "consistently advocated a position that, while seeming to yield all authority, would subvert male power and, quite without appearing to do so, dominate through the force of subtle influence."[25] The wandering female stranger whom Fra Giovanni encounters in the woods does this as well; her subtle yet powerful storytelling undermines Giovanni's set conception of art. That this character occupies the role of storyteller/wanderer, unlike her female counterparts, suggests just how fluid Sachs saw these gender roles. Watson has argued that Sachs's role model Selma Lagerlöf's female characters also, "through the very guise of female servitude, determine the outcome of events. Their agency undercuts the convention of female passivity and illuminates Lagerlöf's submerged feminist agenda."[26] Sachs's characters, however, are not always interested in dominance, or even equal footing. Instead, they value action and self-preservation. This also has relevance outside of purely gender-oriented discourse, in the tradition of resistance to or coexistence with dominant hegemonic forces.

One space in which this struggle plays out in the early twentieth century is the space of words, which was regarded by numerous writers and critics as a reflection of and indeed even as a prescription for national identity. A kind of "nation narration" was at stake in the twentieth century in the perceived symbiosis of literary production and nation. This prescriptive symbiosis began in the seventeenth century, with Martin Optiz's (1597–1639) *Buch der deutschen Poeterey* (Book of German Poetry, 1624), where he suggested that the way to a clearly defined Germany is through the creation of good German poetry. Eighteenth-century thinkers carried the idea forward, most notably Johann Gottfried Herder (1744–1803), who noted in his 1773 essay "Von deutscher Art und Kunst" the incompatibility of antique and Romance tradition with Germanic tradition. The nineteenth-century drive to create and maintain the nation-state placed great value on art and national character, and found expression also in more marginal (often immigrant or diasporic) social groups attempting to secure a voice in a national narrative. German authors, for example, sought to valorize a long "Germanic" tradition in literature; in the wake of social and political reforms, especially in Germany, some Jews, like Heinrich Heine, sought to defend their ability to write "German" literature. Some Jewish publishers and critics, on the other hand, went the other direction and urged writers to resist secularization by writing "Jewish" literature, a position that had various ties to Zionist politics in both Jewish and German-nationalist journalism.[27] This symbiosis of national character and literature appears to play a role in Nelly Sachs's works from the 1910s to the late 1950s, and seems in some cases to account for variations on the motif of language as a landscape, where acts of speech or writing reflect power struggles between dominant and marginal figures or cultures. The construction of a national literature proceeds hierarchically: there are great masters and those who aspire to reach that level of mastery (and thus gain admittance to the presumably stable, sovereign, dominant culture). Nelly Sachs's aesthetic questions probe the viability of that hierarchy. In the prose text "Wie der Zauberer Merlin erlöset ward," from *Legenden und Erzählungen* (1921), the topic of the following chapter, Sachs reframes the mythic material of Merlin the sorcerer in her wandering versus stasis dynamic in order to explore the hierarchy of narration and representation.

3: Sachs's Merlin the Sorcerer: Reconfiguring the Myth as Plural

SACHS HAD A LIFELONG FASCINATION with the figure of Merlin the sorcerer. Although the archive collections contain Merlin fragments and texts she wrote right up to the end of her life, she published only one: "Wie der Zauberer Merlin erlöset ward" (How Merlin the Sorcerer was Saved, from *Legenden und Erzählungen*, 1921). This text allows us an opportunity to contextualize Sachs's authorial interventions within the spectrum of Merlin narratives and consider the significance of her choices. Because we possess so few drafts of texts by Sachs, and because she is frequently understood, as Fioretos recently noted, as a vessel rather than as a writer, this provides rare and important insight into the conscious action of the artist. Sachs's various Merlin pieces suggest that she was aware of different Merlin source texts and also major themes across the generations, especially narration and fiction versus factual history, Merlin's dualistic nature, and Merlin's relevance for addressing contemporary political, national, and social problems. Into the Merlin narrative tradition Sachs weaves strands that engage with German literature and gender roles, and that hint at a concern with the rhetoric of race, national identity, and the power of hegemonic forces to shape myths that define and validate their position at the expense of the voices and experiences of those who are deemed outsiders. Ultimately, "Wie der Zauberer Merlin erlöset ward" makes the point that every "definitive" story, whether it is the legend of an individual or the history of a nation, is the result of interpretative choices that obscure numerous other perspectives.

From the twelfth century onward, regardless of epoch or language, the figure of Merlin has been a complex presence of trustworthy wise man and feared supernatural power, nation builder and outsider, manipulator of events and seeker of justice. He is the son of a virgin mother and a phantom father. He possesses the ability to tell the future, the ability to see and hear across great distances (allowing him to be everywhere at once), and power with words, which is manifested in both his rhetoric and the spells he casts. He foretells the end of King Vortigern's rule by interpreting the battle between the red and white dragons beneath his tower. He brings about dynastic rifts, exposing—either by persuasion or sorcery—concealed motives, jealousy, or disloyalty. Merlin both prophesies and helps orchestrate the accession of Uther and Pendragon, and then the conception of King Arthur. He is responsible for the sword in the stone, and he moves Stonehenge to Salisbury Plain. He helps both Uther and Arthur establish the Round Table and Camelot, a kingdom of fairness, justice, and tolerance. He travels throughout Britain (and later Gaul) involving himself in political and social matters. He has the monk Blaise write down the events and context of his life as a guide and a history of Britain for future generations. Eventually, Merlin meets a nymph, sorceress, or wise virgin called Viviane (also known as Nynianne or Nimuë), who either tricks him into being trapped in a rock or bush, or becomes his consort and they choose to retire together to the *esplumoir*, a kind of pocket in space that is invisible, but which is (at least for a short time) permeable to sound. Merlin remains trapped in this other space forever.

Sachs's Merlin text expands especially on the blurred boundaries and dualities of the Merlin tradition. The significance of the monk-scribe and the play with the boundary between fact and fiction, myth and history are fertile ground for Sachs's interest in the power dynamics surrounding figurative language, while the character of Merlin represents a confluence of many recurring themes in Sachs's body of work. Merlin is a wanderer who possesses power with words as a persuasive counselor and spell caster. He is a wise, marginal figure, like the prophets, sorcerers, seers, and fairytale figures in both her early and later work: he has an all-seeing gaze, like the Baal Shem Tov, the Chassidic master who is referenced in many of her postwar texts; he interprets events and dreams like a sibyl or the Biblical Daniel; and he explicates the folly of human nature, as so many of her postwar poems do. Merlin is made up of dichotomies, a feature that not only resonates with some of the figures who appear in early and later texts (like Melusine or Silenus, who are half human and half beast, or characters who are wise fools or foolish scholars), but also resonates with the fundamental attribute of her postwar poetry: it examines the dialectical relationship of, for example, forgetting and memory, life and death, art and reality, justice and revenge, or even the complex existence of Israel as idea and as place.

The narrative tradition of Merlin also provided Sachs a suitable framework in which to explore the dynamic of wanderer and static forest dweller. Sachs adds to the Merlin context a female character, Gotelind, who is shy and simple and lives in the woods, but is the vessel of a magic song. The Gotelind storyline allows Sachs to push the limits of the tension between myth and authenticity inherent to the Merlin tradition. It also allows her to introduce a reference to Germanic tribes, and allusions to the Romantic symbol of the blue flower and the Faustian trope of two souls. Sachs maintains the convention of a truth claim in Merlin texts, while adding radically new plot developments with the common theme that stories of any kind are often a tool for exercising control or securing dominance.

A Summary of the Story

"Wie der Zauberer Merlin erlöset ward" comprises a very dense nineteen printed pages, and tells the story of how Merlin, through an encounter with a young woman in the forest, loses and regains the "fromme Seele" (pious soul) he inherited from his mother.[1] It begins as Merlin, who carries within him the dark arts of his father and the gentle, pious soul of his mother, is on his way to visit the scribe Meister Blasius (Blaise). Because he can see and hear over great distances, he overhears the Knights of the Round Table speaking ill of him, and sends demons to punish them for their hypocritical behavior. He also intervenes in people's lives beyond Artus's (Arthur's) court to create situations that require people to confront their illusions and the lies they tell themselves. He then encounters a sleeping shepherd girl named Gotelind at the edge of a forest whose goodness and innocence he decides to test. He makes one of her goats disappear, and after watching the trouble this causes between her and her adoptive mother, changes his appearance to that of a handsome noble-man and returns the goat. Gotelind is speechless, and he tells her the only thanks he requires is that she agree to meet him again the next day. Over three consecutive days, Merlin attempts to lull Gotelind to sleep with gentle words and fantastical stories. He gets her to tell him about her life; most importantly, she recounts the tale of how she came to possess inside her a magic song that can protect her, but that she can only sing three times before she must pay with her life. Merlin, who has thought him-self omniscient, has never heard of this song, and so decides to proceed more carefully with Gotelind. As he finally nearly succeeds in lulling her to sleep, the magic song sounds and wakes her up. It also causes the soul Merlin inherited from his mother to fly into Gotelind's safekeeping. He tells her to keep it well because he will need it someday, and he departs.

Without the gentle soul of his mother, Merlin's powers of persuasion are neutralized. Satan calls upon him to go to Gaul and cause discord among the Germanic tribes trying to found a realm of their own race, but without his soul, his attempts fail. He longs to return to Gotelind and his soul, which displeases Satan. Satan provokes Gotelind to attempt suicide, so that he might thus win both her soul and Merlin's, but the song stops her. Unable to overpower Gotelind, Satan instead decides to waylay Merlin by leading him to a white thornbush, where he discovers Nynianne. Merlin fails to heed Nynianne's figurative warnings and in his attempts to gain her favor casts spells he cannot control. He and the white thornbush disappear in fire and lightning. Blasius, who was accompany-ing him in order to write down what happened, returns to Artus's court to beg for help in finding and freeing Merlin. Artus sends his knights with Blasius; only Gavain (Gawain) survives the journey, but he is soon cursed by a woman he fails to properly greet and rides away. Blasius then goes to find Gotelind, the keeper of Merlin's soul. As he and Gotelind arrive in the forest where Merlin disappeared, they hear a crying voice and know it is Merlin's. Gotelind starts her song, and a dark tower made of demons appears before them. The demons fly away to reveal the white thornbush, and within it, a cowering, aged, and animal-like Merlin. As his soul returns to his body, he becomes aware of himself again and Gotelind runs to embrace him. Blasius leaves them alone together.

When Blasius returns the next day, he finds them dead beneath the thornbush. He is saddened and regretful, but praises the wisdom of the Creator for taking Merlin and Gotelind before Satan could. As he digs their grave, a dove flies overhead and drops a seed in the dirt, where first one blue star-shaped flower, and then many such flowers grow. Blasius plucks one to bring to Artus as proof of what happened.

Artus takes the flower and puts it in a golden vase as if it were a holy relic; he declares the flower a sign from God to remember that resisting the devil and bringing souls to holiness only requires the will of a pure and steadfast heart. Blasius returns to his hermitage to finish writing the story of Merlin. His final act as author of the story is to name the miraculous blue flower and the place where Merlin and Gotelind lie buried.

What Sachs Retains from Her Source Texts

Sachs's primary interest appears to be the unresolvable tensions at the core of Merlin's story and Merlin's character; and indeed, Peter H. Goodrich asserts that it is precisely Merlin's many tensions—between authentic and inauthentic narrative, reality and illusion, good and evil, the pagan and the Christian, the chronicler and the storyteller, wisdom and folly, etc.— that account for his longevity and, perhaps more importantly, his cultural adaptability.[2] Although Germany does not have the extensive Merlin tradition that Britain and France have, he does appear in isolated instances in medieval and early modern German literature, but, as Ulrich Müller points out, "the great magician and sorcerer in Middle High German romances dealing with Arthur and the Grail is not Merlin but Clinschor."[3] Clinschor maintains his presence in German literature in the nineteenth-century rediscovery of medieval romances, most popularly in Novalis's (Friedrich von Hardenberg, 1772–1801) unfinished novel *Heinrich von Ofterdingen*, where he is the master storyteller, and Richard Wagner's (1813–83) opera *Parsifal*, an interpretation of Wolfram von Eschenbach's (ca. 1170–1220) epic *Parzival*, where he is the emasculated lord of a magical castle filled with exotic women who distract the knight Parzival from his quest to find the Holy Grail. German Romantics, however, also took up the Merlin tradition, as Goodrich writes, "emphasizing Merlin's demonic inheritance, nation-making powers, and internment by his beloved."[4] Christoph Martin Wieland (1722–1813) brought Merlin back into the literary consciousness with summary and commentary in his *Teutscher Merkur* in 1777, and in 1804 the German translation of the twelfth-century French vulgate, or

"Prose Merlin," appeared, initially claimed by Friedrich Schlegel, but later attributed to his wife, Dorothea Schlegel (daughter of Moses Mendelssohn, the founder of European Jewish "Haskalah," or Enlightenment). Müller notes that "Merlin, as depicted by the Germans of the nineteenth century, was a combination of romantic love for nature and for a woman, of 'Weltschmerz' as well as of male anxiety and panic."[5]

Johann Wolfgang von Goethe (1749–1832), Ludwig Tieck (1773–1853), Ludwig Uhland (1787–1862), Karl Leberecht Immermann (1796–1840), Heinrich Heine (1797–1856), and Nikolaus Lenau (1802–50) all produced Merlin texts that revolve around the wise wild man ultimately trapped by a woman. A handful of late nineteenth-century and early twentieth-century German writers continued working with the Merlin tradition in the vein of the Romantics, among them Gerhart Hauptmann (1862–1946) and Paul Heyse (1830–1914),[6] and of course, Sachs, whose text also deals with Merlin's dualistic inheritance and his role in nation-building, but whose Merlin loses one side of his inheritance, is trapped as a result of ensuing vulnerability, and is then liberated by a woman.

Sachs's Merlin is drawn primarily from Dorothea Schlegel's 1804 "Die Geschichte des Zauberers Merlin," which is a translation of the French vulgate that was composed at least in part by the late twelfth-century cleric Robert de Boron, and from Karl Leberecht Immermann's 1831 drama *Merlin: Eine Mythe* (which was also inspired by Schlegel's translation, as well as by Wolfram von Eschenbach's *Parzival* and by Novalis's *Heinrich von Ofterdingen*). Both texts have distinguishing features that resonate in Sachs's legend, and indeed a number of passages in Sachs's Merlin text are clearly adapted from Schlegel's translation, for example:

Schlegel:
Da stand Merlin auf, entfernte sich ungefähr einen Bogenschuß weit von ihr, *brach eine Ruthe ab, und machte damit einen Kreis um sich her.* Dann ging er wieder hin, und setzte sich neben der Jungfrau nieder. Nach einer kleinen Weile blickte sie von ungefähr nach dem Ort hin, wo er den Kreis gezogen, *und siehe da, es kamen Damen, Ritter, Fräulein und Edelknechte daher spaziert, hielten sich bei den Händen angefaßt, und sangen mit so lieblicher Stimme, und so herrliche Weisen*, als man niemahls vorher dergleichen gehört.[7]

Sachs:
Er erhob sich, *brach eine Rute vom Strauche und zog damit mannigfache Kreise. Und siehe, es kamen Ritter, Fräulein und Edelknechte dahergeschritten, und sie hielten sich an den Händen gefaßt und sangen in süßester Weise* . . . (M, 71)

Da er nun eines Tages ganz schwer-müthig und in tiefe Gedanken versenkt in einen Wald ritt, *begeg-nete ihm ein Fräulein, auf einem der schönsten schwarzen Zelter reitend,* den man sehen konnte. [. . .] Die Dame selber war *in weißen Atlas gekleidet,* und ihr Gürtel von Seide und sehr reich gestickt; *den Kopf hatte sie in einen dicken Schleier gehüllt,* um sich gegen den Sonnen-brand zu schützen[8]

Gavain aber, da er glücklich in den Wald von Broceliande gelangte, *begegnete einem schönen Fräulein, welches einen prächtigen, schwar-zen Zelter ritt. Sie war in weißen Atlas gekleidet und ihr Antlitz von einem dünnen Schleier verhüllt.* (M, 75)

Der schöne Busch aber und die lieblichen Blumen auf den frischen Rasen blieben stehen, weil das Fräulein den Merlin gar sehr darum bat, daß es möchte stehen bleiben, und *sie nannte den Ort: Wonne und Trost.*"[9]

Die Stelle, allwo Merlin und seine traute Freundin unter dem Weiß-dorne ruhen, hieß er: *Wonne und Trost.* (M, 78)

The content Sachs retains that specifically links her text to Schlegel and Immermann relates to the mission of the Knights of the Round Table and the details and significance of Merlin's origin. The de Boron vulgate version that Schlegel translated was the first text to connect the Merlin material with Joseph of Arimathea, whose task of guarding the Holy Grail was passed on to the Knights of the Round Table, and was the first text to introduce the specific detail that Merlin is the son of Satan, rather than the son of an unspecified incubus. Immermann's drama maintains the grail link and amplifies the significance of Merlin's dual heritage in his relationship to Arthur and the knights' mission. Sachs's knights are also the heirs to the grail mission, and Sachs appears to have taken a cue from Immermann and made Merlin's dual heritage one of the central focuses of the story. In all three texts Merlin possesses the supernatural power of his father and the essential goodness of his mother; he is there-fore uniquely positioned to cross magical, moral, and ethical boundar-ies forbidden to Christians. Merlin commits objectionable deeds, but in pursuit of justice in the Schlegel and Immermann texts, and in an effort to expose hypocrisy and self-righteousness in Sachs's text. Both Schlegel and Immermann essentially tell a story of civilizing Britain through the spread of Christianity, aided primarily by the marginalized, demonic-yet-Christian Merlin and his friend the scribe, Blasius. Sachs keeps the roots of these texts, and retains the spirit of the Merlin tradition to highlight the contribution of outsiders to the civilization that condemns them, but casts these in a narrative with vastly different (though contextually appropriate) stakes. Sachs's Merlin text is a story about the power of interpretation and the illusion of a seamless, singular identity.

Sachs's Major Changes to the Merlin Narrative

The Merlin and Gotelind variation of the wanderer versus stasis dynamic bears the hallmarks of Sachs's concern with the power of figurative language and people who can negotiate its use. Language is the common currency of power in the narrative, and most characters in the story are defined by their relationship to it. Merlin's main tools are spells, stories, and persuasion; Meister Blasius is "wohl bewandert in der Schreibekunst" (M, 59; well traveled in [i.e., experienced and good at] the art of writing); Gotelind struggles to speak; Nynianne uses "zweideutig[e] Wort[e]" (M, 71; words with double meaning), which the vulnerable Merlin fails to heed; Kay is an idle boaster and sycophant, Lancelot slanders Merlin and upbraids the knights, and Gavain's curse is the result of his failure to address a lady whose path he crosses. Even the song inhabiting Gotelind speaks to her, we are told, in a wordless language (the nightingale in "Die stumme Nachtigall" speaks similarly to the girl). Where words fail, Gotelind and the song have the power to liberate Merlin from his entrapment. As usual, the entities that are most associated with wandering (Merlin, Blasius, Gotelind's song) possess the most power over others.

However, Gotelind's story also presents an opportunity to challenge Merlin's customary power and authority, not by confronting him with a traditionally competitive adversary, but by confronting him, essentially, with self-awareness. He does not consider Gotelind a threat; she does not possess the attributes he is accustomed to associating with an opponent. Instead, the life story she recounts for him makes him aware that he is not omniscient. Merlin is historically the character that knows all, that others cannot grasp or see through, who is more than is immediately apparent, whose appearance can change, who is unpredictable and cannot be bested. Sachs's addition exposes this fixed belief as a presumption, and introduces a character that, even for Merlin, is an enigma. Because he has never heard of this kind of magic, he does not know how to overcome it. This is very similar to "Die stumme Nachtigall," where the girl succeeds in resisting the efforts of the young scholar, who is then silenced. He, of course, eventually leaves the forest unharmed, while the girl perishes having misinterpreted his figurative expression. In the Merlin text, both Merlin and Gotelind are at the mercy of someone else's figurative language, and in the end, they both die in the forest. In "Die stumme Nachtigall," the girl finds a detour to God in death; in the Merlin text, Merlin is "erlöst," which can mean liberated, saved, delivered, or deceased, all of which apply. "Erlöst" as liberated is often meant in the sense that a fairytale prince liberates a princess; in this story, then, Gotelind functions as the prince who frees Merlin, who occupies the princess role. "Erlöst" as saved means to rescue someone from a dangerous situation or condition, and again, here Gotelind functions as the hero. "Erlöst" as deceased indicates that God has relieved someone of suffering in life, although it is important to point out that in this story, it is not clear how Merlin dies. On a larger scale, we can also interpret Sachs as the liberator, since she has effectively liberated Merlin from his conventional omnipotence, omniscience, and eternal entrapment; ironically, the noun "Erlöser" (Deliverer) is a common epithet for Christ, and Sachs delivers Merlin from the Christianity he serves in other Merlin stories.

Both Merlin and Gotelind draw their power from a symbiotic but contrasting internal duality, which allows Sachs to combine the conventional duality of Merlin with the Faustian trope of two opposing souls, but with an unconventional outcome. Merlin, like Goethe's Faust, has two diametrically opposed drives within him: his father Satan's dark arts and wisdom, and the "fromme Seele" of his mother (M, 62). When Faust tells Wagner "Zwei Seelen wohnen, ach! in meiner Brust, / Die eine will sich vor der andern trennen"[10] (Two souls, alas! reside within my breast, / and each is eager for a separation), he laments the opposing nature of these two souls, or drives, the one earthly and the other spiritual. Immermann also draws on this tension for his Merlin. Immermann's Merlin is an "unglückliches Doppelkind"[11] (unhappy double-child), whose struggle between the diametrically opposed drives within him (demonic and heavenly) forms the foundation of the plot. When the Blasius character (Placidus) tells him to declare who he is, Merlin replies: "Sterbliche Hülle vaterlosen Kindes, / Die arme Waise Himmels und der Erden, / Unsel'ges Fertigsein und Nimmerwerden, / Vom weichen Öl der Schwäche nie gelindert, / Von Liebe nicht befeu'rt, vom Hasse nicht gehindert!"[12] (Mortal husk of a fatherless child, the poor orphan of heaven and earth, unholy completion and never-becoming, never soothed by soft oil of weakness, not ignited by love, not hindered from hate!) This Merlin feels he can never be whole, because he belongs neither entirely to the heritage of his father nor entirely to the heritage of his mother. Early twentieth-century Germanist Harry Maync, the editor of the 1906 edition of Immermann's *Werke*, specifically links this struggle with *Faust I*:

Satan ist der Herr der Welt und der Sinnlichkeit, der Vertreter des bunten Scheins und des Genusses, und als solcher der Urfeind der christlich entsagenden Überweltlichkeit. Er zeugt den Merlin mit einer reinen Jungfrau, um sich durch ihn die Welt von Gott zurückzugewinnen. Aber durch seine Mutter gehört Merlin zugleich Gott an; zwei Seelen wohnen in seiner Brust, wie sie in jedem einzelnen

Menschen leben. Er strebt, die Menschen von diesem Widerspruche zu erlösen, Sinnlichkeit und Sittlichkeit, Leib und Seele, Materie und Geist miteinander in Einklang zu bringen. Damit stellt er sich sowohl über Satan wie über Gott.[13]

[Satan is the Lord of the world and sensuality, the representative of colorful appearance and of pleasure, and as such he is the archenemy of Christian transcendence. He sires Merlin with a pure virgin in order to reclaim the world from God through him. But through his mother, Merlin also belongs to God at the same time; two souls dwell in his breast, as they dwell in every single person. He strives to free people from this contradiction, to bring sensuality and morality, body and soul, matter and spirit into harmony with one another. Thus he places himself above Satan and above God.]

Ultimately, Immermann's Merlin rejects the satanic side in favor of his Christian maternal soul. In his final confrontation with Satan, he is mortified to realize that even when he acts on his Christian intentions, the results benefit Satan. He nonetheless refuses to ally himself with Satan, and dies in the white thornbush declaiming the Lord's Prayer. He has, as Maync explains, the intention of demonstrating that the two sides need not operate at odds. Yet Immermann's Merlin, since he dies embracing only one side of his being, succumbs to the despair that leads Faust to counsel Wagner "Du bist dir nur des einen Triebs bewußt, / O lerne nie den anderen kennen!"[14] (You only know the one driving force, / and may you never seek to know the other!). Sachs's Merlin text approaches the issue of opposing drives from a different perspective.

Maync writes in his introduction that Immermann had planned an "'erlösten Merlin'";[15] perhaps Sachs followed through on that intention. Sachs also brings her Merlin to the realization that his two sides inform one another; but rather than have him struggle to bring them into cooperation, she explores the implications of reducing anything to only one of its constituent parts. Sachs's Merlin's dual inheritance is also oppositional (demonic and pious), but he does not struggle between them; on the contrary, he believes he only acts according to his paternal side. Her Merlin is unaware that the soul he inherited from his mother affects him at all; it appears to sleep "wie eine gefangene Prinzessin inmitten der Dornhecke" (M, 62; like a trapped princess concealed in thorns). Sachs then separates the two parts by having Merlin lose the pious soul of his mother when he attempts to abduct Gotelind. As soon as it is gone, he is rendered nearly powerless. His demonic side requires his pious side, and only when he possesses both irreconcilable parts is he whole.

The coexisting parts are not, as Immermann conceived of the issue, two sides of one coin, but instead two separate entities that come together in one space. Merlin contains both his maternal and paternal heritage, and Gotelind and the magic song form a symbiotic composite in which one cannot survive without the other. When they lose possession of one component, they not only lose their power, they lose their ability to survive, since the power they each possess makes them dangerous outsiders, a threat and an object of envy. Merlin only commands his dark powers and persuasive words, a threat to the moral privilege of the knights and defense against other sorcery, when he is in possession of both his paternal and maternal inheritance. Gotelind's possession of the magic song wards off aggression and saves Merlin, but it also arouses violent jealousy in the village she once called home, and is a threat to Merlin. We are thus led to believe that Gotelind would not survive without the song, and the song cannot survive without a host; even so, once she sings it a third time, it will exit her body to find a new home and leave her lifeless. Merlin loses his sense of self as a result of losing the soul he inherited from his mother. Sachs's Merlin text aims for awareness: of self, of other drives, of other perspectives. Reducing a person to one side of their composite self weakens their impact. Ultimately, this relates to an overarching theme in the story, that any singular identity or narrative (i.e., omniscient, good, evil, simple, Christian, pagan, German, etc.) one constructs for oneself (or others) obscures plurality of elements or perspectives. Sachs's Merlin text goes on to make a similar point about narratives through the addition of the blue flower.

The "blaue Wunderblume" (M, 78; blue miracle flower) becomes a metaphor and a symbol for Merlin and Gotelind's story. First one and then many grow from their grave; Blasius plucks one to take back to Artus as "Beweis" (M, 77; proof) of what happened. The blue flower, then, stands as an abstraction for their story. Blasius could have simply told the story, or presented Artus with the text he is writing, but he instead brings the miraculous new flower as representative for the story, and as a representative example of all the other blue flowers that he did not choose to bring Artus. This flower is one of Blasius's interpretations of the story: it represents what he *thinks* happened. He did not see what happened to Merlin when he disappeared, because he was some distance away; he left Merlin and Gotelind alone after they were reunited and found them dead the next day. Since Merlin and Gotelind are dead, he will never know their story. Tasked with recording all that Merlin says and does, Blasius must act as chronicler as best he can. He tells Artus a story, with the flower as proof; but, since we know he was not there, it is proof of events he cannot know and can only interpret as he thinks right. Artus does the same. He places the flower in a golden vase "gleich einer heiligen Reliquie" (M, 78; like a holy relic), and proceeds to give it his own interpretation: a symbolic reminder to the knights, on which they swear that the will of a steadfast heart is all it takes to bring souls to holiness. Thus the blue flower—one of many, and representative of events for which there is no witness—becomes *the* blue flower. It, and many others, grew from the grave of two outsiders whose lives were largely governed by magical (and therefore difficult to grasp) events, and is now a token in the service of the Christian king. Merlin and Gotelind cannot tell us their stories; they have been mediated for audiences, first by Blasius and then by Artus.

This blue flower is likely meant to allude to the blue flower from Novalis's *Heinrich von Ofterdingen*, which became and remains a definitive symbol of German Romanticism. The texts are certainly related: *Heinrich von Ofterdingen* contains the storytelling Merlin figure Klingsohr, and was one of the inspirations for Immermann's drama. More to the point, Sachs's Merlin story and its blue flower reflect the philosophical and poetical underpinnings of Novalis's unfinished novel, which, as Azade Seyhan has written, is "a configuration of various literary forms which narrate the story of their own historical and formal production."[16] Heinrich's story is a series of encounters, based on mythical and legendary figures, that evoke the uncertain boundaries between creation, reflection, and representation. The blue flower he dreams of at the beginning of the book is the first image in the narrative that represents both memory and interpretation and the tenuous position between them. As Heinrich lies in bed thinking about "[der] Fremde und [seine] Erzählungen"[17] (the stranger and his stories), he desires "die blaue Blume . . . zu erblicken"[18] (to get a glimpse of the blue flower) that he presumably remembers from the stranger's stories. He drifts into a reverie, where he is preoccupied by only one thing: "eine hohe lichtblaue Blume, die zunächst an der Quelle stand, und ihn mit ihren breiten, glänzenden Blättern berührte. Rund um sie her standen unzählige Blumen von allen Farben, und der köstliche Geruch erfüllte die Luft. Er sah nichts als die blaue Blume . . ."[19] (a tall, pale blue flower, which stood beside the spring and touched him with its broad glistening leaves. Around this flower were countless others of every hue, and the most delicious fragrance filled the air. He saw nothing but the blue flower . . .). As he attempts to reach the flower, it begins to change shape, until he is awoken by the sound of his mother's voice. In his dream, countless flowers of many colors surround him, but he sees only the blue flower, an abstraction that he deeply desires to reach. The flower is not only unreachable because it is an abstraction, however; as soon as he tries to approach it, it begins to change. The flower in Sachs's story is reachable, but the story from which it grows and that it represents lies buried in a grave, unreachable. Blasius interprets it, and then hands it to Artus, who reinterprets it; the flower changes meaning each time someone vows to have clearly understood what it represents. The flower is an amorphous representation of Merlin and Gotelind's story; it also represents interpretation and the production of symbols, metaphors, myth, and legend.

Because Heinrich longs to reach the unreachable blue flower, it is widely interpreted as the symbol of the essential Romantic theme of

Sehnsucht (longing). That meaning is also given by Blasius to this blue flower when he names it "Wegwarte" (chicory; the archaic English "way-warden" better reflects the compound German word), although this reference to *Sehnsucht* likely also draws on a German folk etiology for the chicory flower.[20] The folktale tells of a maiden awaiting the return of her lover who dies and becomes a flower waiting along his supposed path. This name bestowed by Blasius represents his interpretation of the longing Merlin and Gotelind felt for one another. Here, too, the version of the story implied differs from an earlier source; Gotelind dies actively saving Merlin, rather than waiting for him, and the narrative suggests that the longing both felt was an effect of magic more than authentic feeling. This blue flower is thus multifaceted. It alludes to a definitive German Romantic symbol, but at the same time evokes a lesser-known German folktale that is an adaptation of the story of Persephone. It is only one of many blue flowers that grow on Merlin and Gotelind's grave. It is interpreted and reinterpreted. For every one definitive blue flower, there are countless others left behind, and countless interpretations. There are likewise many Merlin narratives constructed according to the choice of the scribe or the narrator, all the more significant because Merlin texts, as the myth and history of Britain, often include a discussion between Merlin and Blasius that emphasizes the authenticity and accuracy of the narrative.

The Significance of the Narrator

Whereas in "Fra Angelico" and "Die stumme Nachtigall," the reader can extrapolate the significant power of a narrator from the wandering character, in the Merlin text the narrator is an active part of the plot of the very story he is writing. Through Blasius, Sachs can link her own interest in the power of the author and the agency of the reader with a traditional (and traditionally murky) attribute of Merlin texts: that they insist on their authenticity while recounting a story that, like Merlin himself, is multisided, contradictory, and full of irresolvable tensions. The Merlin tradition is, as noted above, intended as a guide; authenticity is a key value in the educational authority of the text. Toward the beginning of Blasius's friendship with Merlin in the Schlegel translation, for example, Merlin tells Blasius:

> Verfertige ein Buch, darin Du alle Dinge aufschreiben sollst, die ich Dir vorsagen werde. Allen Menschen, welche künftig das Buch lesen werden, wird es eine große Wohlthat sein, denn es wird sie bessern, und sie vor Sünden bewahren.[21]

> [Complete a book in which you shall write down all the things that I tell you. It will be a great service to all who will read the book in the future, because it will better them and safeguard them from sin.]

Toward the beginning of Sachs's story, we learn that "diesem Manne, tat der große Magier seine sonderbaren Erlebnisse kund, daß er sie aufzeichne in einem Buche, zur Belehrung und vielfachem Ergötzen nachmaliger Geschlechter" (M, 59; To this man the sorcerer relayed his amazing experiences, so that he might describe them in a book for the instruction and delight of generations to come). Later, Merlin asks Blasius to accompany him to Gaul to write down "alles, was sich zutrüge, sogleich an Ort und Stelle" (M, 69; everything that might happen then and there, i.e., to be an eyewitness). Most importantly, the story draws to a close with Artus's interpretation of the blue flower, followed by the statement "Meister Blasius aber . . . schrieb die letzten Begebenheiten in seinem Buche nieder, so etwa, wie es hier zu lesen stand" (M, 78; But Meister Blasius . . . wrote the final occurrences in his book, much as they are to be read here). Blasius then names the flower and the location of the grave, which requires him to interpret the events. The end of the story, then, makes the point that what we have been reading is, at least to a large extent, the work of Blasius (who is, as a writer and narrator, an analog for Sachs). It is especially significant that Blasius is described at the beginning of the story as well traveled in the art of writing. There is more to any narrative than is immediately apparent, and those entities in the story that wander (Merlin, Gotelind's song, and Blasius) have the greatest power of expression. Blasius is the least visible and yet the most pivotal character in the story. Ultimately, what we read is under the control of Blasius, a narrator whose task it is, for the instruction and delight of future generations, to accurately relay Merlin's story, but who repeatedly gives the reader hints that stories are rarely consistent and are almost always tools for manipulating others. The lesson of this self-referential Merlin story, then, is that we should not trust Blasius, either; and he (and therefore Sachs) gives us numerous opportunities to be aware that this text (and therefore Sachs's text, and therefore all other Merlin texts) is the interpretation of a scribe-narrator who is always working in the service of an idea, or an ideology. To sway the reader, he (or she) must insist that what is on the page transpired "much as it is to be read here."

The Merlin in the Schlegel translation ultimately counsels Blasius that, although future generations will read his books, they will not believe them, because Blasius is not an eyewitness like Christ's apostles were, and instead only writes what Merlin tells him.[22] This is implicitly addressed in Sachs's text, since the narrator routinely assumes a skeptical position in recounting events. The narrator notes when Blasius was not immediately present, and relates most of the dialogue in subjunctive mood. Most strikingly, the characters that readers are accustomed to seeing represented as flawed but ultimately redeemed are rendered here through a different lens that suggests an outside, marginalized perspective, someone who is not necessarily an objective observer, and who does not share the goals and values of Arthur and the Knights of the Round Table. Sachs downplays the emphasis of her source texts on redemptive Christianity and instead shifts the primary focus onto representing and interpreting peoples' stories. Her treatment of the knights and their missionary work, and Merlin's relationship to it, differ markedly from both Schlegel's translation and Immermann's drama. In both, the Knights of the Round Table are essentially well-meaning men in need of guidance, either by Arthur or both Merlin and Arthur; and indeed, Merlin, in both Schlegel and Immermann, is baptized and becomes a servant of Christ. In both texts, Merlin is conceived by Satan as an Antichrist, and in both, he rejects that role. Sachs's Merlin does not appear to be baptized, does not reject his father, and her knights are not particularly good or well meaning. Lancelot scolds them for their boorish behavior, and even he is not beyond reproach. Sir Kay, who in Immermann's drama is a kind of ne'er-do-well comic-relief figure, is in Sachs's text an essentially bad man whom Merlin bans to hell, "wo er allem Anscheine nach längst zugehörig war" (M, 60; where he evidently had long belonged). The only exception is Gavain, the most polite and moral of knights, and even he fails to live up to his gentle reputation. In the Schlegel text, Gavain quickly rights his wrong and regains his former shape and nature; in Sachs's text he merely rides away, defeated.

The failure to uphold their mission, the knights claim in Sachs's text, is "das Werk Merlins, des argen Zauberers, der auf Luzifers Geheiß in der Welt umherstreifte, das Werk dessen zu vernichten, der auf die Erde herabgestiegen war, die Menschheit durch das Dornengebüsch der Bekehrung zu geleiten" (M, 60; the work of Merlin, the terrible sorcerer, who traveled the world under the command of Lucifer to destroy the work of him who came down to Earth to accompany mankind through the thornbush of conversion). In this sentence there are several notable authorial choices. First, Sachs recounts their dialogue in subjunctive I, implying uncertainty about the validity of the knights' perception of themselves as heroes. Their corrupt behavior and subsequent punishment in the text underscores this shift in perspective. Sachs's story describes Merlin's punishment of Kay, for example, as warranted. The reader is left to wonder whether it really is Merlin's fault that they lost the grail and have become ruffians, or whether the fault is perhaps theirs. Sachs's Merlin, like the Merlin of her source texts, is profoundly interested in drawing attention to human foibles, and does not spare anyone. Although he is in the service of Satan, his interventions are often at least instructive, if not justified.

Also notable in the above-quoted sentence is the mention of conversion. In the Schlegel text, dialogues between Merlin and Uther and between Merlin and Arthur lay out the purpose of the Round Table, to defend Christendom, seek justice for all subjects, never to compel or coerce any subject.[23] There is no talk in either source text of conversion. Sachs has thus reframed the rhetoric of the Knights of the Round Table from that of essential saviors of uncivilized, pre-Christian Europe to that of boastful colonizers. Her use of the word "Bekehrung" (conversion) suggests that this is a mission of force. There are other words she could have chosen, for example "übertreten," or even "konvertieren," which imply a personal choice. "Bekehren" requires an outside agent acting upon an object. (This depiction of conversion also appears in the dynamic between the young scholar and the forest girl in "Die stumme Nachtigall.") In the vulgate version, Arthur and his knights do fight the heathens, but they do not convert them or lead anyone through the thornbush of conversion.

Sachs's use of the thornbush, moreover, expands an image from the Schlegel text into a theme of entrapment. In the Schlegel, Nynianne and Merlin sit down to rest beneath a pleasant "Weißdornhecke" (white thornbush) before he gives her the power to enchant and enclose them there.[24] In the Sachs text, there are three references to thorns or thornbushes: Merlin is ultimately trapped in a white thornbush; the soul he inherited from his mother slumbers like a princess trapped in thorns; finally, there is the thornbush of conversion. Sachs includes conversion, then, as a mode of fairy-tale entrapment. The stakes are the same as with figurative language: taken at face value, uncritically, conversion leads to a loss of self. Other voices, other characteristics of people or events are obscured in the creation of narrative, whether it is the sorcerer, the nymph, the scribe, or the king who is creating and relating it. Sachs's inclusion of the Germanic tribes in Merlin's story can also be read in this context.

After Merlin loses his pious maternal soul, he makes his way to Blasius in Northumberland. While there, Satan calls upon him to travel to the land of Gaul "um Unfrieden zu stiften unter den Stämmen der Franken, Alemannen und Burgunder, welche sich sämtlich mit dem Gedanken trugen, alldorten ein Reich von ihrer Art und Rasse zu begründen" (M, 69; in order to cause unrest among the tribes of the Franks, Alamanni and Burgundians, who had the collective idea to found a realm there of their kind and race). He finds that lacking the soul of his mother, he has lost his powers of persuasion and agitation, and thus cannot perform the (often not unjust) political intrigue he has caused in other similar situations. It seems reasonable to conclude that this addition alludes to the populist rhetoric of racial nationalism, which was widespread by 1921, when Sachs's "Merlin" was published, and aimed to define a common Germanic race primarily to create national historical narrative. That narrative was meant to exclude Jews. While religious anti-Semitism had long been a common feature of European politics, racial anti-Semitism was a cultivation of the nineteenth century that appears to have entered national-scale German politics in the 1890s and remained a familiar though contested feature of right-wing politics until the Nazi regime codified it in the 1930s.[25] It is difficult to imagine that Sachs, in creating a story so focused on the power of two marginalized, powerful individuals, one of whom is composed of two opposing heritages, was not also thinking about the pressures facing nineteenth- and early twentieth-century Jewish Germans. The German nationalism of the nineteenth century informed the ongoing discussion of whether Jews could ever be both Jews and Germans. Throughout the early twentieth century, the political as well as journalistic arenas saw a consistent stream of pamphlets, papers, articles, and editorial debates that ran the spectrum of advocating total assimilation (which meant losing a Jewish identity), advocating political Zionism (which meant the loss of a German identity), and descriptions of a sometimes positive, sometimes negative middle position of being unable to be either completely Jewish or completely German.[26] The themes of the Merlin text suggest Sachs leaned toward the middle position; Merlin and Gotelind both are only whole when their selves are divided between two separate entities (unlike Immermann's Merlin, who feels that he can never be whole). While the text makes no specific mention of Judaism, the added element of Germanic "race," with its unavoidable implications for Jewish Germans, suggests that it is not far from Sachs's mind. Ultimately, her addition of race rhetoric fits with the pattern of her other additions, which imply that singular representatives (i.e., one blue flower, one side of a person, one race) always obscure multiple components or voices. Here, the three Germanic tribes that are named have the collective plan of creating one realm of their race; in addition to the fact the validity of race was doubted already in the late nineteenth century, this brief allusion obscures the violent conflicts between the Germanic tribes that ultimately resulted in the Frankish subjugation of the Alamanni and the Burgundians.[27]

The establishment of hegemony requires the erasure of difference, which can be accomplished through war, but also through narrative. As archeologist Malcolm Todd writes regarding the Franks, "the creation of a past is often as important as the past itself";[28] myths and legends are every bit as vital to nation as military and cultural conquest. Merlin stories that arose beginning in the twelfth century, a golden era of Christian civilization, used Merlin and the Knights of the Round Table to promote and valorize the Christian conquest of the heathens. Sachs's Merlin text instead draws attention to the work of creating legends.

Rather than being a story about the redemption of heathens through Christianity or about the love of nature or the dangers of uncontrolled women, Sachs's Merlin is a story about the question of who has the power to dictate a narrative, and about awareness of the perspectives that are obscured or interpolated in the process. It is a story in which the power to affect events, often wielded by marginalized figures, is subject to the power to control the narration of events. The marginal protagonists are composite creations who draw their power from this multiplicity and are weakened and ultimately lost when they are reduced to one of their parts. Merlin, forced in this version of his story to lose one side of his dual inheritance, loses first his power to affect the foundation of a nation and then finally himself. The only figure who can save him is an outcast young woman, in possession of a magic song that she inherited, who can restore his dual inheritance. How their stories are represented, however, is at the discretion of a narrator. It is a story that draws attention to the presence of numerous blue flowers, and to the different sources from which one blue flower can grow.

Because this text is so different from others that tell the story of Merlin, and calls attention to the work of creating and interpreting stories, it encourages the reader to step back from familiar myths and narratives and consider the power a storyteller can have over an audience. Through her changes and additions, Sachs throws light on the task and the challenges that face the chronicler, on the power of a narrator, on the often obscured process of choosing what to represent and what to leave out, and, through her protagonists, the damage done when people, who are by nature conflicted and complex, are whittled down to one feature. The definitive German cultural moments she weaves into the Merlin context suggest that the story is intended to point out that symbols that are read as definitively German are made that way by obscuring sources, voices, contexts, and conflicts that they contain. Sachs liberates Merlin by accentuating his plurality and building extensively on the adaptable, multicultural historical framework of the Merlin tradition.

4: Poetic Space after the Abyss

S ACHS'S SENSE OF UNEASE in the space of words intensified and took on greater urgency after the Second World War. Fascinated with and mindful of the power of figurative language already since the 1920s, Sachs experienced increasing confirmation of the need to retain critical distance to figurative language throughout the 1930s and 40s. First, Nazi propaganda introduced a new vocabulary of exclusion and obfuscation; then, upon hearing in the early to mid-1940s of Nazi atrocities, Sachs was confronted with the ethics of using figurative language to react and respond to mass murder; and finally, between 1945 and 1949, she was confronted with the need of both Germany and the newly founded State of Israel to rely on writers to help define national identity and national narrative. She understood that there is a clear link between nation and text, but it is a link that she chose to problematize rather than validate. Sachs's poetics continue after the war to posit the text as a deceptive and dynamic landscape that both reader and writer traverse; the need for the individual reader to be aware of this is magnified by the violence done to and with figurative language during the Nazi genocide. Both Germany and Israel sought through literary voices to re-create unified cultural identities, and this depended on a longing for reconciliation and return, to a place as well as to a tradition. Sachs had an embattled relationship to both.

The construction of unified identity and the celebration of wholeness and singularity through longing for reconciliation that dominate the postwar Zeitgeist are often attributed to "Emigranten-" or "Exil-Literatur," of which Sachs was considered part; in Sachs's work they are, however, the object of critique, not the goal. Sachs's postwar poetics suggest that the idea of the nation as an exclusive, sovereign topographical body, and the defense or even mythologizing of this body through poetic language, reinforce an ontology of conflict, whereas a more fluid encounter between differences would allow for individual awareness that prevents overidentification with the state. The two poems I focus on in this chapter, "Wenn im Vorsommer" (When in Early Summer) and "Völker der Erde" (Peoples of the Earth), problematize the need for poetic language to heal cultural and national rifts by showing that it cannot, and compel readers to confront not only the damage done to poetic language, but also, and perhaps more importantly, the agency each individual has in the reality he or she shapes with words.

Stephen Brockmann, in his book *German Literary Culture at the Zero Hour*, recently expressed just how important Germany's literary legacy was in the immediate postwar effort to heal and cultivate a German identity:

> In addition to its traditional function as a fill-in for unavailable political power, German *Kultur* now also served an exculpatory function: for many Germans, the *Kulturnation* as represented by its highest achievements was to provide a cultural counterweight to the nation's heavy moral and political sins.[1]

Postwar Germany had to redefine itself, either as the revived *Kulturnation* of Goethe, or as something completely new; writers were viewed as the key to this task. The basis for both solutions is a sense of cultural cohesion, a unified identity that is represented in the work of celebrated writers who can speak for the people. At a meeting of writers that took place in Berlin between October 4th and 8th of 1947, the writer Ricarda Huch (1864–1947) remarked on the central importance of the writer in reestablishing a unified national identity:

> Die Dichter und Schriftsteller haben eine besondere Beziehung zur Einheit, nämlich durch die Sprache. Die Sprache scheidet ein Volk von anderen Völkern, aber sie hält auch ein Volk zusammen. Die Schriftsteller sind die Verwalter der Sprache. Sie bewegen durch ihre Sprache die Herzen und lenken die Gedanken.[2]

> [The poets and writers have a special relationship to unification, namely through language. Language separates one people from other peoples, but it also holds a people together. The writers are the trustees of language. They move hearts and steer thoughts through their language.]

The writer thus has a great deal of power to create a bond through shared experience and shared language. The tension lay, however, in which direction to steer and how to unify people who had essentially been turned *against* one another to create the Nazi unity that depended on a culture of mutual suspicion and subjugation of the self to the state. Further complicating matters were the roles of the occupying forces, which determined what could be and was published.

Emigrant and refugee writers had a significant but contentious role to play in rebuilding German national identity after the Second World War. When Thomas Mann left Germany in 1933 in political protest, he became the leading representative of what at first was known as "Emigranten-Literatur," later Exil-Literatur. The intellectual community that emigrated to a number of countries and was referred to as "das andere Deutschland" and even as "das wahre Deutschland" (respectively: the other Germany;

the true Germany), constituted, in theory, the continuation of humanist tradition that was not able to continue under National Socialism.[3] There were those, like refugee and scholar Walter Berendsohn, who considered Mann and the other emigrants and refugees to be cultural warriors who essentially rescued German cultural tradition, and thus the real Germany, from Nazi control and preserved it as a landless abstraction, waiting for a time to return the true Germany to its homeland.

Berendsohn, the first major academician to call for serious examination of "Emigranten-Literatur" and one of Sachs's first major postwar promoters, published part one of his *Die humanistische Front* (The Humanist Frontline) in 1946, in which he suggested that the main task of emigrants was "die Verteidigung und Pflege des großen deutschen und europäischen [Kultur]Erbes" (the defense and care of the great German and European [cultural] heritage).[4] They could then return, and bring "das wahre Deutschland" with them, in order to revive Germany's cultural tradition. Berendsohn's insistence on this "frontline" was an appeal primarily to the non-Soviet sectors of occupied postwar Germany, which were proving, immediately after the war, to be extremely unwelcoming to the "emigrants" and their literature.[5] The citizens of West Germany themselves opposed these writers, expressing anger and a sense of betrayal, especially with Thomas Mann.[6] The Soviet zone was much more willing to allow publication of what it considered antifascist texts or material critical of Nazi Germany, as Ralf Schnell has written:

> Von einer Repatriierung der Exilliteratur kann allenfalls im Blick auf die damalige Sowjetische Besatzungszone, die spätere DDR, die Rede sein. Nur hier konnten die Exilautoren an politische und literarische Traditionen anknüpfen, die bis zu den politischen Kämpfen der Weimarer Zeit zurückreichten, zur Mitgliedschaft in der KPD und im Bund proletarisch-revolutionärer Schriftsteller (BPRS). Nur hier entstand, freilich von der sowjetischen Besatzungsmacht gelenkt, eine Öffentlichkeit, die für ihre Erfahrungen aus der Zeit des Faschismus—KZ und Gefängnis, Flucht und Exil, Widerstand und Krieg—Interesse zeigte. Nur hier waren die Exilautoren ebenso willkommen wie ihr literarisches Werk, denn sie wurden hier gebraucht, auch aus Gründen einer politischen Kontinuität in der Tradition der Volksfront.[7]

> [One can speak of a repatriation of exile literature in view of the then Soviet-occupied zone. Only here could exile authors draw on political and literary traditions reaching back to the Weimar time, to membership in the KPD and the Association of Proletarian Revolutionary Writers. Only here did a public space emerge, steered, obviously, by the Soviet occupying force, that showed interest for their experiences during the time of fascism—concentration camps

and prison, flight and exile, resistance and war. Only here were the exile writers as welcome as their literary work, for they were needed here, too, on grounds of a political continuity in the tradition of the people's front.]

While the ideological constraints of the Soviet narration of history, which emphasized the destruction incurred by National Socialism in order to present Soviet Communism as the antidote, eventually became a hindrance to artistic production, in the immediate postwar era Soviet encouragement of political engagement provided writers more open ground than did the Allied program of denazification, which discouraged engagement with the recent past. Refugee and exile writers were not likely to unify the people, because on the one hand, they did not share the same experiences, and on the other, many of them—despite the call to preserve German and European tradition—wrote confrontational texts the public was not ready for. Sachs remarked on this situation in her letter to Johannes Edfelt from September 24, 1953: "In Deutschland lehnt man bei fast allen Verlegern Dichtung ab, die noch über Rilke hinaus eine Form für diese unsere zerbrochene Welt sucht. Es soll alles glatt und harmonisch im früheren Sinne sein. Wie ist das möglich, fragt man sich, aber das Publikum gibt die Antwort und kauft neue Dichtung nicht." (In Germany nearly every publisher rejects poetry that seeks a form beyond Rilke for this, our broken world. Everything is to be smooth and harmonious like it once was. How is this possible, one asks oneself. But the public gives the answer and does not buy new poetry.)[8] Sachs's *In den Wohnungen des Todes*, for example, one of the earliest works to deal with the Nazi genocide against the Jews, was published in the Soviet zone—by Aufbau Verlag in 1947.

On the opposite end of the spectrum from Berendsohn's *Humanistische Front* was Alfred Andersch's (1914–80) *Deutsche Literatur in der Entscheidung* (German Literature in the Balance), also published in 1946. There is an echo of Berendsohn's optimism for the future in Andersch's text, but whereas Berendsohn, a refugee in Sweden, was fighting for the integrity and valor of the emigrants, Andersch, who had been a socialist before being drafted and had undergone trial efforts of "re-education" in an American POW camp, primarily attacked the "innere Emigration" and called for a break with tradition. For Andersch, who also became a very close friend and promoter of Nelly Sachs, the humanism (also called "bürgerliche Klassik") of writers like Ricarda Huch, Gertrud von Le Fort (1876–1971), Hans Carossa (1878–1956), and Gerhart Hauptmann (1862–1946), had failed to prevent the rise of National Socialism, and he called for the writers of postwar Germany to bring Germany back to "Reinheit" (purity). Both Andersch and Berendsohn saw the twelve years of NSDAP rule as an "Irrtum" (losing one's way, a mistake), a break between where Germany had been headed until 1933 and where it would end up, suggesting that there was no connection between the German Reich of Bismarck or Wilhelm II or the Weimar Republic and National Socialism, a discussion that remains unresolved to this day. In Berendsohn's view, the emigrants could carry on where Germany left off. The postwar poets associated with the desire to revive classical tradition were nature poets who followed in the footsteps of Oskar Loerke (1884–1941), like Wilhelm Lehmann (1882–1968), Elisabeth Langgässer (1899–1950), and Karl Krolow (1915–99).[9] For Andersch, the break with tradition was final, and Germany had to start over entirely. Writers like Andersch, Wolfgang Weyrauch (1907–80), and Hans Egon Holthusen (1913–97) were associated with terms like "Kahlschlag," "Stunde Null," and "tabula rasa," the notion that the poets were starting from a completely blank slate.[10] Between the two extremes was "Trümmerliteratur," in which, as Ralf Schnell puts it,

> die Wirklichkeit gegenwärtig [ist], durch welche diese Literatur geprägt wurde, die Realität des Schutts und der Ruinen—nicht nur der Städte und Häuser, sondern auch der Ideale und Ideologien—, die Realität des Krieges, des Todes, des Untergangs und des Überlebens inmitten von Trümmern.[11]

> [the reality is present that molded this literature, the reality of debris and of ruins—not only of cities and houses, but of ideals and ideologies—the reality of war, of death, of downfall and of survival in the midst of rubble.]

The official stance in western occupied Germany was to establish a "return" to stability, under the slogan "No experiments," which included a resistance to openly political art.[12] This ran parallel to a preference for "the conservative tradition and the re-enthronement of a culture that eschewed politics, reflected in Gottfried Benn's *Statische Gedichte* (Static Poems, 1948) . . . with . . . stress on rigorous form and the expunging of quotidian concerns from literature."[13] Poetry quickly became the major genre of contention.

Rudolf Hartung, later an editor at the Willi Weismann Verlag in Munich, published an article in 1947 in *Die Fähre* (also known as *Literarische Revue*) in which he criticized poetry currently being published in Germany as "unzeitgemäß" (untimely), or absolutely out of sync. Here he takes on a question primarily associated with Adorno's much later work on the culture industry, namely "the question of the right of poetry to exist in a time of the most extreme material need."[14] It was not poetry per se, but the untimely poetry that was being produced in 1947, with its drive for a "timeless aesthetic" or "lyrical flower-picking," that was the problem for Hartung (as it would remain for, among others, Ingeborg Bachmann and Hans Magnus Enzensberger). But it was not untimely because of its content, which in some cases indeed dealt with current topics. Rather, the immediate postwar poetry manifested in its form a conception of representation that was borrowed from the turn of the century or earlier, a conception that was problematic for Hartung because "Jedes Wort und jeder Satz sind auf höchst fatale Weise zur rationalen Aussage geworden und mit Erschrecken stellt man fest, daß alle Wörter abgegriffen und verbraucht sind." (Every word and every sentence have become a rational expression in the most disastrous manner and with shock one determines that all the words are worn out and used up.)[15] That is, such poetry was conventional in a manner that could no longer be considered poetic, and moreover aimed for a reconciliation with the past that was simply impossible. As late as 1981, Klaus Weissenberger suggested "was nun die Nachkriegslyrik betrifft, ist der primär restaurative um einen Ausgleich bemühte Charakter der Lyrik von Exil und Innerer Emigration bis Mitte der 60er Jahre vorherrschend" (concerning postwar poetry, the primarily restorative, conciliatory character of poetry from exile and inner emigration dominates until the middle of the 1960s).[16] It was thus largely the "Exil" and "Innere Emigration" writers who appeared interested in—or were at least interpreted as being interested in—restoration, reconciliation, and preservation of form rather than in a tabula rasa or "Stunde Null." Sachs's poetry is often assigned to this category, although it generally problematizes or outright undermines the tendency, exemplified by Berendsohn's invocation of a "humanist frontline," to see literature as a servant or representative of the nation; but neither does Sachs eschew more traditional poetic vocabulary. Rather, her work is a kind of *Trümmerliteratur* that captures the tension between needing to find a new vocabulary, new imagery, and yet being neither willing nor able to entirely break free of the ruins.

In this way, Sachs's postwar poetics in general demonstrate the archaic and simultaneously avant-garde style Ehrhard Bahr ascribed to them.[17] On the one hand, she created poetic texts that fulfill a traditional function of poetry: to create, as Culler and Bachelard remind us, a textual reality (beyond but not disconnected from empirical reality) in which words are pushed beyond their conventional limits. How and why she does this, however, is notably avant-garde. She draws on well-established poetic traditions in order to show their bankruptcy, or even their culpability; she does so in a very subtle way that demands close attention and involvement of the reader—an urgent skill in the wake of fascism. Like a number of twentieth-century poets, she conceived of language and text as its own landscape, created with images and tropes adapted from cartography, geography, and astronomy. It is not a landscape of return, reconciliation, or refuge; it is a landscape of illusion, rift, and harm, where the reader is confronted with "diese apokalyptische Zeit . . . aber auch die ewigen Geheimnisse dahinter" (this apocalyptic time . . . but also the eternal secrets behind it).[18] Bahr, writing in 1980, suggests that readers preferred to see in her work something soothing or sentimental.[19] Sachs, however, did not seem to conceive of poetry as a medium for soothing or unifying a people; she conceived of it as a medium that creates a landscape meant to destabilize an empirical reality that gives a false sense of cohesion and therefore security. This space of words compels readers to confront a hybrid, disjointed empirical and literary reality they themselves create.

Two of Sachs's poems that unambiguously tackle the complications of poetic language for the postwar era and their implications for national identity and unity are "Wenn im Vorsommer" (When in Early Summer) and "Völker der Erde" (Peoples of the Earth). The traditional tropes in these poems have been read as characteristic of texts by "emigrant writers" who wish to preserve the humanistic tradition. Readers like Michael Braun, Ehrhard Bahr, and Hilde Domin see Sachs's use of poetic tropes as essentially innocent, at times inappropriate, and as expressing longing for a return to a more innocent, pristine poetic tradition. Sachs does not, however, so much preserve the tropes she uses as place them in question and restructure them, a literary act that constitutes her contribution to literary-political discourse in the immediate postwar era.

"Wenn im Vorsommer" and "Völker der Erde" were composed between 1946 and 1948, and were intended for publication in the 1949 volume *Sternverdunkelung*. This was the first volume of Sachs's postwar poetry not to be published by a Soviet-backed publisher, appearing instead through Bermann-Fischer, a German publisher in Amsterdam that specialized in exile and refugee writers. Interestingly, these two poems, as well as two others also intended for the collection ("Im Lande Israel" and "Wir üben heute schon den Tod von morgen"), were not included in *Sternverdunkelung*. They did appear, apparently under Hans Magnus Enzensberger's direction, in the 1961 collected poems edition *Fahrt ins Staublose*, in a separate section called "Zur *Sternverdunkelung* gehörig" ("Belonging to *Sternverdunkelung*").[20] Before *Fahrt ins Staublose*, however, "Völker der Erde" and "Wenn im Vorsommer" were first published in 1950 in the Soviet-zone journal *Sinn und Form*. Why these four poems were not included in *Sternverdunkelung* is uncertain. It may, however, be because they are among the most obviously ideologically critical and intentionally political poems in Sachs's body of work, which may have drawn the attention of the American military censors.[21] Such content may have presented a challenge to the forward-looking stability pursued by the West German government, but would have been less of a problem in the Soviet zone. Neither poem provides an optimistic vision of a cohesive and peaceful future; rather, they are two different wake-up calls. "Wenn im Vorsommer" confronts the reader with the struggle for a new poetic voice; there is no return to an innocent past, because innocence has been destroyed. "Völker der Erde" confronts the reader with the individual's agency; there is no return to an innocent past because an innocent past was always a fallacy. The skepticism regarding the innocence of figurative language is easier to recognize in light of her earlier texts, in which figurative language is often a mask or trigger for harm.

"Wenn im Vorsommer" has the appearance of a poem that tries to recapture Romantic poetic tradition, but as the poem unfolds it becomes a nature poem that shows how untimely nature poetry is. The Romantic enchantment is interrupted by an amazed voice that admonishes the world for avoiding the reality of war and genocide by trying to immerse itself in the poetic traditions of a more innocent era. Yet even as the voice is critical of these more innocent tropes, it cannot escape using them. The result is a poem that exhibits the simultaneously archaic and avant-garde style described by Ehrhard Bahr, which makes Sachs's work more complex than it may seem on the surface.

Wenn im Vorsommer der Mond geheime Zeichen aussendet,
die Kelche der Lilien Dufthimmel verströmen,
öffnet sich manches Ohr unter Grillengezirp
dem Kreisen der Erde und der Sprache
der entschränkten Geister zu lauschen.

In den Träumen aber fliegen die Fische in der Luft
und ein Wald wurzelt sich im Zimmerfußboden fest.

Aber mitten in der Verzauberung spricht eine Stimme klar und
                                                      verwundert:
Welt, wie kannst du deine Spiele weiter spielen
und die Zeit betrügen—
Welt, man hat die kleinen Kinder wie Schmetterlinge,
flügelschlagend in die Flamme geworfen—

und deine Erde ist nicht wie ein fauler Apfel
in den schreckaufgejagten Abgrund geworfen worden—

Und Sonne und Mond sind weiter spazierengegangen—
zwei schieläugige Zeugen, die nichts gesehen haben.[22]

[*When in early summer*

When in early summer the moon sends out secret signs,
the chalices of lilies scent of heaven,
some ear opens to listen
beneath the chirp of the cricket
to earth turning and the language of spirits set free.

But in dreams fish fly in the air
and a forest takes firm root in the floor of the room.

But in the midst of enchantment a voice speaks clearly and
        amazed:
World, how can you go on playing your games
and cheating time—
World, the little children were thrown like butterflies,
wings beating into the flames—

and your earth has not been thrown like a rotten apple
into the terror-roused abyss—

And sun and moon have gone on walking—
two cross-eyed witnesses who have seen nothing.[23]]

"Wenn im Vorsommer" drew much attention, in particular for the lines "Welt, wie kannst du deine Spiele weiter spielen / und die Zeit betrügen— / Welt, man hat die kleinen Kinder wie Schmetterlinge, / flügelschlagend in die Flamme geworfen—." Ehrhard Bahr summarizes the problem engendered by what he sees as an inappropriate simile:

Es besteht . . . bei Nelly Sachs' Vierzeiler die Gefahr, daß der Leser den unermeßlichen Unterschied zwischen Schmetterling und Mensch geflissentlich übersieht und über die Schmetterlinge weint, aber darüber die Wirklichkeit der sechs Millionen Menschenopfer vergißt. Zweifellos ist darin der Grund für die Popularität dieses Vierzeilers während der sechziger Jahre in der Bundesrepublik zu finden. Er ermöglicht durch ein eingängiges Naturbild die sentimentale Distanzierung von dem historischen Geschehen.[24]

[The danger . . . exists in Nelly Sachs's two couplets that the reader deliberately misses the immense difference between butterfly and human and cries over the butterfly, but then forgets the reality of the six million human victims. Doubtless this is the reason for the popularity of these four lines during the 1960s in the Federal Republic of Germany. Through an accessible nature image, it makes a sentimental distance from the historical occurrence possible.]

Bahr reads this poem as a misdirected critique of nature, because "der Ausdruck des Entsetzens über die Neutralität der Natur ist als verfehlte Erwartung an die Natur zu kritisieren . . . und höchstens als mytische Erkenntnis, daß Gott sich aus seiner Schöpfung zurückgezogen hat, zu rechtfertigen" (the expression of horror over the neutrality of nature is to be criticized as a misguided expectation of nature . . . and at most to be justified as mythical realization that God has withdrawn from his creation).[25] That is, this poem is understood to be a nature poem in which

nature is confronted with the fact of genocide and ignores it. The two
couplets in particular are significant for Bahr for two reasons. First, he
finds the comparison of children to butterflies "ein unzulässiges dich-
terisches Gleichnis" (an inadmissible poetic comparison) that is not only
sentimental, it also "stellt . . . eine bestürzende Dehumanisation dar"
(represents a disturbing dehumanization).[26] Second, he finds that the iso-
lation of these lines seems "in der Bundesrepublik auf ein ideologisches
Bedürfnis zur sentimentalisierten Distanzierung von der Wirklichkeit der
Vernichtungslager hinzudeuten" (to indicate an ideological need in the
Federal Republic of Germany for sentimental distancing from the reality
of the death camps).[27] Sachs evidently eventually distanced herself from
the poem. Bahr acknowledges that his interpretation is the result of reading those lines out of context, though he does not articulate how the lines
might work in the context of the entire poem. The entire poem, I suggest, puts forth the very critique Bahr lays out.

The first stanza sets a nighttime forest scene reminiscent of the work of
poets like Friedrich Gottlieb Klopstock (1724–1803), Friedrich Hölderlin
(1770–1843), or Novalis, who depict the poetic "I" in a heightened state
of consciousness in nature, where it can perceive otherwise obscured wisdom and impulses. "Manches Ohr," that is to say, the occasional individual,
is open to the sounds of the earth turning, and to the language of spirits.
Sachs's poem evokes the trope of the poet as a being who can perceive and
communicate the secrets of nature or the beyond. Intriguingly, this sensory experience takes place "unter Grillengezirp" (beneath, or also, more
idiomatically, amidst the chirping of crickets). The sound of the cricket in
folklore and in poetic tradition often signals the approach of an unpleasant change;[28] but if the ear perceives the crickets' chirping, it does not pay
attention to it, choosing instead to listen to distant spirits and the turning
of the earth. The second stanza also has a foreboding air. The "aber" suggests again that something is not as it should be, as if in dreams fish should
not fly, or a forest should not take root in the floor of a room, although sur-
real dreams are hardly unusual poetic material. Like the voice of the cricket
in the first stanza, the "aber" of the second stanza intrudes in the atmosphere of the poem, signaling an unarticulated objection. Through the
three stanzas, the interruption becomes increasingly prominent: the cricket
occurs somewhat buried in the middle of the longer first stanza; the shorter
second stanza has the cricket-like "aber" closer to the beginning of the line.
A repeated instance of "aber" begins the third stanza, in which the objection signaled by this word is finally made clear. In the midst of this poem's
persistent enchantment, a voice speaks "klar und verwundert," clearly and
amazedly. This voice is one of reality, interrupting the concerted effort in
the first two stanzas to create a traditional poetic space outside time—or re-
create one, since we learn from the voice that the sort of idyllic atmosphere
at the beginning of the poem is untimely.

It is important to note that the speaking voice addresses "Welt" (world) rather than "Erde" (earth). In this poem, "Erde" is used to depict the planet and nature; "Welt," then, is used to address the people, the society that occupies Earth. The voice admonishes the world for ignoring reality in favor of a more enchanted space of play, reminiscent of a more carefree time, represented by the attempt to create nature poetry. In so doing, the world "betrügt" (betrays, even swindles) time. The poetic tradition evoked in the preceding stanzas depicts the world trying to immerse itself in another time, or rather, an enchanted world outside of time: a conventional poetic space of words, poetic landscapes of forests, magic moons, and distant spirits. This clear, amazed voice asks how the world can continue on in an illusory state of innocence and play when actual innocents have been murdered in a way that suggests the perversion of a game. Throwing butterflies into flames recalls childish malevolence of the sort Shakespeare evokes in the line from *King Lear* "as flies to wanton boys are we to the gods; they kill us for their sport."[29] Sachs uses the impersonal pronoun "man," akin to English "one," so that agency is obscured, yet here it is clearly not the gods who kill human beings for sport. Sachs's line captures the hubris of playing with life and death in the manner of cruel gods of myth or drama and unwillingness to accept responsibility for it. Because such cruelty has become the reality rather than mythology or the stuff of imagination, it is hard for the voice to believe that any kind of escapism or play of other times can continue to exist. Not only has this cruelty become a documented reality, the vague impersonal pronoun "man" means "someone" has perpetrated the act, but no one is accepting responsibility for it. In the stanza that follows, the voice can barely believe that the world's planet ("deine Erde") even continues to exist. The passive construction of the fifth stanza ("geworfen worden") progresses logically from the passive substitute "man" of the fourth stanza; since "man" threw children into the fire, it seems amazing to the voice that the planet was not thrown into "den schreckaufgejagten Abgrund," the abyss that was roused (aufgejagt) into existence through terror. Whether this dense and provocative metaphor captures a crisis of faith in the divine or in the world, or communicates a sudden shock at the amorality of nature and the cosmos, the voice suggests that the just resolution to what has happened would be the disposal of "deine Erde," by whose hand it is unclear, in an abyss generated by the terror of the "Welt" itself. As improbable as the voice finds it, the Earth, sun, and moon continue to revolve, and the world tries to move either back in time or outside of time, through the now untimely medium of the idyllic poetic landscape.

Most of the voice's statements are broken off with a dash. The only statement it can bring itself to complete is the last line of the poem. The Earth in the poem keeps revolving; the sun and moon, at a distance, are pretending not to have seen anything. Only the description of unaffected nature ends with a period. Where the voice attempts to describe what it sees on Earth and in the world, it can only speak in incomplete thoughts, as if it is struggling to find words, and cannot continue using the words it is finding to describe what it sees. The four lines singled out above are problematic, and because the poem is concerned with the illusion of poetic refuge and is comprised of more traditional poetic imagery in utterances that are repeatedly broken off and left incomplete, it is logical to conclude that these lines are meant to be unsettling. The voice breaks through the idyllic nature poem to admonish the world for escaping into untimely distractions; yet the only words the voice can find to describe the reality it sees come from the same untimely vocabulary it is trying to disrupt and critique, with one prominent exception.

The closest the voice comes to breaking out of tradition is the phrase "schreckaufgejagten Abgrund." Most of the other images in the poem can in some way connect to poetic tradition or give rise to a mimetic image. "Schreckaufgejagte[r] Abgrund" is an abrupt change from the more conventional poetic images around it. The "schreckaufgejagt[e] Abgrund" is not mimetic, nor is it easily categorized. It is an attempt to describe something that has no precedent or conventional signified. Auschwitz is certainly part of it; but the abyss image goes far beyond that, into uncertain territory of the reality that has emerged in the wake of war and genocide. The absence of an agent makes it impossible to determine whether this abyss was roused through "schrecken" as an action or as a feeling. The poem begins with the evocation of a poetic landscape, which is mirrored at the end of the poem by a new poetic landscape that, rather than communicating a magical beyond, an innocent past, or a healed future only poets can help us find, communicates the reality that we would prefer to avoid and that only poets can make us first see and then confront. The voice speaking is a new poetic voice, no longer the poet-prophet of the opening stanza who communicates the mysterious, but the poetic voice that must intercede to force the reader to confront the reality that defies the senses, that is difficult both to grasp and to bear.

In using the kind of images one might find in conventional poetry or folklore, for example children as butterflies or comparing murder to torturing insects, to describe something that happened in Auschwitz, the poet shows just how incapable traditional poetic language is of describing the reality of the post-Holocaust Earth. To write the kind of idyllic verse that begins this poem is to follow along with the moon and sun, as witnesses who saw nothing. The world before this time cannot be re-created completely; any attempt to re-create that tradition will be obviously disingenuous, and any attempt to describe the new reality in traditional terms is inappropriate. Literary language cannot create stability or heal the damage; such language can only compel the reader to consider how unviable it has become.

The poem "Völker der Erde" takes up the problem of language after the Nazi genocide as well, but from a different perspective. Whereas "Wenn im Vorsommer" exposes the impossibility of re-creating prewar poetic spaces of innocence, "Völker der Erde" more directly admonishes people for trying to insulate themselves in passivity or behind a veneer of innocent language. People create their own story, their own reality, with constellations of words; yet they persist in assigning the power to, for example, muses, or poets, or politicians. The poem ultimately urges the people to acknowledge and respect the source of their words; based on the agency repeatedly assigned to people in the poem, I suggest that the source here is the individual consciousness. In contrast to the indirect "man" and "Welt" of "Wenn im Vorsommer," Sachs uses the traditional poetic device of a vocative "ihr, die ihr" (all you, who . . .) to call out all the peoples of Earth. All peoples, not only Germans, and not only poets or politicians, fail or refuse to acknowledge how mutable, dangerous, and even violent language has always been—not only in the twentieth century, and not only in or as a result of Nazi propaganda, but for anyone in any time.

The position explicated in the poem is to some extent reflective of a mindset Brockmann describes:

> In the immediate postwar period what is now called the Holocaust was seen as one particularly horrific part of a general panoply of horrors, not as a unique and incomparable event. It was seen not from the perspective of late twentieth-century identity politics, but from the perspective of a generally idealistic universalism that potentially included all human beings.[30]

Sachs's position on literary tradition in the aftermath of the Holocaust as we see it in her correspondence indicates that she did see the Nazi genocide as a uniquely extreme event; yet as many of her poems attest, she was also preoccupied by it as a particularly extreme and disturbing example of power dynamics that have existed for millennia, the "Urzeitspiel von Henker und Opfer"[31] (Age-old game of hangman and victim). Its consequences are thus applicable to everyone, everywhere. Nazi manipulation of language compels us to be more conscious of how anyone uses language, and compels each individual to be more cognizant of his or her power with words. As Michael Braun writes, "Das Wort eines jeden einzelnen ist verantwortlich für die Sprache aller."[32] (The word of every individual is responsible for the language of all.) The poem communicates an idea similar to the call for skepticism Aichinger presented in her 1946 essay "Aufruf zum Mißtrauen," pushing readers to question any feelings of nostalgia or moral superiority. Ultimately, the poem urges peoples of the Earth, collectively but ultimately as individuals, to acknowledge their active role in creating and changing meaning with words, and thereby in the violence words cause or validate.

Völker der Erde
ihr, die ihr euch mit der Kraft der unbekannten
Gestirne umwickelt wie Garnrollen,
die ihr näht und wieder auftrennt das Genähte,
die ihr in die Sprachverwirrung steigt
wie in Bienenkörbe,
um im Süßen zu stechen
und gestochen zu werden—

Völker der Erde,
zerstöret nicht das Weltall der Worte,
zerschneidet nicht mit den Messern des Hasses
den Laut, der mit dem Atem zugleich geboren wurde.

Völker der Erde,
O daß nicht Einer Tod meine, wenn er Leben sagt—
und nicht Einer Blut, wenn er Wiege spricht—

Völker der Erde,
lasset die Worte an ihrer Quelle,
denn sie sind es, die die Horizonte
in die wahren Himmel rücken können
und mit ihrer abgewandten Seite
wie eine Maske dahinter die Nacht gähnt
die Sterne gebären helfen—[33]

[*Peoples of the earth*

Peoples of the earth,
you who swathe yourselves with the force of the unknown
constellations as with rolls of thread,
you who sew and sever what is sewn,
you who enter the tangle of tongues
as into beehives,
to sting the sweetness
and be stung—

Peoples of the earth,
do not destroy the universe of words,
let not the knife of hatred lacerate
the sound born together with the first breath.

Peoples of the earth,
O that no one mean death when he says life—
and not blood when he speaks cradle—

Peoples of the earth,
leave the words at their source,
for it is they that can nudge

the horizons into the true heaven
and that, with night gaping behind
their averted side, as behind a mask,
help give birth to the stars—³⁴]

"Völker der Erde" has been read as an "Aufruf" (a calling out or call to arms)
of a kind that is seldom found in Sachs's work.³⁵ Michael Braun argues that
Sachs calls upon the peoples of the Earth not to forsake language in the wake
of Nazi propaganda, because for Sachs there was no completely destroyed
or unusable word.³⁶ Other analyses shy away from attaching this poem to
any specific reference point(s). Hilde Domin's reading skirts the issues of the
Holocaust and National Socialism, focusing on the poem's intended resonance for the future. The poem's importance for future generations, however, is perhaps even clearer when the reader considers the climate in which it
was written and the venues in which it was published. Whereas most poems
composed for *Sternverdunkelung* were composed in 1948, "Völker der
Erde" appears to have been composed already by November 12, 1946,³⁷ the
same time during which Andersch and Berendsohn wrote their treatises on
the need for writers to heal or re-create German literary language, Hartung
wrote his essay about the right of poetry to exist, and Victor Klemperer was
readying his *LTI*, a journal in which he had tracked Nazi manipulation of
language, for publication.³⁸ Concerns about the ruined German language,
where some words even took on their opposite meanings, were in the air.
This particular consequence of Nazi rhetoric comes through in the second-
to-last stanza of the poem. Such an extreme shift in meaning was especially
troubling for poetic language, because it obviated the boundaries between
truth and lies, and thus destabilized the boundary between euphemism and
metaphor. Because the language of the camps—of both perpetrators and victims—radically changed what it meant to be alive, or to die, to be free or
to be a prisoner, and Nazi German manipulated many culturally significant
terms, conventional poetic language in particular became suspect. This problem is present in the version of "Völker der Erde" printed above (first printed
in the anthology *Fahrt ins Staublose*, 1961), but the version of the poem that
was published in *Sinn und Form* in 1950 begins with a stanza not included
in later editions that, to my mind, alludes more clearly to literary language in
the postwar era:

Völker der Erde,
die ihr den Geheimissen ein paar Blätter und
zerrissene Blumenkronen abgelistet habt,
euren sterbenden Welten sind für immer die Wurzeln abgewendet.³⁹

[Peoples of the Earth,
you who have tricked out of the secrets
a pair of leaves and ripped-up flower crowns,
from your dying worlds the roots are forever turned away.]⁴⁰

This stanza suggests that the poem had as one of its impulses writing and writers. "Geheimnisse," secrets, most often carry a creative connotation in Sachs's work, even as early as 1921, for example in describing Fra Giovanni's desire to paint the "Geheimnisse" of heaven and earth (FA, 7) as the unspeakable that seeks expression in art. "Blätter" and "Blumenkronen" belong to the canon of traditional metaphors for poetic expression and are words Hartung might have categorized as belonging to the problematic "timeless aesthetic." They reflect the bucolic imagery associated with poetic tradition and also with the postwar poets who attempted to return to that tradition, and thus evoke a more idyllic style of poetry that is now no longer accessible. The peoples of the Earth have tricked a few beautiful expressions out of "den Geheimnissen," but will no longer be able to do so. Implied in the phrase "euren sterbenden Welten" is a divide between mortal, dying worlds and the traditional claim of poetry to eternity. The poet might once have been inspired by an eternal divine, or may once have lived on after death in his or her words; but whatever eternal or divine root connected the peoples of the Earth to the ability to coax and cultivate these "Blätter" and "Blumenkronen," that is, these poems, has now turned away from the mortal worlds of the people. Their worlds will no longer live on in words. The stanzas that follow explore, on the one hand, what it can mean that the mortal worlds will henceforth simply die, and on the other, that there is an essentially circular problem of language confronting the peoples of the Earth. Words like "unbekannt[e] Gestirne" (unknown constellations), "Geheimniss[e]" (secrets), and "Quelle" (source) imply that there is an unknown powerful force that is the ultimate source of meaning; yet the subjective force in the poem is the peoples of the Earth, and ultimately the individuals who make up the peoples of the Earth. The later version of the poem begins with "der Kraft der unbekannten Gestirne" (the power of unknown constellations), but then ends with "Sterne gebären helfen" (help give birth to stars); the "Sterne" (stars) are present in the sky, but it is the peoples who help them bear expression, who create "Gestirne" (constellations), the meaningful grouping of stars. It is thus also the peoples who create the different "Himmel" (heavens), "Welten" (worlds), and "Wurzeln" (roots), the "Weltall der Worte" (the universe of words), by bestowing meaning onto "Sterne" (stars). The peoples are the "Quelle" (source) of words. The peoples, then, are able to destroy the mutable universe of words, either through rigid insistence on absolute meaning or through the eradication of subjectivity—either giving it up willfully, or actively taking it from others.

One of the key elements of "Völker der Erde" is the use of plural forms of words that most commonly signify something singular, sovereign, and unified: "Welten" instead of "Welt," "Horizonte" instead of "Horizont," and "die wahren Himmel" instead of "der wahre Himmel."

The use of these plural forms stands out all the more clearly because of the second line of the final stanza: "lasset die Worte an ihrer Quelle" (leave the words at their source); if there are worlds, horizons, and heavens, what is "the" source? Owing to the agency of the peoples of the Earth depicted in the poem, the poem lays bare the uncomfortable truth that they prefer to believe the "Weltall der Worte" (universe of words) is a natural occurrence, or even a mystical entity, when in fact it is something they create and manipulate according to need. Perhaps this is one of the eternal secrets shimmering behind the apocalyptic time of the mid-1940s.

The *Sinn und Form* version's depiction of conventional poetic tropes that are no longer accessible is representative of Sachs's assessment of postwar poetic language in her letters, where she writes that the words and styles of the "*Vor*martyrium-Tradition" (tradition before the martyrdom, that is before the genocide against the Jews) are "verbraucht," used up, and no longer valid in a time ripped open like a wound, after the abyss.[41] Traditional poetry is no longer possible, but its legacy and destruction must be borne in mind. I believe Michael Braun's reading, that the poem calls upon the peoples of earth not to forsake language, is accurate; but not because no word has been rendered unusable. Rather, the peoples of earth should not forsake language because it is our creation. We must own up to our creation and to the responsibility of how we wield it. The poem's ancient and modern imagery highlights the mutability and subjectivity of words: they are what individuals use to weave and reweave their stories; words are necessary in the establishment of a sovereign self. They are therefore also not absolute. "Sprachverwirrung," language confusion, is the norm, not the exception. The peoples of the Earth, and the individuals that make up the peoples, are capable of deception and harm with language. All people bear the same burden as the poet to create their reality with their constellations of words.

Each stanza of "Völker der Erde" explicates a particular relationship to language, and makes clear that all the peoples, and thus all the individuals who make them up, possess a certain amount of power with words and have a tendency to pay it little heed, or to place the responsibility for those words' meaning with someone else. The first stanza immediately lays out the subjective nature of the power of words through the reflexive pronoun "euch." There is a small but distinct nuance contained in the "ihr euch": it is possible to read the "euch" as "each other" (i.e., one people wraps up another in the power of unknown constellations), and as "yourselves" (i.e., the peoples wrap themselves up in the power of unknown constellations). "Unbekannt" suggests that the constellations may be visible, but are unfamiliar. To wrap themselves and each other up in the power of unknown constellations, however, means that someone must know them, since wielding that power would require some knowledge. In likening the unknown constellations to "Garnrollen" (spools of thread, but also balls of yarn), the poetic "I" associates the power of words with constellations and the complex of weaving and sewing, both traditional metaphors and analogs for narrative. Constellations represent a culture's distinct mythological tales and mark important agricultural phases; the "Garn" in "Garnrollen" suggests the sewing together or weaving of tales, but also introduces a sense of deception and entrapment. The verb "umgarnen," extending from the act of entrapping an animal in a net, means "to beguile," "bewitch," or "befool"; "ein Garn spinnen" means "to spin a yarn," in the sense of telling an untrue, fantastic tale. In wrapping themselves and others up in the idea of mystical, unknown constellations like "Garnrollen," they deceive themselves and others in the comforting mindset that a distant, greater power beyond them controls meaning.

The line immediately following takes up the textile theme begun with "Garnrollen," and points out that it is the plural "you" (ihr) that not only sews (näht), or creates a cohesive, meaningful fabric by joining pieces together, it then also undoes what it has sewn or created (auftrennt das Genähte). The wide variety of ancient associations with weaving, sewing, and creating narrative, for example the Fates or Norns, or Penelope, or any number of Greek myths involving tapestries, carry within them also the idea of control over fate. Philomela, for example, takes control of her fate when she weaves the tapestry communicating her rape and mutilation to her sister Procne. The thread spun by the Fates controls the destiny of the world; when it is cut, humans determine their own. Penelope weaves and unweaves Odysseus's father's death shroud night after night, thus maintaining her sovereignty and holding off her would-be suitors. The "ihr," in that it wraps "euch" in mystical constellations like "Garnrollen," controls destiny; it can also create and re-create that destiny according to will. Any unifying mythology or narrative is tenuous and dependent on the needs of those who hold the strings. The variety of associations also asserts that this control can happen on a grand or smaller scale. Constellations yield a sense of a larger power governing a group. The sewing and cutting what was sewn, however, is more relatable to a story of a single person who is creating a narrative and deceiving a group of people in order to protect herself. The power to create a narrative is both great and small, and anyone who creates a narrative, whatever the motivation, has the potential to undo it. This stanza places the agency in the hands of "ihr," the peoples of the Earth.

It then makes clear that the "ihr" includes everyone. From constellations, thread, yarn, and fabric, the second-person plural "ihr" then climbs into "Sprachverwirrung" (literally "language confusion"), which is likened to beehives (Bienenkörbe) where everyone stings and is stung. In the lines "um im Süßen zu stechen / und gestochen zu werden—" is a nod to a consistent theme in Sachs's early and later work, namely that sweetness often brings with it a sting, that is that figurative, beautiful language can sugarcoat malice or an unwanted reality. In her early texts, the sting concealed in the sweet is the loss of subjectivity or even life. This poem adds another possible sting of an uncomfortable reality: every individual carries responsibility for words and the violence that can be accomplished with them. Linking "Sprachverwirrung" to "Bienenkörbe" creates an association of droning, thoughtless, reactionary movement. The narratives one weaves affect others, but so do the words one uses in common, unreflective daily activity. This can as easily apply to a nation of people embracing Nazi German as it can to the crush of modern life, in which people, like worker bees, are absorbed in the rush, too busy or brainwashed to think about the words they use. The Grimms' *Wörterbuch* listing for "Bienen" gives two examples that suggest both readings are possible. Their hierarchical social structure makes bees a provocative metaphor for people. One entry reads: "gleich den menschen halten diese thierchen fuer noethig sich einen herrn zu setzen, der ueber sie gebiete" (just as people, these insects consider it necessary to set themselves a master, who rules over them); the other is a quote from Goethe: "nur die dem staat am treusten dienen, dies sind allein die bessern bienen" (only those who serve the state most loyally, they alone are the better bees).[42] In both of these examples, bees are associated with a devotion to service and authority that for the postwar era could have been immediately related to the Nazis and those who supported them. The bee is not only a loyal servant, it is also capable of doing harm as it goes about its regulated business. Inculcated in their collective culture in this stanza, the "ihr," like drones in a buzzing hive, sting and are stung, surrounded by sweetness. The violence is perhaps obscured by the sweetness, or perhaps it is an accepted component of being part of the hierarchy. Finally, Sachs's clear familiarity with the canon of Greek literature makes it entirely possible that the link between poetry, honey, and politics found in Hesiod's "Theogony" plays a role here, as well. In Sachs's poem, there are no muses to honey-coat the tongue of poet or politician; rather, it is the people who create the honey as well as the language confusion.

The poem's second stanza articulates the extent of the damage that can be done. Returning to the cosmic theme from the opening verses, the poetic "I" urges the people not to destroy the "Weltall der Worte," the universe of words, a space that encompasses all the constellations, worlds, and heavens, every description that has ever been or has the potential to be. The poetic "I" then reframes this destruction in the context of violence done to a person. It is one thing to sew and unravel a fabric; the strands can be rewoven or resewn. It is another to cut to pieces ("zerschneiden") with the knives of hate the sound that was born together with the first breath ("den Laut, der mit dem Atem zugleich geboren wurde"). Breath and the power to express oneself with the voice are the essence of life in this poem. The poetic "I" sets even the smallest sound of the voice ("den Laut") equal to breath; as they are born together, the implication is that cutting the one is to cut the other. The image evokes a sense of silencing a speaker by cutting her or his throat. Silencing someone's voice with the knives of hate is equated with murder. Each individual voice has cosmic importance, since this stanza equates the destruction of the universe of words with the silencing of the sound of the voice.

The third stanza stands out for its brevity, and is, I think, the most challenging. It is the one most clearly linked to Nazi propaganda generally and to the concentrationary universe specifically, where words and concepts took on opposite meanings. Again the poetic "I" brings the problem down to the importance of the individual voice, to the individual ("Einer") choosing what he says. At issue here is not so much that words have absolute meanings, but rather that the meaning of a word is the prerogative of the individual. He can choose, for example, to use a sweeter word to mask what he means. He can also choose to use a word in an unusual way, and it can be what he means. On the other hand, he can choose to thoughtlessly repeat a euphemism created by someone else, in which case he surrenders his own subjectivity not only by not saying what he means, but also by reproducing someone else's disingenuous words. He may, however, be stripped of choice, and forced to use words he does not mean. The operative word of the verse, and indeed of the poem, is the verb "meinen": what the individual means.

The final stanza tempts the reader to believe that words should be left to mean what they originally meant, but that comforting belief in an absolute original meaning is steadily unraveled by the poem. How are we to determine such a thing when the entire history of words consists of interpretation and reinterpretation? How likely is it, moreover, that a poet, whose profession depends on stretching and pushing words beyond their conventional meanings, would advocate a return to an absolute source or a singular meaning? Furthermore, Sachs is a writer who has proven to be consistently preoccupied with figurative language. She says what she means; it is the work of the reader to carefully study the words for what they can mean in their constellations, with the awareness that the entire history of textual creation depends on words being malleable enough to signify things that defy easy description and even things that do not exist. The source of words is the individual consciousness. The corruption of language perpetrated by Nazi propaganda and the ensuing unease surrounding poetic language threatened to destroy the "Weltall der Worte." In that destruction, the poetic "I" sees nothing less than the eradication of the individual, the extension of a National Socialist principle as a consequence of attempting to overcome the legacy of National Socialism. "Völker der Erde" is a complex and far-reaching poem that neither aims to return to an (illusionary) innocent past, or to start from a blank slate; either of those aims obscures the damage done by and to language and the individual. The poem aims to preserve both the ruins left in the wake of Nazi control and the culpability of every people, and every individual; it, like Aichinger's essay, is an "Aufruf zum Mißtrauen."

The critique of language and authority in "Wenn im Vorsommer" and "Völker der Erde" carries important implications for the conventional notion represented by Ricarda Huch's faith in writers as the "Verwalter der Sprache," and for Andersch and Berendsohn's conviction that the twelve years of National Socialism represented an "Irrtum" in an otherwise healthy and innocent Germany. Much like writers at the turn of the century and during the Weimar Republic, writers and critics of the 1940s such as Berendsohn, Andersch, and Huch believed that language and literature were tightly linked to the development of a healthy, independent, and strong German nation. The idea that writers steer thoughts of the reading public is one of the problems that Sachs repeatedly places under scrutiny in many of her poems and early prose works. From a German-Jewish perspective that confronts and questions the viability of *Geist* in relation to the nation, there are two potential problems with the postwar rhetoric of literature and nation. First, it presumes that prewar Germany regarded virtually all poets writing in German as essentially German poets. This view obscures the manifold political and sociological problems that modern poetry exposed and was exposed to. The well-meaning assumption of universality neglects the open hostility and censure encountered by nineteenth- and twentieth-century Jewish German-language writers like Heinrich Heine (1797–1856), Ludwig Börne (1786–1837), Arthur Schnitzler (1862–1931), or Karl Wolfskehl (1869–1948), whose "Germanness" was openly questioned, as well as the double marginalization of Jewish women like the Salonnière Rachel Levin Varnhagen (1771–1833), the poet and playwright Else Lasker-Schüler (1869–1945), or the poet and writer Gertrud Kolmar (1894–1943). It also presumes that humanist universality was a defense against National Socialism rather than part of the problem. Second, the same drive to connect a *Geist* with a geographical place or *Heimat* that was so central to National Socialism (and was indeed widespread before the Nazi period) had retained its hold after the war.

The *Kulturnation* was not a counterbalance to the crimes of National Socialism for Sachs. Her postwar poetry attempts to depict the postwar world, to make it possible for the audience to place it in question, but not to heal it; instead, its wounds should be kept present and open. Unifying a people risks validating the national consciousness at the root of the war, and at its extreme, persecution of outsiders. But whose voice determines the unity, and whose voice determines who are seen as outsiders? These were questions that occupied Sachs, not only in assessing German history, but also regarding the postwar world generally, including the establishment of the State of Israel. The creation of the State of Israel proved both a joy and a concern for Sachs. Israel was a place for those who needed refuge; and yet the growing Israeli nationalism worried her.[43] On September 17th, 1948, barely four months after the establishment of the State of Israel, Swedish Count Folke Bernadotte, who negotiated the release of thousands of Jews from Nazi camps during the war and then became the United Nations mediator in the Israeli-Palestinian conflict, was assassinated in Jerusalem by Jewish nationalist extremists. In a letter to Gudrun Dähnert of October 9th, 1948, Sachs wrote in response to the assassination: "Man kann nur bitten und flehen, daß die Verfolgten niemals Verfolger werden."[44] (One can only beg and plead that the persecuted will never become the persecutors.) Such extreme nationalism, she believed, was the result of immeasurable suffering, but begat only more violence.

Sachs's work and correspondence suggest that she was wary of identification with a parcel of land. She never became a poet for Germany; she rejected the idea of being a poet of Israel in the national sense.[45] Her poetry does not valorize a national narrative or lament a lost tradition; it preserves the rubble and the cultural strata, calls for acknowledgment of culpability, and ultimately attempts to create a textual space that requires the reader to actively confront uncertainty and explore philosophical terrain beyond the guidelines and boundaries we use to define a familiar and reassuring empirical reality. The space of words was for her a space between return and starting over, or as she wrote in a letter of November 24, 1948 to Walter Berendsohn, "Ich weiß, daß meine Worte oft dort stehen, wo der Strand zu Ende ist und das Ungesicherte beginnt" (I know that my words often stand where the beach ends and the uncertain begins).[46] Her work as a poet was not tied to country, but rather began at the edge of solid ground and aimed to reflect the experience of uncertainty, wandering, and the long tradition of writing and rewriting history.

5: Israel Is Not Only Land: Diasporic Poetry

IN SACHS'S POSTWAR POETRY, the poetic text is not a refuge, but rather a space in which the reader's conventional associations and beliefs about language are destabilized. The reader is confronted with obscured perspectives, exposed fallacies or states of denial, and most of all, with his or her own agency. Sachs accomplishes this in particular through her use of cyclical structure, her primary mode of composition after the war. Writing in cycles allowed her to create an extended textual landscape in which the reader moves from poem to poem, that is, from textual space to textual space. The reader is called, upon entering the landscape of a cycle, to pay close attention to the continuously shifting terrain that he or she must map out. As many of Sachs's images of cartography and astronomy suggest, an individual uses constellations and maps to shape space and thus create meaning.[1] As the reader wanders through each poem, he or she finds intertextual references and recurring semantic, structural, and grammatical features whose meanings unfold with each poem. The changing terrain allows words to appear differently and to be redefined; the cycle is often its own lexicon. In mapping the terrain of the cycle as he or she reads, the reader also *creates* the cycle by arranging constellations of meaning. Another dimension is added when the reader follows the logical form of the cycle: proceeding from the final poem of a cycle around to the first poem creates an entirely new reading experience, in which the reader reads not in a closed circle, but in a spiral, rearranging the constellations previously constructed, building from experience but reshaping the space of words. This process is very much akin to the images of cosmic constellations, weaving, and sewing from "Völker der Erde"; we join individual pieces together in a way that is meaningful to us, yet each spiral requires us to rearrange the pieces. The cycle can repeat in perpetuity, and has the potential to appear different each time for each reader.

This cyclical spiral structure mimics the Jewish conception of time, which is not a linear progression moving away from a point of origin, but rather a spiral that passes its point of origin even as it moves away from it. Past events are both past and present; they are not commemorated, but are rather reexperienced. This occurs in the rituals and liturgy, but is also intrinsic to the experience of the Jewish text, in the tradition of exegesis, commentary, and law. Each engagement with the text is simultaneously an engagement with others who have engaged with the text, whether in the form of modern scholars responding to medieval commentaries, the congregant interpreting the psalms, or in the form of interpreting the law in the diaspora. Jewish time keeps all things present; to a large extent, this is the result of scattered people, that is, of diaspora. When Jonathan Boyarin writes that "we [Jews] remind ourselves of what we are by reminding ourselves of what we miss,"[2] he is recalling precisely this constant presence as a result of loss. And indeed the poetic cycle's potentially endless and eternally shifting landscape mimics the experience of diaspora. Wandering in this textual space, across the ever-shifting landscape filled with gaps and evidence of loss, the reader must interpret and reinterpret with each reading. This is diasporic poetry: it performs the diasporic condition in the space of the text, and it correspondingly demands that the reader also exist in the condition of diaspora within the space of the text. The diasporic reader connects with other sources and readers, but exists in the present moment, and dynamically engages with the poetic images, which often defy sense or categorization, as they change. These were the attributes demanded of Sachs's early protagonists Fra Giovanni; the girl in the woods with her nightingale; Chelion; and Gotelind: we the readers are now in the position of those protagonists. We are now called upon to actively navigate the space of words. In this chapter I intend to show how diaspora, rather than exile, is a productive perspective for reading Sachs's cycles. Because the text resists closure, I present a viable new reading of a cycle, but by no means a closed or definitive reading. The nature of the diasporic text is to invite discussion and reinterpretation.

Sachs's work reflects a relationship to language that moves between, and often crosses, borders. Her poems are both archaic and avant-garde; her prose characters often find themselves caught in a moment between conventional word usage and uncertain or obscured figurative usage. In the postwar era, Sachs connected the sense of wandering in the space of words, which had long been a consistent pattern in her work, with the stakes and vocabulary of diaspora. In November of 1948, six months after the establishment of the State of Israel, Sachs wrote to Walter Berendsohn, "Ich weiß, daß meine Worte oft dort stehen, wo der Strand zu Ende ist und das Ungesicherte beginnt; aber steht Israel nicht jetzt und immer dort?"[3] (I know that my words often stand where the beach ends and the uncertain begins; but doesn't Israel stand now and always there?) Here, she positions her words in an in-between state; they exist at the margin of a landscape that is still familiar, but at a point where the uncertain and unstable begin. The description acknowledges the capacity of her writing to position the reader in a somewhat familiar poetic landscape that nonetheless blends into a formless and unstable space. The reader thus has familiar anchor points, but must simultaneously confront unfamiliar, ambiguous, and unstable poetic constructions. She justifies this conception of words by likening it to a diasporic conception of Israel, an idea and a diverse people, not *Eretz Israel*, the land of Israel. For Sachs, Israel was always engaged in wandering, always aware of the lack of a permanent home, and this instability actually afforded Israel the unique power to breach conventional limitations, to continually cross borders of time and space, and to maintain relevance because it was by necessity always being written and rewritten. Israel occupied a position on the margins, on the brink of the uncertain, always in the present tense, and never completely defined. Sachs saw the establishment of the State of Israel as an important step in creating a safer world for Jewish refugees,[4] but at the same time, she was apprehensive that securing national borders and establishing a national identity would undermine what she saw as the essence of Israel.

Central to Sachs's postwar poetics is her sense of reverence for the experience of *galut* understood as diaspora, which is not dependent on a longing to return to a homeland, as opposed to *galut* as exile, which is based precisely on that longing. The creation of the State of Israel in 1948 presented a new context in which Sachs saw an urgent need to create a space of words that resisted valorizing the concept of a return and emphasized instead the significance of constant wandering and uncertainty. In her immediate postwar poems, Sachs demonstrated that a return to a more innocent past in German literature was impossible and disingenuous. Similarly, she problematized the idea that the establishment of the State of Israel meant a return to an originary or corrective, innocent existence; such a belief not only obscured thousands of years of meaning, it ultimately threatened to eradicate the very meaning of Israel. Sachs explored the significance of diaspora and the danger of valorizing the nation-state in numerous poems, for example "Land Israel" in *Sternverdunkelung*, "David" and "Wie viele Heimatländer" in *Flucht und Verwandlung* (1959), and "Überall Jerusalem" from *Noch feiert Tod das Leben* (1961); but the cycle "Flügel der Prophetie" from *Und Niemand weiss weiter* does it in a way that brings the major themes of nation, literature, and the space of words to the forefront.

Sachs's position on the State of Israel contains elements of a branch of Zionism associated with Martin Buber, whose works Sachs read and incorporated into "Flügel der Prophetie," a branch that was more focused on Jewish values than on politics, and that resonates with the diasporic interpretation, rather than the exilic interpretation, of *galut*. Finding uniquely keen awareness of detail and therefore insight in the disorientation of wandering and the marginality that comes with existence in the diaspora, she found a similar power in diaspora to that which Jonathan and Daniel Boyarin argued for in 2002, to that which Moritz Goldstein argued for in 1912, and to that which Erich S. Gruen has argued was an essential feature of Jewish thought and practice even in the ancient world.

The nation of Israel is fundamentally tied to, and created by, texts both read and spoken. The canon of the Hebrew Bible, the Tanakh (consisting of the Torah [Five Books of Moses], the Nevi'im [Prophets], and the Kethuvim [Writings]), and in particular the Torah, was compiled largely in the Babylonian exile of the 6th century BCE, and serve as a bond and an ersatz homeland to a diverse group of people driven from the place they once occupied. The lack of a physical homeland coupled with a strong cultural and textual history of questioning of and dialogue about ritual, history, and meaning make the necessity of constantly asking and discussing what Israel is the strength, or power in the Boyarins' words, of diaspora. Identifying very strongly with a parcel of land risks losing the uncertainty that is the very source of the dialogue and irresolvability that make up the ever-shifting parameters of Israel. Sachs was wary of the temptation to view *Eretz Israel* as the solution to the problem of anti-Semitism or anti-Jewish sentiment, as an antidote to Europe's ills, or as destination that would put an end to *galut*. The roots of the nation of Israel are, moreover, semi-nomadic; biblical figures too attached to place, like Abraham's nephew Lot or Noah's great grandson Nimrod, are punished. In the creation of an Israeli state, Sachs saw the threat of a diverse group of people unlearning the paradoxical essence and meaning of their existence in a potentially damaging effort to adhere to the structure of the "nation-state," the very structure that persecuted them. In "Flügel der Prophetie," Sachs brings to light Israel's fragmented, multicultural history and the essentially unclosed, diasporic meaning it contains. In bringing the diasporic meaning out in this cycle, she reminds Israel of what it, Israel, is as a result of loss and scattering. Rather than aiming for return and healing, Sachs suggests that the open, unhealing wound of diaspora creates a powerful, even physical link to Israel's history, which has been repeatedly threatened by states insistent on what is ultimately a destructive ideal of the nation-state. In the postwar world, the diasporic existence is a new way that Israel can be a "light of nations" (*Jewish Study Bible*, Isa. 42.6, 49.6), providing an alternative model for a postwar world trying to rebuild itself.

"Flügel der Prophetie" revolves around the meaning of Israel, as a word, as a concept, and as a nation-state. It consists of eight poems: seven that appear to have been composed together: "Chassidim Tanzen" (Hasidim Dance), "Nicht nur Land ist Israel!" (Israel Is Not Only Land!), "Später Erstling!" (Late Firstborn!), "Dieses Land" (This Land), "Abraham der Engel!" (Abraham the Angel!), "Immer noch Mitternacht auf diesem Stern" (Still Midnight on this Star), "Daniel mit der Sternenzeichnung" (Daniel with the Mark of Stars); and an eighth poem appended to the end, "Mutterwasser" (Maternal Water), which is the prologue to Sachs's play *Abram im Salz* (Abram in Salt).[5] The essential conceptual image that runs like a red thread through the cycle, both thematically and structurally, is the "Rand," a word that can be rendered in English as margin, border, boundary, brim, edge, verge, seam, fringe, or brink. A number of images in the cycle are related through their significant edges or borders, like the edge of wounds, or the edge of the beach, the rim between earth and sky, the boundary between death and life or dream and waking, or the imprint in the earth of long since dissolved bones, roads, structures, or civilizations. In a structural sense, we straddle and cross borders and spaces literally between poems or as we turn the page. We also stand at the margins of texts and cross their borders as we connect ideas and references from texts such as books of the Hebrew Bible, legends by Buber, myths from the ancient world, or with Sachs's transplanted prologue. The "Rand" is essential in the cycle because it is both important to take heed of and important to breach. No border is impenetrable, but neither are borders erased; on the contrary, readers are encouraged to rediscover long-forgotten borders they have simply learned to overlook although they still exist. Sachs worked the sense of standing at the edge of the beach, just at the beginning of the uncertain, into the cycle both literally (in the poem "Abraham der Engel!") and structurally. The content of the poems flows between images of breaching boundaries and images of trapping oneself within limitations; the structure forces the reader beyond conventional imagery and conventional limitations of text on a page.

The cycle resonates with the atmosphere of the biblical book of Genesis and is dominated by images related to the human body, agriculture, and wandering. Scattered throughout the cycle are symbols for the cultural legacy of civilizations and cultures, from ancient Greece and Israel to the high point of Jewish mysticism in the eighteenth century, that inform the present world. Their symbolic meanings reverberate in the twentieth century; they represent the work of thousands of years of writing and interpretation that shape the empirical and political world we occupy. Markers of time are present in terms of the periods of the days (night, midnight), while what we would consider longer-term time coalesces into a constant present. The cycle throws into relief the multicultural history of defining Israel (culturally, semantically, politically, geographically), resists closure, and emphasizes the work of wanderers who recognize the power of their own bodies to sense and then shape the space around them, and to ultimately define (and continually redefine) the space with words. In particular the relationship of the body to the creation and transmission of meaning is juxtaposed with self-important overidentification with a single geographical location.

The cycle proceeds from a Chassidic (Jewish mystical) principle of experiencing the divine in the world, that is, in sacred as well as banal tasks. An important aspect of this principle is the power of the word. The individual has power with words to shape the empirical world and to connect generations in real time. Martin Buber gives the example in his introduction to *Tales of the Chassidim* (1949) of a lamed man telling a story about his teacher, the Baal Shem Tov (Israel ben Eliezer, ca. 1700–1760; founder of Chassidism). As he described how the Baal Shem Tov danced and jumped when he prayed, the lame man himself danced and jumped: in recounting the tale, he himself experienced the tale physically. This Chassidic principle is an intensely literal reflection of diasporic life. As one is not in Israel, Israel must exist within the person, or within the Torah. Holy days are not days to remember events long past, but rather to experience events of the past as if they were happening in the present; the Sabbath is a suspension in time. Jews come together, across generations, in and through texts. Sachs worked this into the cycle by including references to ancient myth as well as more modern texts. Martin Buber's story "Abraham der Engel," the source text of the poem "Abraham der Engel!,"[6] gives a representative example of this deep connection to text in a character that has the ability to exist in a state between earthly and divine. This Abraham is a wanderer, who, through the word, experiences and shapes time and space in the present. The Book of Daniel (from the Writings section of the Tanakh) is the source text for "Daniel mit der Sternenzeichnung"; we are encouraged to recognize his skills for reading long-forgotten language and script as well as his messages regarding earthly power and apocalypse. "Mutterwasser" and the text that provided its original context, *Abram im Salz*, emphasize land as a readable text: "Bei den Ausgrabungen in Ur fand man oft auf der Erde den Abdruck und das Muster von Gegenständen, die selbst gänzlich in Staub zerfallen waren. Es war die Schrift des schon unsichtbar Gewordenen, die man zu lesen versuchte."[7] (During the excavations in Ur the impression and pattern of objects that had themselves fallen completely to dust were often found in the earth. It was the writing of that which had already become invisible that they were trying to read.) These impressions are the symbols of the past, written into the earth; the objects are gone, yet their writing in the earth remains. They are therefore as much a part of the present as they are of the past: they are reminders of what we miss and lack. Within the scope of the cycle "Flügel der Prophetie," the suggestion is that we not only learn to read these texts, but also learn to experience them ourselves as we read. The readers depicted in the cycle, like Abraham and other Chassidim, Daniel, and the excavator of "Mutterwasser," are marginal, displaced figures, and because of this, they carry knowledge of different cultures, are aware of their surroundings, and are capable of seeing boundaries and patterns to which the dominant culture remains blind; they experience and are open to experiencing shifting landscapes across time, and they contribute to its continued creation and re-creation. The experience of the text is eventually inscribed in the body itself, and bodies merge with or dissolve into different forms of land and text.

The first poem in the cycle sets the reader up to consider experiencing and creating the world, first through sense and then through words. It also sets in place the link between body and land.

Chassidim Tanzen

Nacht weht
mit todentrißnen Fahnen

Schwarze Hüte
Gottes Blitz-Ableiter
rühren das Meer auf

wiegen es
wiegen es aus

werfen es an den Strand
dort wo das Licht
die schwarzen Wunden ausgeschnitten hat.

Auf der Zunge
wird die Welt geschmeckt
abgesungen
die atmet mit der Jenseitslunge.

Auf dem Sieben-Leuchter
beten die Plejaden—8

[*Hasidim Dancing*

Night flutters
with flags torn from death

Black hats
God's lightning rods
stir up the sea

weigh it
weight it out

cast it upon the shore
there where the light
has carved black wounds.

The world which breathes
with lungs of the beyond
is tasted on the tongue
chanted out.

The Pleiades pray
on the seven-branched candelabra—9]

A group of Chassidic men dancing, represented by their black hats, "wie-gen" (the verb can mean either "to weigh" or "to rock") both night and the ocean; in their movement, they also resemble night and ocean, in their black hats and swaying back and forth. They are God's lightning rods, suggesting that they are able to channel the power of the divine and bring it to earth. The second stanza describes something the reader might see, whereas the first and third stanzas place the reader in the moment: we sense the "wehen" (translated as "flutters" but carrying also a more audial character of blowing, to which we will eventually return), while the dactylic rhythm of the third stanza helps the reader experience the dance of waves being moved and bodies moving like water. Although the subject is presumably carried over from the second stanza (black hats, God's lightning rods), the possibility exists to feel a part of the subject of the third stanza, as well. Because the conjugation "wiegen" matches the pronoun "they" (sie) as well as "we" (wir) and the formal "you" (Sie), and because no subject is written into the third stanza, we the readers can also read ourselves as subjects of "wiegen," a reading that is in line with the implication of the generalized body resulting from the passive voice of the fifth stanza. The fourth stanza introduces the potential to conceive of land as body, since the light has cut black wounds into it.

The light of the fourth stanza presents a complication, because it inflicts wounds. The Chassidim (and potentially we) throw "das Meer" (the sea) onto the beach, where light, perhaps from lightning channeled by the lightning rods, has cut black wounds. This may represent man-made light, something as banal as an electric light casting shadows on beach, or the power of humans to cut, that is to divide up, the land. Sachs wrote that the image was inspired by a moment in which she observed Chassidim dancing under lights from her window.[10] It may also be a reinterpretation of the light from the Book of Isaiah (from the Prophets section of the Tanakh). The final stanza of the poem invokes the seven-branched menorah, which today represents Israel because it symbolizes Isaiah's metaphorical light. Israel as the light of nations (Isa. 42.6; 49.6), paradoxically, derives from the idea that light is not a violent force; yet the menorah image suggests a conceptual link. The light-wounds-menorah link draws a connection between the violent light, the wound, and the light of nations, as do other poems in the cycle. This is all the more surprising because it means that this violence must then contain some positive element.

Whether its violence originates with humankind or the divine, the light requires transmission, mediation, and interpretation by people, for example the dancing Chassidim, or indeed the reader. Whichever way "light" is interpreted, there is a sense of permanence, since wounds, even if they heal, leave scars. "Black" suggests deep, burnt wounds etched into the body of the land. The Chassidim throwing the sea on the beach would shape the sand, affecting also the shape of the wounds cut into it; they are shaping the empirical world through their experience of the divine, which is detailed more particularly in the fifth stanza. The world is tasted, in essence sensed, on the tongue, and then sung, in essence created, from the tongue. If we the readers read the poem aloud, which would be "absingen," we, with the dancing Chassidim, are creating the world. As with the third stanza, the verbs suggest that Chassidim are not alone in their task. In using the passive voice ("wird geschmeckt," "wird abgesungen"), tasting and singing the world become a prescription for everyone. The final line of the fifth stanza makes clear which world: the one that breathes with the "Jenseitslunge," the lung of the beyond. Also the "Jenseits" (the beyond), then, is described in terms of the body. Since the Chassidim channel and convey divine input, they are very much like poets. That they (and we) can sense and sing the world that "breathes with the lungs of the beyond" suggests "inspiration," etymologically the creative impulse resulting from divine breath.

Because their physical experience of inspiration affects the empirical world, then, there is little separation between earthly experience and spiritual experience. The first poem leads the reader into a secular, poetic experience through mystical practice: we all sense the world, we all also create the world, in action, and, as the final stanza suggests, with the meanings we ascribe to the symbols we create. The final stanza is made up of two multivalent and intercultural symbols brought together. The "Sieben-Leuchter" (literally "seven-lamp") is the literal German translation for the seven-branched menorah, the ancient symbol of Judaism. The seven-branched menorah evokes also the destruction of the first and second temples; since the first and second temple menorah had seven branches, its use was discontinued after the destruction of the second temple in 70 CE. It also became the symbol on the seal of the State of Israel, representing simultaneously the State of Israel, the nation of Israel, the commemoration of the destruction of the temple, and the goal of Israel to be a light of nations—an ancient goal, and one with added significance in the post–Second World War world. But the menorah is not a sovereign object in this poem; atop the seven-branched menorah sit the Pleiades, the seven sisters, praying. The Pleiades are also invested with a number of meanings: in Greek mythology, they are the seven daughters of Atlas, who carries the night sky on his shoulders; they are also a constellation in the night sky that is important for the agricultural calendar. As they are associated primarily with night, and are praying, they mirror the Chassidim of the title. As stars, they are a guiding light; their story of transformation and the resulting constellation define part of the night sky. The myth of the Pleiades contributes to how generations have defined the shape of the night sky, and it in turn contributes to how generations have navigated, shaped, and worked the earth. Because many Greek myths and their resulting constellations have these functions, it seems reasonable to ascribe the particular significance of the story of the Pleiades to their number. Both the Pleiades and the menorah are seven lights from ancient cultures that guide spiritual and geographical wanderers. They are perhaps even appropriately linked through the history of flight and loss they represent. The story of the seven sisters is a story of pursuit and flight: they flee the lustful hunter Orion, until "Zeus intervenes . . . not to resolve the relationship of pursuit and flight but to freeze it forever in a different form."[11] While their story is of a different nature than that of Israel, the result is relevant for the cycle: they are frozen in a state of unresolved flight from pursuit. Their story and constellation reflect a state of incompleteness and flux.

The choice of a Greek myth at the outset of the cycle has one other potential point of significance. The Greek Pleiades praying are presumably the light of the menorah, that is, they activate this major Jewish symbol with their act of vocalization. It was Hellenistic Greek culture that gave rise to much of how we define the cultural productivity of *galut*, and indeed that culture gave us the word "diaspora," meaning "scattering." These unresolved states of being, translation into different forms, the perpetual existence in flight in foreign climes, all these are part of the scattering, the diaspora. The importance of Greek and other foreign influences for Sachs's diasporic conception of Israel will continue to appear in the cycle. Finally, it is important to note that the poem "Chassidim Tanzen" itself will never resolve, is never completed, because the final line is never completed. Although these lines are made up of ancient symbols, they are symbols whose meanings have multiplied over time; they continue to evolve, unceasingly if we continue to actively intone them.

Whereas "Chassidim Tanzen" places the reader actively in the cycle, "Nicht nur Land ist Israel" provides an orientation for reading it. The poem is comprised of a set of sentence segments, like variations on a theme, that describe what Israel is in addition to land. It begins with lack and longing, moves through historical sequence, defeat, wandering, and comes to a divide between the tortured desert-heaven on the ground and an open "Gotteswunde" (wound of God) in the plumage of the air. The series of variations represents a microcosm of the cycle, which is a set of variations on the theme "Flügel der Prophetie" (line seven). Each poem brings out a different aspect of the theme of the cycle, explicates certain words or concepts that are introduced in other poems. This poem, using language reminiscent of the Book of Daniel, makes the land a body that is carried by words of prophets, and exists in words of spoken prayer. It also hints toward carefully woven-in references to Jacob in the next two poems. There is only one conjugated verb in the entire poem: "ist" (is). Everything expressed in the poem is what Israel is, always in the present tense. Like "Chassidim Tanzen," it breaks off with a dash at the end, allowing for the list to continue.

Nicht nur Land ist Israel!
Vom Durst in die Sehnsucht,
von der rotangeheizten Mitternachtswurzel
durch die Türen des Ackerkornes
zu den geisterblauen Hauchtrinkern
hinter der Gnade zuckender Blindenbinde.
Flügel der Prophetie
an der Schulter aus Wüstensand.
Deine Pulse im Nachtgewitter reitend,
die erzenen Füße
deiner Ewigkeit-schnaubenden Berge
galoppierend
bis in der Kindergebete
milchweißem Schaum.

Deiner Fußspuren kreisende Meridiane
im Salz des Sündenfalls,
deine grüne Segenswurzel eingeschlummert
im gemarterten Himmel der Wüste,
die offene Gotteswunde
im Gefieder der Luft—[12]

[*Israel is not only land!*

Israel is not only land!
From thirst into longing,
from the red-heated midnight-root
through the doors of the field's seed
to the ghost-blue drinkers of breath
behind the grace of the twitching blindfold.
Wings of prophecy
by the shoulder of desert sand.
Riding your pulses in the night-storm,
the iron feet
of your eternity-snorting mountains
galloping
even in the milk-white foam
of children's prayers.

Circling meridians of your footprints
in the salt of original sin,
your green root of blessing fallen asleep
in the tortured desert sky,
the open wound of God
in the plumage of air—[13]]

Although there is only one conjugated verb in the entire poem, this is a poem of movement. It lacks a consistent meter, but occasionally reintroduces the swaying dactyl to trochee progression of "Chassidim Tanzen," for example "vom Durst in die Sehnsucht," or "Mitternachtswurzel." Lacking complete sentences or resolution, it is also a poem of fragmentation. The sentence segments divide the poem into five variations. Line one, "Nicht nur Land ist Israel!," sets the theme. Line two is the first variation: from thirst into longing. Lines three through six are the second variation; it resembles the first variation as a "von" statement, but it is a different, more specific description of the history of the nation of Israel. The first variation asserts that Israel is fundamentally rooted in a lack and in a longing for something. The second variation (lines three through six) is a cycle of agricultural life that can also be read as a sequential history. It begins with a root that maintains the theme of night and is an analog to the lightning rods of the first poem. Night is increasingly marked as a time of great potential. The next line describes the evolution of the root to "Ackerkorn," a seed that is then a doorway to the next stage, something more ambiguous and less earthly. The "geisterblauen Hauchtrinker" (ghost-blue drinkers of breath) maintain the theme of thirst, and also mark a transition from thirst to consumption, behind the "Gnade" (which can mean grace or mercy) of "zuckender Blindenbinde" (twitching blindfolds). This sequence describes at least three progressions. First, from its beginnings in agricultural terms to its end in more abstract, spiritual terms, it describes the life cycle: life takes root, grows, emerges, and then is transformed to the beyond, a possible reading for "Hauchtrinker," as if the breath of the earthly body is drunk into a different realm. The thirst and desire of Israel transforms ultimately not in finding satiation, but in the process of being drunk itself. The other realm exists behind "der Gnade zuckender Blindenbinde," a plausible metaphor for judgment; in this context it would make more sense to read "Gnade" as mercy, since justice is meant to be blind and merciful. This possibility provides a thematic link to the first poem, since the image of justice as a blindfolded woman is of Greek origin, and is also reflected in the constellation Virgo. This sequence also reflects the progression from spring planting, around the time of Passover, to the time of judgment and atonement, from Rosh Hashanah through Yom Kippur, that is, the span of the agricultural calendar between the most significant holidays that mark exodus and divine judgment in the Jewish liturgical calendar. Finally, the sixth verse suggests a particular historical moment. The image of the slipping blindfolds reflects the medieval icon of Judaism, "Synagoga" (a Greek word that appears in the next poem), a blindfolded, stooped, defeated woman. The second line of the poem describes ancient expulsion; the third through sixth lines essentially trace growth to a period of demise. In this context, it makes sense to read "Gnade" as grace, a word largely associated with Christianity. "Hauchtrinker" coupled with medieval Synagoga suggests that the firm establishment of Christianity as the dominant ruling power during the Middle Ages, eventually even establishing the Kingdom of Jerusalem, drained Israel of its life force and thus depicted it as a defeated queen who cannot see the light (in direct opposition to the Chassidic dancers of the first poem, who internalize and transmit light).

The seventh and eighth lines bring together body, word, and land. Here is the body of Israel, represented by a shoulder that is made of desert sand. Appended to the body are wings of prophecy. Although the translation says "by the shoulder," it is grammatically possible to read "an der Schulter" as "*on* the shoulder," as well, and so these verses present the body as the land in the diaspora, carried by wings of prophecy, that is by the words that make up the story of Israel. Israel is the body in the diaspora; it is also the words that define it in the diaspora (i.e., the Tanakh). The word-body-land complex continues into the next variation, lines nine through fourteen. Since lines seven and eight established Israel as a body, line nine introduces the poetic "I" addressing the body; but, since it does not say "Deine Pulse, *Israel*," the poetic "I" can also address the reader in "Deine Pulse." Encapsulated in two words, the poetic "I" creates a dynamic link between Israel and the reader. The "Deine Pulse" directly addresses the body of Israel, which has multiple pulses: this can be read as the people who make up that body, and as the collage of impulses that have infused it with life and meaning, from Greek mythology to medieval iconography, the Prophets and Writings of the Tanakh and the stories of the Chassidim; but the "deine" also turns a sense of familiarity toward the reader. The pulses of this body are "yours," that of the singular, now familiar ("du") reader. The first poem already establishes the involvement of the reader's body in the creation of the text. In "Nicht nur Land ist Israel," the text, the land, and the body are moving together.

Variations three and four (lines seven and eight, nine through fourteen) incorporate references to the subject of the seventh poem, "Daniel mit der Sternzeichnung." The dynamic landscape resembles the monsters of Daniel's night visions, all of which are symbols for the rise and fall of kingdoms, thus providing an example of the wings of prophecy carrying the body-text of Israel, and foreshadowing the warnings in later poems. These verses expand into prayer, a subjective and sometimes spontaneous speaking experience learned from childhood. The experience of prayer is the experience of this moving ("reitend" and "galoppierend," riding and galloping) body and land; all of these variations follow boundary crossings, from thirst into desire, from root to the realm behind "Gnade," galloping "bis in der Kindergebete / milchweißem Schaum" (even into the milk-white foam of children's prayers). Like the prayers of the Pleiades, the prayers of children are coded with power. Even the child is connected to the experience of Israel, who continues to create him- or herself as Israel through spoken prayer, allied with a sense of life-giving power through the image of the milk-like foam.

The final stanza comprises two final variations, lines fifteen through eighteen and lines nineteen and twenty, which bring the significance of the lines together with the establishment of a nation-state. The list begins with the long history of wandering ("Deiner Fußspuren kreisende Meridiane," circling meridians of your footprints) and continues with a green root of blessing that recalls lines three through six; but this root is "eingeschlummert." The root is asleep in the "gemarterten Himmel der Wüste," which the translation renders as "tortured desert sky," but can also be rendered as "tortured heaven of the desert," not a possessive but rather a metaphorical link between heaven and desert. Because there is no body part in the phrase, it appears this is not the desert that otherwise has been carried in body and word, but rather the desert as a place to which one returns. "Himmel" can appear less in the sense of sky, but in the sense of a heaven, a place one longs to finally reach. Israel is "kreisende Meridiane," diasporic paths around the world and throughout time, made of the impressions of feet in the salt left behind by a mix of original sin with the great flood ("im Salz des Sündenfalls"). Its root is slumbering in a tortured ("gemartert") desert heaven, tortured, perhaps, in that it has been fought over, carved up into territories, and indeed engineered for agriculture. Above the land, in the "Gefieder der Luft," the plumage of the air (recalling the wings of prophecy that carry Israel), we find the "offene Gotteswunde," the open wound of God. There is no clear sense of what this might be; but the open wound of God in the air suggests that the vibrant, present need for attention is not in the land, but rather all around beyond the land. The same kind of wound appears in *Abram im Salz* as a wound in the sky that gives birth to Abram's covenant with the God of Israel; another iteration will appear in the poem "Abraham der Engel!" The "Gotteswunde" in this poem offers no sense that it can be closed or healed. Because the poem is in the present tense and is, since it comes to an abrupt end with Sachs's characteristic dash, also incomplete, this "Gotteswunde" will always remain open, like the poem will always remain unresolved. The cycle encourages the State of Israel not to lose sight of the nation of Israel, which is in its essence an eternally incomplete complex of sojourners of different times, traditions, languages, texts, calendars, and icons, sharing a bond to a wound. What unites them is this continually emerging experience, not a parcel of land. The next five poems continue to weave text, body, and land to explicate Israel for a postwar world, beginning with a "Später Erstling!"

"Später Erstling!" contextualizes the sojourner returning to *Eretz Israel* within the land-body-text complex. The poem is a deconstruction of home, tradition, prophecy, and ritual, as indicated by the title, a patronizing, emphatic address to someone who self-identifies as a first-born, but who, the poetic "I" points out, is a latecomer.

> Später Erstling!
> Mit dem Spaten heimgekommen
> ins Ungeschachtete,
> Ungezimmerte,
> nur in die Linie,
> die läuft wieder
> durch die Synagoge der Sehnsucht
> von Tod in Geburt.
>
> Dein Sand wieder,
> deiner Wüste Goldmaske
> vor der Engelskämpfe
> heruntergebogenem Himmel,
> vor den flammenden Früchten
> deiner *Gott* sprechenden Nacht.
>
> Später Erstling,
> Rose aus Salz,
> mit dem Schlaf der Geburten
> wie eine dunkle Weinranke
> hängend an deiner Schläfe . . .[14]

[*Late firstborn!*

Late firstborn!
You have come home with the spade
into the unexcavated,
the unconstructed,
but into the line
that leads again
through the synagogue of longing
from death into birth.

Again your sand,
golden mask of your desert
facing the bent-down sky
of angels' battles,
facing the flaming fruits
of your night which says *God*.

Late firstborn,
rose of salt,
with the sleep of births
like a dark tendril of vine
hanging at your brow . . .[15]]

Where the first two poems contained a significant amount of movement, this poem focuses more on stasis. It is the first poem in the cycle
to introduce the concept of home, in the word "heimgekommen"; the
participial construction creates a sense of stasis that is at odds with the
conceptual collage of Israel in the first two poems. There, even seem-
ingly inanimate objects like mountains or footprints are described
as "galoppierend" (galloping) or "kreisend" (circling), whereas the
"Segenswurzel" is "eingeschlummert / im gemarterten Himmel." The
participle is static and the slumbering state is unobservant. In "Später
Erstling!" the returning sojourner is connected grammatically to the
slumber in the tortured desert. The work he is doing is fundamental,
but the poetic "I" suggests his work is limited and misguided. This conflict is depicted as a reinterpretation of the foundational Genesis story
of Jacob and Esau. Jacob becomes the namesake of Israel; but he comes
to a blessing and a birthright that was originally the property of his twin
brother Esau, who was the actual, chronological firstborn. Esau's significance in the family history as firstborn is erased as Jacob outwits and
robs him. Jacob, who ends up with Esau's birthright and blessing, is the
late firstborn, a "Später Erstling." On the one hand, the poem presents
a critical depiction of the mindset of the man returning to *Eretz Israel*;
on the other, the poem concedes that moral ambiguity is part of the
foundation narrative even of the nation of Israel.

The "später Erstling" of the poem has returned to a home that,
having brought his spade, he expects he must build from nothing. It
is the "Ungeschachtete, / Ungezimmerte" (unexcavated, / unconstructed), essentially a home that is not there, and so he must build,
partition, and define. However, he has entered a space that is well traveled: "nur in die Linie, / die läuft wieder / durch die Synagoge der
Sehnsucht / von Tod in Geburt" (but into the line / that leads again
/ through the synagogue of longing / from death into birth). The
"nur" (but, only) and "wieder" (again) underscore the contradictory
"late firstborn"; he is not the first, but rather following in a line of
wanderers who travel and have traveled the meridians of the earth that
run through the "Synagoge der Sehnsucht." "Home" is the unend-
ing meridians that run through the synagogue, a Greek word meaning
"place of meeting," here not a building where Jews come together,
but instead a *concept* where Jews come together, a place of meeting
in and of "Sehnsucht," in and of longing and wandering. The previous two poems establish that the "place of meeting" is in the space of
the word, both textual (the words of prophets and seers) and spoken
(prayer). The phrase "von Tod in Geburt" will be explicated further in
later poems, but at this point in the cycle builds on an emerging theme
of fragments (of fabric as in "Fahnen" or pieces of text or prayer) that
breach the boundary between death and life.

The second stanza of the poem fuses Jacob's dream at Bethel with the night when he strives with the divine being at the Jabbok ford to describe the late firstborn's moment of return to the land of Israel. The body-land complex sets the scene for the nighttime encounter in the poem. "Dein Sand wieder" (again your sand) suggests a return to the land that was once the land of the Jews. If we recall, however, from "Nicht nur Land ist Israel" the lines "Flügel der Prophetie / an der Schulter aus Wüstensand" (wings of prophecy / on the shoulder made of desert sand), we see "Sand" as a component of the diasporic body, which is not the desert itself, but is made of desert sand. "Dein Sand wieder" also reflects the body of the "Erstling" himself, who has returned to the sand he already in effect physically is. In the next line, his sand is covered with the idolized desert, "deiner Wüste Goldmaske" (golden mask of your desert). The material nature of the golden mask ("Goldmaske"), analogous to the false idol of the golden calf, the poetic "I" suggests that the firstborn conceals his own actual self behind an overidentification with the land ("Wüste"). The mask is "vor," in front of, what is happening in the night sky above him. The translation renders this as "facing," but the preposition "vor" also means that the mask acts as a barrier between "Dein Sand" (the body of the late firstborn) and the low-hanging night sky, heavy with the impending "Engelskämpfe," between him and the "flammenden Früchten deiner *Gott* sprechenden Nacht" (flaming fruits / of your night which says *God*). The participial adjective "sprechenden" recalls the active motion and vibrant presence introduced in the final variations of "Nicht nur Land ist Israel!," juxtaposed against the static "heimgekommen" late firstborn. The night is heavy with hot, violent images, and is speaking, which should, following the logic of the source narrative, be Jacob's moment of becoming Israel, as he strives with the being and becomes Israel; the mask he possesses seems to prevent or shield him from the experience of the night. In Genesis, Jacob comes away from the encounter with the name Israel and a significant wound to the hip. Whether or not that happens for the figure in this poem is unclear; the visual form of the final stanza, however, offers a clue.

The final stanza bears two unusual visual cues in the cycle: it begins with an indentation, and rather than breaking off at the end with a long dash, it trails off with an ellipsis. The indentation occurs only one other time in the cycle, in the poem "Abraham der Engel!" The indented stanzas follow a potential encounter. The added visual delay reads as a mark of force in the body of the text, a visualization of a wound after an encounter, or the mark, like a footprint, of evidence of an editorial choice. It reminds readers that they are actively within the cycle, performing the acts of reading and interpretation of figures in the poems themselves. Given the visual similarity of the indentation to the wound, the boundary, or the imprint, there are several meaningful ways to interpret it; however, there is no certainty in assigning meaning to the indentation, a mark left in the body of the text. This in itself is consistent with the presence in the cycle of recognizable symbols imbued with numerous coexisting interpretations.

Such a symbol occurs in the next stanza. The image of the "Rose aus Salz" recalls the postflood salt landscape of the preceding poem, while the striking cultivation of the rose seems to return to Christian iconography. The person as a rose suggests the symbolic link later made between the Rose of Sharon and Christ; it may also be the fruit of his labor in cultivating the land. Such an elegant and striking agricultural image coupled with the paradoxical title "Später Erstling," in contrast to the more simplistic agricultural images of root and seed, indicates that the person returning with his spade unreflectively considers himself something of a progressive, evolved representation of Jewishness or even a savior bringing the millennia of wandering to an end. The remaining three lines draw together the themes of agriculture, body, and tradition in the form of the land-body carrying the potential to bear fruit. At his "Schläfe," rendered in the translation as "brow" but meaning "temples," hangs the "Schlaf der Geburten," the sleep of births, like a "dunkle Weinranke," a dark tendril of vine. The image draws on the tradition of Israel as a vineyard, metaphorically a body that bears fruit; the vines at his temples also suggest the male tradition of wearing ear locks, that is, not cutting or cultivating the locks of hair that grow at the temples. Yet this traditional gesture is linked with slumber, which has the meaning in this cycle of ignorance. The stanza is heavy with potential, but it appears the late firstborn may still be unaware of the past upon which he unwittingly builds yet simultaneously obscures, of the turbulent presence from which he shields himself, and also of the future before him. Casting the late firstborn in the role of Jacob underscores that he is laying claim to things that are not his, which will go on to have lasting, divisive consequences. The poem then trails off in thought, lingering on the intersection of body and land. This is then taken up immediately in the next poem, "Dieses Land," which functions as a transition in the cycle between established themes and their resonant waves from the distant past into the present.

Stripped to a sparer, more elemental form, "Dieses Land" gives the reader an opportunity to focus on the physical experience of the word introduced in the tasting and intonation in "Chassidim Tanzen."

Dieses Land
ein Kern
darin eingeritzt

Sein Name!

Schlaf mit Sternenzähnen hält ihn fest
im harten Apfelfleisch der Erde

mit Psalmenknospen
klopft er Auferstehung an.

Dieses Land
und alle seine Pfade
umblüht blau
mit Zeitlos

alle Spuren laufen außerhalb—

Sand vulkanisch zitternd
von Widderhörnern
aus dem Traum geschaufelt.

Prophetenstunde eilte schnell
die Toten aus der Leichenhaut zu schälen
wie des Löwenzahnes Samen
nur beflügelt mit Gebeten
fuhren sie nach Haus—[16]

[*This land*

This land
a kernel
on it carved

His name!

Star-toothed sleep holds him fast
in the hard apple-flesh of earth
with buds of psalms
he taps out resurrection.

This land
and all its paths
blossoming blue
with timelessness

all tracks run outside—

Sand trembling volcanically
shoveled from the dream
by rams' horns.

The hour of the prophets hastened
to peel the corpse-skin from the dead
like dandelion seed
but winged with prayer
they traveled home—[17]]

The sparseness of the lines and images allows, for example, for patterns of alliteration and assonance to become more visible, and more audible as the text is read aloud. The "s" and "z" of lines one, three, and four, gradually add "sch," "h," "f," and "pf" alternations, for example, creating an increasingly dynamic physical reading experience. Sudden recognition of simple physical resonance is also the zenith of the poem itself, in the sixth stanza where sand is shivered and shaken awake by rams' horns.

The relative sparseness of detail and punctuation, combined with neologism and semantic blurring, also create a profoundly disorienting textual space. Many of the other poems in the cycle have enough detail or recognizable intertextuality to allow readers to initially orient themselves in the text. This poem is so vague and so minimalist that the reader is compelled to become more active in shaping its meaning. Agricultural imagery in particular disorients the wandering reader as he or she attempts to orient him- or herself in the scale and relationship of seeds to soil, in relation to time, or even in relation to the location of text or words. In essence, it becomes nearly impossible to completely separate body and land.

The poem begins with a demonstrative: "dieses" land ("this" land). This land is then possibly reinterpreted as "ein Kern" (kernel, seed, core, but also essence or heart), or possibly has the "Kern" "darin eingeritzt" (scratched, cut, or carved into it). The line breaks leave both possibilities open. This land or the "Kern" (and possibly both "Land" and "Kern") then becomes a text. Taking the conceptual place in this poem of the wound cut into the beach is "Sein Name!" (His name), cut into the land or "Kern." What exactly is carved where is also unclear, since "Sein Name" only indirectly describes the inscription. The name may, furthermore, be carved into the "Kern," but since "Kern" contains the meaning of "essence," it is also possible to read the "Name" as the "Kern."

The already unclear semantic boundaries are then further blurred in the next stanza, where the masculine pronouns (ihn, er) without clear antecedents can refer to "Kern" or "Name." Both have the potential to be firmly held in the "harten Apfelfleisch" (hard apple-flesh) of earth, as the one is a buried kernel, seed, or core, and the other is etched in a surface. How precisely "Erde" is different than "Land" is also left undetermined, and further complicated by the semantic transformation of land, which should produce fruit, into fruit itself (Apfelfleisch der Erde). The apple suggests that earth contains something forbidden, either knowledge or awareness, and represents a choice reflective of the story of Adam and Eve: the insulation of blissful oblivion versus expulsion from that oblivion through awareness.

"Land," "Kern," and "Name," never clearly distinguished from one another, are held in place by force of slumber, here accompanied by an astronomical-body entity, "Sternenzähnen" (teeth of stars). Stars as teeth suggests night as a mouth, always potentially in a position to consume the earth; since there are no clear boundaries that distinguish where a mouth begins and ends, it is also uncertain what that consumption could be, or what it would mean if the apple does carry biblical significance. Stars often appear in the cycle in a more traditionally mythological form; here, however, they are stripped of a known myth, and are presented in a more naked and immediate, yet still mythologized form. They are not organized into a meaningful constellation, but are rather countless, fixed, and oppressive. Within this nebulous context, "er" (the masculine core, essence, or name, and by extension the land) is knocking on or for (anklopfen) "Auferstehung," a word that is largely associated with the Christian concept of resurrection, but that here appears to draw its significance from the slumber, since there is so far no hint of death. The circular logic, obscured boundaries, and dislocated conventions in the poem are dizzying. We are then abruptly displaced to the next stanza, which begins with the same formula that begins the poem, but introduces a completely different landscape in which we must orient ourselves.

In the next stanza, "dieses Land" is not trapped by oppressive stars, but rather is a space free of stars, free of time, free of traces of any kind. The "blau" of this stanza recalls the "geisterblau" that resolves the agricultural life-cycle variation in "Nicht nur Land ist Israel," suggesting that the land-seed-fruit of the previous stanzas has been consumed. Not only this land, but also "seine Pfade" (its paths), are surrounded "blau / mit Zeitlos" (blue / with Timeless; "Zeitlosigkeit" would be timelessness). The land with its paths hearkens back to the lines and meridians of the previous poems, yet they are paths with no "Spuren" (traces, footprints). Those are found, however, in the next line, a stand-alone verse that emphasizes the "Spuren," the traces of presence, which are in the present tense, and "laufen außerhalb" (are actively moving outside, presumably outside of this land). The second "dieses Land" stanza is no less perplexing than its predecessor. It suggests a kind of emerging diasporic awareness for the land: the stanza collapses time into the nominalized adjective "Zeitlos," it has paths, and the land and paths are surrounded by blossoms, which, building on the previous stanza, must also come from "Sein Name" and "Psalmenknospen." The stanzas that follow, however, indicate that this is a false consciousness. The "Spuren" run outside it, and this thought is then interrupted by way of a dash, stanza break, and the return of "Sand," a participial adjective, and the multicultural symbol of rams' horns. The blossoms and resurrection continue perhaps in the vein of the "Rose aus Salz" from "Später Erstling"; the rams' horns shake the "Sand," that is both body and land, volcanically out of an insulated dream.

A ram's horn is another multicultural symbol tying a constellation together with a significant Jewish object. While Aries is the constellation aligned with spring planting, and thus the awakening of slumbering life, the ram's horn in Jewish tradition, the shofar, is sounded for Rosh Hashanah, the Jewish New Year, also a kind of awakening, but in the autumn. Both meanings of the symbol mark a moment in time, in different cultural calendars—even within Jewish practice—that can nonetheless coexist in this reference. The resonating sound waves of the shofar bring Jews throughout time together, marking another liturgical cycle; the exact amount of time the year lasts is dependent, however, on geographical location as well as the era of Jewish tradition. The duration of a year is often determined in relation to a particular incarnation of Israel or Jerusalem. The calendar year once had its origin in the destruction of the temple, not the creation of Earth, and the days and months in Jewish tradition can be calculated mathematically, or according to lunar phases, by lunar month and solar year, or translated to the Gregorian calendar. The boundaries of time and calendar are crossed, but they are not erased. This stanza suggests that "Zeitlos" masquerades as a Jewish concept, but is not. A breakdown of linear time is, on the other hand, a Jewish concept, but as these calendar and constellation references show, multiple conceptions of time coexist and play significant roles in Jewish history and the meaning of Israel.

The final stanza gives one further incarnation of time, provides a diasporic counterpart to the numerous oppressive stars, and breaks off with a destabilization of the concept of "home." A "Prophetenstunde" (hour of the prophets) returns us to a body-agriculture image that breaks "die Toten" (the dead) free of the more static fruit-seed image. The hour of prophets peels ("schälen") the dead from their "Leichenhaut" (corpse-skin, as if they were trapped in fruit rind), and rather than apple-like seeds that stay relatively close to their location, held down by countless "Sternenzähnen," the dead are like "Löwenzahnes Samen" (the dandelion seeds), which scatter far and wide. These dead that are scattered traveled "nach Hause" (home)—but what does home mean in this context? They are carried by prayers, which, throughout the cycle, serve primarily to enliven Israel. The Pleiades pray atop the menorah; children pray and keep the stories alive for coming generations. The dead are part of the land-body-text complex, as well. They are dissolved into the words of others, words that become part of the body, land, and experience of Israel, which is everywhere. "Nach Hause" is not a specific location, but rather many locations, wherever the seeds land and grow, along the meridians, across generations. "Home" is wherever Jews read and experience the words with their own bodies. The poem gives each reader the experience of extreme disorientation in the space of words. It also depicts two responses: that of stasis, in which the reader is either stuck by sheer force of being overwhelmed or in a dream state, or that of movement, in which the reader engages the feeling of the text and allows for multiplicity of meaning. The latter is the diasporic mode that is then further explicated through the example of the next poem, "Abraham der Engel!"

Abraham is an extreme example of the potential of diaspora Jews to experience the meaning of Israel. In this poem, we return to the work of the cycle to reinterpret other texts. We have so far encountered reinterpretations of Isaiah and Jacob; this Abraham does have a namesake in the first convert to monotheism and the subject of Sachs's play, but the Abraham of this poem is a legendary Chassidic rabbi, living in Eastern Europe. This poem also introduces two radical boundary crossings that will transform the character of the cycle.

> *In der Nacht, im Tauchbad die vier Erzmütter*
> *in Strahlen badeten mit seiner Mutter.*
> *Dann empfing sie ihn aus des Maggids Sternenkraft*
> Chassidische Schriften

Abraham der Engel!
Anders gehorcht er
und in schrecklichem Befehl,
wie mit Stricken geworfen durch die Nacht.

Und das Licht wie eine ausgerissene Palme
zerknüllt in der Hand.

Der Traum ist ihm gehorsam,
er durchbricht ihn—
ein Meteor der Sehnsucht—
und langt immer bei Gott an.

Kreist um sein Stück Ewigkeit
wie der Adler um die goldgefärbte Himmelsbeute.
Seine Blutbahn überschwemmt alles Gesagte,
er antwortet nicht auf den sorgenden Anruf der Erde.

Läßt die Geliebten allein,
silberne Schmuckstücke der Trauer.

Schweigt erzene Türen in die Luft
und reißt sie auf
mit einer Wunde als Wort.

Abraham der Engel!
Schrecklicher!
Im Geheimnis
nimmst du dein Tauchbad.

Deine Fußsohle ist immer an den Rand gestellt,
Wo die Unsicherheit zu rauschen beginnt
und die Flügel für die Außer-sich-Geratenen liegen—

Den Tod biegst du aus seiner gläsernen Haut,
bis er bluterschrocken an dir
zur Rose wird
Gott zu Gefallen—[18]

[In the night, in the mikvah, the four matriarchs
in beams bathed with his mother.
Then she conceived him from the Maggid's cosmic power.
Chassidic Writings

Abraham the angel!
He obeys differently
and in the terrible command,
thrown as if with ropes through the night.

And the light like an uprooted palm tree
crumpled in hand.

The dream is obedient to him,
he breaches it—
a meteor of longing—
and always reaches God.

Circles his piece of eternity
like the eagle circling gold-colored heavenly prey.
His bloodstream floods all said things,
he does not answer the concerned call of earth.

Leaves loved ones alone,
silver gems of grief.

Silences primal doors into the air
and tears them open
with a wound as word.

Abraham the angel!
Terrible one!
In secret
you immerse yourself in your mikvah.

Your foot's sole is always placed on the brink,
where uncertainty begins to rustle
and the wings for those who have emerged beyond themselves lie—

Death you bend from its glass skin,
until it, terrified to its blood by you,
becomes a rose
for God's sake—[19]]

The epigraph summarizes the anecdote that begins the story of "Abraham der Engel," in which Abraham's mother gains access to her monthly immersion in the mikvah (ritual bath) through the midnight intervention of the four "Erzmütter" (arch-mothers, presumably the four matriarchs Sarah, Rebecca, Rachel, and Leah). Her encounter with them creates the condition for her to conceive Abraham. He does not appear to be the result of conventional fertilization, but rather the result of the power of the matriarchs, cosmic force, and the fertility of the human body. He is conceived and born into the world, but has supernatural qualities and abilities that make him both wonderful and terrible. He is a model Jew capable of an extraordinary level of insight and piety, but that same devotion means that he neglects the empirical world around him. The poem explicates his power to wander between realms, to breach conventional boundaries, and his powerful connection to words. Much of the imagery of the poem sets Abraham as a counterexample to the "Später Erstling," although the figures and their poems do share certain characteristics: the Jacob-like first-born is morally paradoxical, like Abraham, who is devout but negligent; both appear in a position to have a potentially violent encounter with a divine or cosmic force; and both poems include the indented stanza immediately following the position of potential encounter. Both resist clear judgment or singular meaning, but whereas the firstborn is linked with stasis and obliviousness, Abraham is a constant agent in motion.

He obeys differently ("Anders gehorcht er") than the biblical Abraham, who is tested by God. It is unclear whether this Abraham is only taking commands ("in schrecklichem Befehl") or whether he himself is the source of commanding power, because he, like the "Befehl," is described as "schrecklich." He is thrown through the night, as if he were a cosmic puppet on ropes or strings ("wie mit Stricken"), at the mercy of an outside force, and yet he overpowers most limitations and symbols. It is worth noting briefly that this poem intensifies the feminine gender of night ("die Nacht"), the single most important time in the cycle, by marking it as the time of the power of the four matriarchs, who are the root of Abraham's creation. If we read the line "wie mit Stricken geworfen durch die Nacht" as a passive construction in which "night" is read as the agent (thrown as if with ropes *by* the night, rather than the literal *through* the night; both are grammatically possible), it is the feminine night that is the only entity that can overpower Abraham.

Abraham can dislocate and mangle symbolic objects like the palm tree or the light, rendering them rootless, shapeless, and therefore meaningless.

He breaches ("durchbricht") the conventional boundaries of dream and waking, of life and death, and whatever boundary divides earth from the divine realm. He is a "Meteor der Sehnsucht," a forceful, cosmic object of longing that "langt immer bei Gott an" (always reaches God). The "immer" (always) suggests that this is a frequently repeated journey; if he always reaches God, he must always be starting that journey from elsewhere. There is no mention of a final destination or longing for return in the poem, only a longing that is so strong a force that it drives him beyond any boundary. That longing remains unfulfilled. Though he has no deep connection to a geographical location, however, he tends toward the opposite extreme. The late firstborn has a "Wüste Goldmaske"; Abraham circles a parcel of eternity as if it were "die goldgefärbte Himmelsbeute" (gold-colored heavenly prey). He is so intently focused on the eternal that "er antwortet nicht auf den sorgenden Anruf der Erde" (he does not answer the concerned call of earth). It is worth briefly noting that earth (Erde), like night (Nacht), is feminine, and may stand here in part for his concerned wife. In the source text, Abraham comes to his widow in a dream after he has died and asks for her forgiveness for having been so neglectful. He asks no one else. It is, moreover, his wife who barters with the cosmic ancestors for Abraham to remain among them for twelve earth years. Six women who also seem to easily cross borders and challenge or negotiate earthly limits shape Abraham's existence. Feminine power, in fact, becomes increasingly evident in the cycle, and as this happens, the boundaries of the conventionally impermeable male body are made more porous. This is clearest in the seventh stanza, in which Abraham immerses himself in the mikvah; the sixth stanza appears to describe the act he can perform that would require a cleansing ritual bath. It is also the stanza where the land-body-text complex is confirmed.

Abraham creates "erzene Türen" in the air through silence; "schweigen" is used as a transitive verb that produces the doors of "Erz." "Erz" appears in "Nicht nur Land ist Israel!" as the "erzenen Füße / deiner Ewigkeit-schnaubenden Berge" (the iron feet / of your eternity-snorting mountains), where it makes sense to render "Erz" as ore or iron. The epigraph of "Abraham der Engel!," however, establishes instead the meaning of the prefix "Erz" in "Erzmütter": arch, preeminent, or prime. Abraham "silences" these fundamental, matriarchal doors into the air, and then tears them open "mit einer Wunde als Wort" (with a wound as word). Here, finally, the wound and word are brought together. The wound in the air, the "Gotteswunde," is a word; the name carved into the land is a wound. The wound is a mark that binds air and land, and the wound is a powerful link and conduit only when it is open and experienced. This point in the text opens a conduit across time and space between Abraham and the "später Erstling," whose golden desert mask is between him and the "Engelskämpfe / heruntergebogenem Himmel, / vor den flammenden Früchten / deiner *Gott* sprechenden Nacht" (the bent-down sky / of angels' battles, / facing the flaming fruits / of your night which says *Gott*). The "später Erstling" is on the other side of the word-wound created by Abraham.

Having opened the wound, Abraham must cleanse himself. The source text does not include an instance of Abraham immersing himself in the mikvah, although pious men must also ritually bathe. This is the poet's addition, and since the mikvah is specifically introduced in the epigraph, Abraham's "Tauchbad" binds him textually to his mother, and by extension, to the four matriarchs. It is during her ritual bath that Abraham's mother absorbs the power of the matriarchs; Abraham is in a position to have the same experience. The indented stanza follows the mikvah stanza. In "Später Erstling!," the indentation follows the potential encounter under the heavy sky and flaming fruit of "deiner *Gott* sprechenden Nacht." The indentation after Abraham's ritual bath may also visually suggest a physical mark left by a powerful encounter. It also appears to mark an encounter between these two poems. As so much of the cycle deals with the visibility, interpretation, and reinterpretation of symbols and traces, the indentation ultimately presents an opportunity for the reader traveling the shifting landscape of the text to encounter a visual representation of the "Spuren" (traces) of writers and readers who were there before us, traces that mark encounters across time and space.

In the penultimate stanza of the poem, Abraham is given that attribute Sachs used to describe her own words and Israel: "Deine Fußsohle ist immer an den Rand gestellt, / Wo die Unsicherheit zu rauschen beginnt" (The sole of your foot is always on the brink, / where the uncertainty begins to rustle). The late firstborn comes home with his spade to the "Ungeschachtete, / Ungezimmerte," things that are lacking in borders and boundaries of ownership; Abraham stands at the border of the uncertain, a space that is not only unformed, but also unstable. It is also where the "Flügel für die Außer-sich-Geratenen" (the wings for those who have emerged beyond themselves) lie. Abraham is always in a position to engage with the uncertain and unshaped, actively shaping space and creating connections with the creation of the "Wunde als Wort." The wings for those "Außer-sich-Geratenen" recall the "Flügel der Prophetie," those words that carry the body of Israel through time and space, connecting them with others, and perhaps more importantly, compelling them to engage, reinterpret, and shape and reshape reality. In the story of the Chassidic Abraham, the terms and boundaries that conventionally delineate concepts like life and death, earthly and divine, home and away, dreaming and awake are broken down. To reach God does not require death, but rather attention; time and space do not separate people or their experiences, obliviousness does; death does not separate one from life, negligence does; dreams need not trap or isolate the sleeper. Abraham is the hyperliteral example of the power of diaspora. He can cross all boundaries, even those of gender and being, is always in motion, and is deeply connected to the physical experience of the word. He is always poised at the brim, where forms become unclear, and where the body transforms into the text that will be experienced by others. The poem closes with the reaffirmation that death is just a term like any other that can be redefined, in this case as a rose for the sake of, or as a favor to, God: "Gott zu Gefallen." Like most of the poems in the cycle, this, too, breaks off, resisting closure.

Our vision is then brought one last time to a larger scale in the poem "Immer noch Mitternacht auf diesem Stern."

> Immer noch Mitternacht auf diesem Stern
> und die Heerscharen des Schlafes.
> Nur einige von den großen Verzweiflern
> haben so geliebt,
> daß der Nacht Granit aufsprang
> vor ihres Blitzes weißschneidendem Geweih.
>
> So Elia; wie ein Wald mit ausgerissenen Wurzeln
> erhob er sich unter dem Wacholder,
> schleifte, Aderlaß eines Volkes,
> blutige Sehnsuchtsstücke hinter sich her,
> immer den Engelfinger
> wie einen Müdigkeit ansaugenden Mondstrahl
> an seine Schwere geheftet,
> Untiefen heimwärtsziehend—
>
> Und Christus! An der Inbrunst Kreuz
> nur geneigtes Haupt—
> den Unterkiefer hängend,
> mit dem Felsen:
> *Genug*.[20]

> [*Still midnight on this star*
>
> Still midnight on this star
> and the hosts of sleep.
> Only a few of the great despairers
> have so loved
> that the granite of night burst
> before the white-cleaving antlers of their lightning.
>
> Thus Elijah: like a forest with torn-out roots
> he arose beneath the juniper,
> dragged, bloodletting of a people,
> bloody bits of longing behind him,
> the angel's finger,

like a moon-ray which sucks weariness in,
always touching his weight,
drawing the shallows homewards—

And Christ! On the cross of passion
only a bowed head—
the jaw hanging,
with the rock:
Enough.[21]]

This poem gives one final mosaic of words and bodies alternating between stasis and movement. Here, the "Heerscharen des Schlafes" (hosts of sleep) are juxtaposed with the definitive prophets of Judaism and Christianity respectively, Elijah and Christ. Elijah, who is associated with circumcision (the ritual covenantal wounding of Jewish males), and whose stanza breaks off with a dash, left bloody tracks and is still "heim-wärtsziehend" (drawing homeward). There is no resolution to his homeward movement, and it is unclear what that home might be. Christ, on the other hand, who is associated with the arrow of history that culminates in the birth, death, and resurrection of the messiah, hangs motionless on the cross. His stanza resolves with the biblical quote accompanying his death, and a period, a grammatical full stop. The poem seems to serve primarily as a reminder that although "einige von den großen Verzweiflern" (a few of the great despairers) have had the courage or love to have faced the turmoil of night awake, the majority is still asleep.

The final warning and reaffirmation for Israel in the cycle is the seer Daniel, whose book is contained in the Writings section of the Tanakh, not in Prophets, and is the only apocalyptic text in the Hebrew Bible. The poem reminds us of the relevance of his story as a warning to the nation-state, but more particularly as a reminder of what Daniel is. Daniel is a multilingual, multicultural reader and sharer of stories. The poem begins with content images of stasis from which he arose, and closes with a grammatical image of stasis, a period, in which he is arising.

Daniel mit der Sternenzeichnung
erhob sich aus den Steinen
in Israel.
Dort wo die Zeit heimisch wurde im Tod
erhob sich Daniel,
der hohen Engel Scherbeneinsammler,
Aufbewahrer des Abgerissenen,
verlorene Mitte zwischen Anfang und Ende
setzend.

Daniel, der die vergessenen Träume noch
hinter dem letzten Steinkohlenabhang hervorholt.

Daniel, der Belsazar Blut lesen lehrte,
diese Schrift verlorener Wundränder,
die in Brand gerieten.

Daniel, der das verweinte Labyrinth zwischen
Henker und Opfer durchwandert hat,

Daniel hebt seinen Finger
aus der Abendröte
in Israel.[22]

[*Daniel with the mark of stars*

Daniel with the mark of stars
arose out of the stones
in Israel.
There where time grew to be at home in death
Daniel arose,
the high angels' gatherer of fragments,
keeper of things torn down,
setting a lost center between beginning
and end.

Daniel who fetches forgotten dreams
even from behind the last slope of coal.

Daniel who taught Belshazzar to read blood,
this script of lost edges of wounds
which took fire.

Daniel who wandered through the tear-stained labyrinth
between hangman and victim,

Daniel lifts his finger
from the evening-red
in Israel.[23]]

The Book of Daniel, Sachs's source text, is a compilation of episodes about foolish Babylonian kings who require the insight of their Jewish courtiers, whose diasporic existence makes them much better readers and interpreters than the static imperial rulers. Daniel distinguishes himself among the courtiers as a particularly insightful reader, capable even of recognizing texts obscured to others' eyes. These attributes are brought out in the poem, along with the resulting abilities. Daniel emerged "aus den Steinen" (out of stones) and "wo die Zeit heimisch wurde im Tod" (where time grew to be at home in death), that is, wherever establishment, stasis, is limiting and blinding. Where time is singularly established as "heimisch," other boundaries and meanings, the "Scherben" (fragments), the "Abgerissenen" (things torn down), "verlorene Mitte" (lost center), "vergessene Träume" (forgotten dreams), and "verlorene Wundränder" (lost edges of wounds), are discarded. Daniel is the preserver of this discarded knowledge.

Here again, text and wound are brought together with the body, in that Daniel taught Belshazzar to read blood, "diese Schrift verlorener Wundränder" (this script of lost edges of wounds). The settled ruler has lost the ability even to perceive the wound, although, as Daniel helps him see, it is still there, still open, and still relevant. It is, like the "*Gott* sprechende Nacht*," in flames, suggesting urgency and radiant power.

Daniel also has experience navigating ambiguous and changing terrain. A "Labyrinth zwischen / Henker und Opfer" (labyrinth between hangman and victim) is another image of circular logic. A labyrinth has only one entrance, which is also its exit, and only one path to its center. Although "Henker" and "Opfer" are diametrically opposed entities, as a labyrinth the only thing distinguishing them is interpretation. They are the same path, the same entrance, the same exit. This particular iteration of Daniel is the one who, after an enjambment, lifts his finger "aus der Abendröte / in Israel" (from the evening-red / in Israel). The "Abendröte" (evening-red) is moment of potential; it is not quite night, it resembles the flaming word-wound, and the poem ends in grammatical stasis in Israel. Following the logic of the source text, Daniel is in a position to make the "verlorene Wundränder" (lost edges of the wound) and its script clear, to set the "verlorene Mitte" (lost middle), the core, between "Anfang und Ende" (beginning and end). One further figure is introduced in the cycle that can read the obscured scripts of the body of Israel: an excavator who is the frame narrative for the play *Abram im Salz*.

"Mutterwasser" is not simply, seamlessly added to the cycle, but rather is clearly marked as a displaced piece of text. In it, an excavator reads the text of the land, through which we are then introduced to Abram's experience of reality under a king too obsessed with owning land, word, and time. The poem also emphasizes the feminine gender of the conditions for both destruction and creation, and makes clear that the land is both text and body.

Vorspruch zu Abram im Salz

Mutterwasser
Sintflut
die ins Salz zog—Gerippe aus Sterben—
Erinnerungsstein
gesetzt
unter des Mondes Silbertreppe

in Ur
da wo das Blut der Nachtwandlerschar
zu Chaldäa
stürzte
durch die blaue Ader der Finsternis.

Da liest der Ausgräber
in der Bibel des Staubes
eingeküßtes Muster
königlich Gewebtes
und
sieht die Kette
golden
den Staub sonnen.

Der Hals der traulich
zwischen dem Geschmeide einging
in seine Nachtexistenz
ließ immer noch
nebelgraues Gedenken zurück.

Musizierende Gestirne
rauschten wie Wein
in Abram's Ohr

bis er rückwärts stürzte
abgerissen
getroffen
von einem Tod
der kein Tod ist—[24]

[*Maternal water*

Prologue to Abram in the salt

Maternal water
deluge
that soaked into salt—skeleton made of dying—
stone of memory
set
beneath the moon's silver stair
in Ur
there where the blood of the sleepwalking crowd
of Chaldea
fell
through the blue vein of darkness.

There the archaeologist
reads in the Bible of dust
kissed-in pattern
royal wove
and
sees the chain
light
the dust with gold.

The jeweled neck
which passed smugly
into its nocturnal existence
still leaves
a mist-gray memory behind.

Music-making constellations
roared like wine
in Abram's ear
until he fell backwards
torn down
struck
by a death
that is no death—[25]]

"Mutterwasser" is both destructive and fertile. It is the overwhelming force of "Sintflut," the word used for the biblical flood that destroyed humanity, but it also became the salt, "Gerippe aus Sterben" (skeleton made of dying), into which the story of diaspora is written. The remainder of the stanza sets the scene of the end of Nimrod's reign in Chaldea. He is building ziggurats to reach the sky, penetrate it, and own it as part of his moon cult, but is frightened by a prophecy that someone else will claim his throne. The moon-cult members will fall into darkness, fade into the earth, and disappear like Nimrod.

Their story, however, is being read in the next stanza by an "Ausgräber" (rendered as "archeologist," but literally "excavator"). The "Bibel des Staubes" (bible of the dust) literally understands the earth as a text in which we can read the "eingeküßtes Muster" (kissed-in pattern), the traces and impressions, left by the lives and matter of people. The "Ausgräber" reads the pattern of textiles and finds a golden chain that illuminates the dust. From these, he can discern the human form that must have been wrapped in both. The bible of the dust he is reading is a transformed human body. The gold in which the person, presumably Nimrod, took comfort has remained, but does not appear to have improved his longevity or secured his hold on the land; if he is being disinterred, he will certainly not be left there. His text can be read, preserved, and passed on, however; we the readers must only be aware of its presence. Nonetheless, the experience of this body text is difficult to interpret: it "ließ immer noch / nebelgraues Gedenken zurück" (leaves a mist-gray memory behind). The impressions in the dust are evidence of presence, but the adjective "nebelgrau" gives the sense that they are hard to clearly discern. Sachs leaves them for the reader to interpret.

The next stanza jumps to the protagonist of the play, Abram, who hears "musizierende Gestirne" (music-making constellations). In the play, this is a cosmic voice calling him, from which he will hear the word that Nimrod covets. In the context of the cycle, it recalls less the "*Gott* sprechende Nacht" than the praying Pleiades from "Chassidim Tanzen," the first constellation we encountered, and one that gives fire to the symbol of Israel. It is this sound cue that increasingly occupies him until we reach the enjambment, and takes us to the final stanza of this edge of the cycle, at which Abram (and the reader) stands, until the fall and transformation.

The concluding lines of the poem, "getroffen / von einem Tod / der kein Tod ist—" (struck / by a death / that is no death—), reinterpret death as a state decree that can be defied. In the play and in midrash, Nimrod orders Abram thrown into a grave and declares him dead, but Abram emerges, effectively defying the official state version of history. Nimrod's decreed narrative is rewritten, like all state narratives can be by outsiders who can fluidly cross borders and challenge convention. Abram is a wanderer and border-crosser, unlike Nimrod. Nimrod's major transgression, Boyarin suggests, is that he chooses

> to use the power bestowed upon him to fix the place for "us," a city whose boundaries will be that of "us." Endowed with greatness, the gentile paragons typically deny the Bestower and solipsistically project themselves in space. They exult in presence, taking power to be an attribute of themselves.[26]

Sachs's interpretation of Nimrod and Abram transcends the notion of divine power to emphasize the role of humans in the stewardship of tradition. In this cycle, power and possession apply to the meaning of words, since the interpretation of symbols of all kinds can be used to create a narrative of ownership and stasis. The cycle actively highlights that meaning is never static. Built into the concept of Israel is the multiplicity of meaning. Israel is not a mode of progress where one interpretation is considered an improvement or replacement for another, but rather depends on coexisting cultural difference. Diaspora rejects the corrosive, exclusionary unity of the nation-state ideal in favor of the unresolved wound that fosters a much richer nation that has long outlived the states that have persecuted it. There is room in the concept for *Eretz Israel*, but Sachs's cycle urges Israel not to abandon its poetic potential to radically rethink the way we shape our world.

In both the play and the poem "Mutterwasser," Abram fell (rückwärts stürzte) into uncertainty, though not obscurity. Ultimately, he is rewritten, literally from Abram to Abraham. He is the father born of the maternal water; his story is experienced, heard, tasted, and then sung. The dash that breaks off the poem prevents closure, suggesting that we wait for, or create, a continuation. If we return, as the "musizierende Gestirne" (music-making constellations) and Jewish textual year would have us do, to the point of origin, here the beginning of the cycle, "Chassidim Tanzen," we discover that it does take up where "Mutterwasser" left off in a number of ways that reveal new semantic depths that change the textual landscape we have just traversed.

"Chassidim Tanzen" begins: "Nacht weht / mit todentrißnen Fahnen," which can be reinterpreted using the insight we gained from the initial reading of the cycle. Night is both a feminine entity and a condition of the highest potential power and fertility. We have seen examples in the cycle where adjectives are made nouns ("Zeitlos"), verb structures are changed ("schweigt"), and multiple figurative and literal meanings are interwoven; it thus becomes contextually and grammatically possible to read "weht" as the nouns "Wehen" (birthing pangs) and "Weh" (pain) made into an active, vibrant, wounding verb. Night is birthing, painfully and vocally, all the discarded fragments ("Fahnen," "Binden," "Gewebtes," "Abgerissenes") that have been caught, read, preserved, "todentrißen" (torn from death) and passed on by the seers, prophets, excavators, "angels" like Abraham, the Chassidim, and us the readers. The Chassidim dance, and "wiegen" (rock, like one does a child) all that is born through the wound that is the link across time and space. They pass on the words, aggravating and reinvigorating the wounds in sand by tossing the salty water of the sea, the "Mutterwasser," onto the beach. "Mutterwasser" is deadly ("Sintflut"), and yet can also (with salt) preserve and reinvigorate the wound in the bodies that read, experience, and pass on the story of Israel. The lexicon of the cycle allows us to rethink individual words and concepts, such as "land," "wound," "angel," or "seed," and as we do, we can reconsider their interaction in the cycle. Subsequent journeys through the landscape of the cycle allow readers to rethink the roles of masculine and feminine entities, explore the land as a body, explore the way the body is dissolved and redistributed, explore the differences between sand, desert, salt, and water. We are compelled to consider the meaning and transfer of force and power, and rethink the interpretations of symbols, rituals, and acts. Each journey through the cycle is a new exercise in orienting oneself in the textual landscape, by shaping the constellations of meaning allowed by the ambiguous and sometimes palpably disorienting terrain of the poems.

Sachs valued the capacity of the nation of Israel to discover and theorize, to think beyond limitations or borders of every kind, and advocated this same potential in art, as she described regarding a festival for the State of Israel in 1957:

> Warum sollte man in Israel außer den eigenen Stimmen, die ihres Landes heutigen Stand besingen, nicht auch einer Stimme Raum geben, die dort einsetzt, wo des jüdischen Volkes Entdeckertat sich außerhalb der sichtbaren Grenzen bewegte und für die Menschheit eine der wenigen ewigen Geisterrevolutionen vollbrachte, die heute noch eben so wirkt "bis in der Kindergebete milchweißem Schaum."[27]

> [Why shouldn't one in Israel, besides the [national] voices that sing of the current condition of the country, give space to a voice that comes into play in that place where the Jewish people's discovery moved, outside the boundaries of the visual, and humankind accomplished one of the few revolutions of mind, one that even today has an effect "even into the milk-white foam of children's prayers."]

Poetry can reflect what happens inside borders; Sachs asserts here, however, that it has the power to do something much greater, namely to explore beyond borders and limitations in a way that obliterates the stasis of location or time and remains perpetually in play. "Flügel der Prophetie" describes the significance of learning to read the different kinds of texts that surround us, and that furthermore make up who we are. Through a Chassidic principle that advocates experiencing physically the texts we read and retell and the prayers we say, the cycle weaves terminology of body and agriculture together with myths, constellations, iconography, symbols, and biblical texts that make up "Israel" as a concept. The cycle shows that we are the stories and prayers we recount. Because the body tells the story of Israel, the body becomes the land whose story it tells; we ourselves are Israel, and create Israel, whether it is (a) land or not. Sachs encourages us to explore the uncertain and find new ways to conceive of ourselves and the world we inhabit.

6: Relearning to Listen: Sachs's Poem Cycle "Dein Leib im Rauch durch die Luft"

SACHS'S EMPHASIS ON "ISRAEL" as more than land hinges on her conception of and uncertainty about memory, in particular memory of the immediate postwar era, and grows out of her problematizations of memory and memorialization in earlier texts. When an object, for example a blue flower or a parcel of land, is made the representation of an event (for example Merlin's and Gotelind's death) or of something more abstract, for example "Israel," the event or abstraction can seem contained. "Nicht nur Land ist Israel" suggests that a projection of whatever else Israel can be as land does away with any need to be mindful of the history of wandering, to question, or to discuss. The same apprehension can apply to Holocaust memorials. A projection, for example a nation-state, or an object, for example a memorial or monument, runs the risk of obscuring or even replacing the meaning or significance of the thing being represented. With a concrete object, there is a sense of closure. Closure implies that the questions have been answered; that any lack has been fulfilled. If the blue flower stands for Merlin's and Gotelind's death, then we need not worry about telling the story. Unsatisfied with Arthur's relic, Blasius goes home to write a story, one that the reader knows conflicts with other accounts of Merlin's story. Where there is uncertainty, there is no closure, which means that questions remain: there is an absence of answers, and a presence of discussion. "Nicht nur Land ist Israel" warns that the closure implied in the State of Israel blinds us to the unanswered questions and lack of certainty that, as Jonathan Boyarin asserts, are the very powers of diaspora;[1] those same powers of diaspora play a role in Sachs's poetic confrontations of Nazi genocide.

As so many of her postwar poetry cycles deal in some way with a discussion or depiction of a time ripped open like a wound, it is possible to see her work as a critical voice on remembering and memorializing the Holocaust. Several of her postwar cycles examine the meaning and significance of different kinds of memory, often reinterpreting or reinscribing poetic forms associated with reminding in ways that resist the closure of a standard memorial and insist, as we see also in her correspondence, on "suffering through" *in* the moment rather than remembering something past. As she wrote in a letter in 1947: "Nur darum geht es, denke ich, nur

darum, und deswegen unterscheiden wir uns von den früheren, denn der
Äon der Schmerzen darf nicht mehr gesagt, gedacht, er muß durchlitten
werden." (It is only about this, I think, only this, and it is in this way that
we are different from those [writers] who came before, because the aeon
of pain may no longer be said, or thought; it must be suffered through.)[2]
She draws on the Western literary canon as well as Jewish ritual to create
texts in which events and traditions of all times and places exist concurrently. In so doing she evokes wounds of the past that have not healed
to keep them open and ensure that they never will heal, allowing for a
poetic—textual as well as aural—examination of humanity and its modes
of memory.[3]

Sachs's first postwar poetry cycle, "Dein Leib im Rauch durch
die Luft" from the 1947 volume *In den Wohnungen des Todes* (In the
Habitations of Death), arguably her best-known cycle, introduces us
to the perplexed and desperate tension between memorial and memory
in the immediate wake of the war and the Nazi genocide against the
Jews. It consists of thirteen poems, each one laying bare an experience
of confronting murder and loss, as well as the poet's struggle to find a
justified poetic response. Each poem approaches the problem from a
different perspective, ranging from reacting to the camps and mourning, to imagining the voices of the victims and the moment of death, to
asking how it happens and who is responsible. Only three of the thirteen have separate titles, "An euch, die das neue Haus bauen" (To You
That Build the New House), "Ein totes Kind spricht" (A Dead Child
Speaks), and "Ihr Zuschauenden" (You Onlookers). The sparing use of
titles is not unusual in Sachs's cycles, and most often appears to be a
kind of direct address to the reader. The title of the entire cycle, on first
reading, addresses the body of the nation of Israel, but after the first
pass through the cycle, the "Dein" (your, singular) can have the feeling
of applying to the reader, as well.

Taken as individual, isolated poems, it is easy to conceive of "Dein
Leib im Rauch durch die Luft" as an elegiac, healing collection of texts.
Read as a cycle, however, what is instead reflected is the "durchleiden,"
the suffering through, that Sachs referred to in 1947 (and continued
to refer to in 1957).[4] Similar to the poems "Wenn im Vorsommer" and
"Völker der Erde," in which Sachs explored the impossibility of poetic
convention healing the damage of war and genocide, the cycle "Dein Leib
im Rauch durch die Luft" explores the inadequacy of more conventional
methods of representing pain and death in words. At the same time as it
compels the reader to suffer through the wounds left by genocide, this
cycle sometimes depicts and sometimes describes the destruction of traditional metaphors and poetic conventions, including numerous tropes and
images readers will recognize from Sachs's earliest prose texts. Reading
"Dein Leib im Rauch durch die Luft" in the spiral manner encouraged by

Sachs's cyclical writing ultimately demonstrates her radical reinscription of the metaphor of the nightingale and the poetic convention of the vocative "O" to reflect the struggle to express something that overwhelms traditional poetic tools and devices.

In creating these poetic experiences of suffering, Sachs has created something like what James E. Young termed "countermonuments," which reject art's redemptory function and demand active intervention, interaction, and confrontation of the reader.[5] The few poems in the cycle that reflect more conventional healing and mourning are entirely overpowered by those that reflect the present suffering of which Sachs speaks. "Dein Leib im Rauch durch die Luft" clearly demonstrates how not only poetic conventions, but also traditional approaches to mourning and memorializing offer an inadequate or inappropriate perception of poetry and the empirical world. A nebulous "ihr" (second-person plural familiar pronoun, for example "ihr Finger" [you fingers] or "ihr Zuschauenden" [you onlookers]) appears in most of the poems, woven together with complex agricultural and nature imagery and a destabilization of linear time that ultimately directs a probing, admonishing eye and finger at the reader—whoever, wherever, and whenever the reader may be. This sense of collapsed time and reexamination is represented especially by the shofar that appears in the poem "Einer war," at the center of the cycle. This poem evokes and performs the blowing of the ram's horn at Rosh Hashanah. The shofar becomes a space where events that occurred throughout time are present, calling the hearer (or reader in this case) to examine his or her own deeds. This is very much linked to the diaspora. The horn that dissolves geographical or chronological distance between Jews simultaneously evokes absence from a geographical and temporal center, traditionally Jerusalem and events in Jewish history; in this poem, the shofar performs an additional task, to dissolve geographical and chronological distance between the reader, the poet, and events in Jewish history, including the Nazi genocide. This does away with any need to "remember," because nothing can be forgotten that remains present. Present, for example, in the shofar blast or present in prayer or discussion, while also absent: the Temple, which remains present although it was destroyed, or Jerusalem, which is present in thought although one is not physically there, or the missing or dead individuals, who are absent, but who are present in thought or by way of their initials, or even, as the cycle repeatedly forces us to acknowledge, in ash, dust, and sand beneath our shoes and in the air we breathe. The shofar cries and wails, evoking and confronting wounds that do not heal.

Read as a complete cycle (as opposed to isolated poems) that calls forth questions pertaining to mourning and memorialization, "Dein Leib im Rauch durch die Luft" aggressively pursues the politics of memory and literature's role within it, since, as I have argued elsewhere,[6] Sachs seems keenly aware that the *kleos* (renown, immortal fame) of traditional, conventional poetry is rendered sterile by the mass murder that makes mourning and remembering more urgent than ever before. Literary convention, which privileges closure, and Jewish ritual, which emphasizes presence through absence and therefore precludes closure, are brought into juxtaposition in the cycle, drawing on the trope of hearing inherent in both *kleos* and the shofar, but also in Sachs's own early prose, in which hearing is routinely the tripwire of remembering, the marker of the presence of absence. Hearing and listening, historically linked to perception (i.e., sense) and heeding, are woven into a complex system of agricultural references that ultimately link human drives, intentions, and creation, pushing the audience to learn to perceive again through the confrontation and assessment of deeds in a textual Rosh Hashanah. The nexus of the Classical tradition of *kleos* and the Jewish tradition of the shofar captures the diasporic consciousness that manifests itself in Sachs's political unease as Israel takes on its nation-state form and Germany looks to its authors to define its new, cleansed, and innocent national incarnation.

Sachs's prose texts of the 1920s and 1930s already demonstrate a critical distance with regard to memory or memorial, particularly with regard to the philosophy of history, subjectivity, and authority, and indeed identity. In "Wie der Zauberer Merlin erlöset ward" (1921), for example, a blue flower is (re)appropriated as a relic by King Arthur, prompting Blasius to write his story. In "Eine Legende von Fra Angelico" (1921), the painter monk is troubled that his memory of events is called into question by the other monks; and it is the sound of the nightingale's song that transports the young scholar in "Die stumme Nachtigall" to a long-lost *Heimat*.[7] Although "Dein Leib im Rauch durch die Luft," and in particular the poems "O die Schornsteine" (O the Chimneys) and "An euch, die das neue Haus bauen" (To You Who Build the New House), are frequently read as ultimately healing, the representation of memory in the cycle contains a more complex consideration of the desire or need to remember and memorialize (not only on ethical grounds but based on purely personal drive) and skepticism vis-à-vis the ethical mandate to remember in a contained, memorial manner. The cycle contains a handful of poems that evoke conventional poems of mourning and comfort, but these are then answered by a series of poems that capture the reader in the unmistakable truth that that kind of writing is sterile at best and uncomfortably sentimental at its worst. I suspect this is precisely what Rudolf Hartung referred to in his critique of poetry of the mid-forties that uses tropes and words that, at one time, were pointedly metaphorical.[8] In the context of this cycle metaphorical turns of phrase like "wie im Tod / das Leben beginnt" are thrown into carnivalesque relief by the not terribly metaphorical feeling of being followed by the inescapable eyes of the dead, an ironic and yet apparently realistic depiction of the Zeitgeist. Memory in this cycle is cast largely as a specifically Jewish historical memory, in the chimneys, the new house, the Rosh Hashanah ritual of blowing the shofar, drawing on recent as well as ancient events. Past and future—which exist on top of one another and not as progressive entities, that is, all present—are captured in the bell and then the sound of the shofar. In each of the poems, even those that do not exclusively depict Jewish historical memory, the past continues to exist as part of the present in the smoke that becomes part of the air and drifting landscape ("O die Schornsteine"), the fluids of death and mourning that become part of the shroud ("An euch die das neue Haus bauen"), the confusing remains of past poetic or textual objects of value (the nightingale, the wisdom of Solomon, the bitter truth of wormwood in "Wer aber"), the place of the mother now filled by the terrible nursemaid ("O der weinen-den Kinder"), the child's hands still present in the hands of the adult ("Hände"). These images present a tension between evolution and sta-sis, echoing Walter Benjamin's sense of the "jetzt," the *now*, represented in his "Theses on the Philosophy of History," and captured in the gap-ing mouth of Klee's *Angelus Novus*: when time marches forward—or in Sachs's formulation "rieselt" (trickles away)—it takes the mounting pile of rubble, ash, dust, and sand with it. At the center of the cycle is the poem "Einer war," which performs the New Year ritual of the blowing of the shofar. The ritual/poem transforms past into present through sound cues, cleverly forming and performing the work of the cycle, which on closer examination can itself be read as the resonant sound and events that emerge from the ritual at its center. From the shofar the sounds ema-nate that unite past, present, and future in continuous, cyclical, unend-ing reverberation. Read linearly, the poems progress; read cyclically and repeatedly, the poems inform each other concurrently. The poet thus is the "Einer" who blows the shofar, the poem is the shofar she blows, and the encircling cycle is the absent presences evoked by the three distinct shofar blasts. This sort of cyclical structure with an anchor poem at the center is characteristic of Sachs's first postwar poetry volume.

"Einer war" is the seventh of the thirteen poems in the cycle, and therefore the center of the circle. It is the only poem in the cycle that is not broken into strophes. It is the anchor poem of the cycle, toward which all the poems move, from which all the poems emanate. It liter-ally and metaphorically encapsulates the themes under examination, and keeps them in a resonant presence that marks an absence (i.e., the poem resonates in all the other poems, and is thereby both absent and present). It is the Rosh Hashanah ritual of the shofar blast, marking the beginning of the calendar year (but occurring in the month of Tishrei, the seventh month of the ecclesiastical year), and set off with the Zoharic epigraph "Und das Sinken geschieht / um des Steigens willen" (The sinking occurs for the sake of the rising). It begins in the past tense, but then changes to the present tense, and ends with the dash so characteristic of Sachs's poetry, signifying broken thought, the continuation of the poem's structure, lack of closure, and resonance *ad infinitum*.

> *Und das Sinken geschieht*
> *um des Steigens willen*
> Buch Sohar

Einer war,
Der blies den Schofar—
Warf nach hinten das Haupt,
Wie die Rehe tun, wie die Hirsche
Bevor sie trinken an der Quelle.
Bläst:
Tekia
Ausfährt der Tod im Seufzer—
Schewarim
Das Samenkorn fällt—
Terua
Die Luft erzählt von einem Licht!
Die Erde kreist und die Gestirne kreisen
Im Schofar,
Den Einer bläst—
Und um den Schofar brennt der Tempel—
Und Einer bläst—
Und um den Schofar stürzt der Tempel—
Und Einer bläst—
Und um den Schofar ruht die Asche—
Und Einer bläst—[9]

[*Someone blew the Shofar*

> *The sinking occurs for the sake of the rising*
> Book of Sohar

Someone
Blew the Shofar—
Threw back his head
As the deer do, as the stags
Before they drink at the spring.
Blows
Tekiah
Death departs in the sigh—
Shewarim
The seed descends—
Terua
The air tells of a light!
The earth circles and the constellations circle
In the Shofar

Which someone blows—
And round the Shofar the temple burns—
And someone blows—
And round the Shofar the temple falls—
And someone blows—
And round the Shofar the ashes rest—
And someone blows—[10]]

Rosh Hashanah prompts remembering as well as reexamination. The shofar is an instrument that has a vocative task, to call out and set the individual to action. The *Tekia* is an unbroken sound; the *Schewarim* is a wailing sound broken into three parts; the *Terua* is a sobbing sound broken into nine parts: all together, a total of thirteen sounds.[11] The significance of these wailing sounds echoes in the thirteen poems here, each of which is broken, sobbing, and represents an articulated but inarticulate expression of horror, madness, grief, and desperation; this process of expression is mirrored in the oft-cited image of the nightingale sobbing from the final poem of this cycle. The reexaminative function of the shofar blasts is represented in a number of incriminating and searching questions posed in the cycle that can be read as a prompt to all readers to reexamine their deeds. In a liturgical sense the shofar calls out to all Jews; if we extend this to a textual metaphor, then the poem calls out to activate all readers to hear, or read, that is, to perceive. This possibility is supported by the ambiguous use of the pronouns throughout the cycle, which leaves no one unexamined as a bystander, or even as a potential perpetrator or victim. Finally, we ought not overlook the aural nature of memory at play here, so integral to Jewish practice. The shofar calls through articulated if inarticulate broken sound to "remember," and as we see in this poem, events past, present, and future are made present through the sounds. In "Einer war," the shofar sounds, and "the temple *burns*"; the shofar sounds, and the temple *falls*; the shofar sounds, and the ash *settles*. All remain in the present tense here: the blowing, the burning, the collapsing and the settling, and owing to the broken-off end of the poem, this process conceivably keeps going into eternity. None of the wounds of the past are realizably past, and none of them are healed. The listener perceives from the sound that those wounds are always present, in the present tense on the page, and made tangibly present by the current of sound waves striking the eardrum. The wounds are therefore absent and present at the same time: present in sense, represented by sensory input.

The poem/shofar performs this function for the wounds resulting from Nazi atrocity, be they personal, communal, or literary in nature. "O die Schornsteine," the first poem in the cycle, is a resonant ripple of the shofar, casting on the page the wound of the poetic text, keeping it present rather than healing it, ironically capturing the impossibility of the vocative poems of *kleos* and Romantic death that once characterized mourning in literature. The thirteenth poem of the cycle, "Lange schon" is a vocative call to poetic action, to "sob out / The throat's terrible silence [that exists before or stands before] death," which if we connect it with the rest of the cycle and the last line of the preceding strophe ("Namenlos geworden," "Her name lost"), can be read as a call to make clear the obscured absence—make clear that we do not and cannot know, make clear the gap that cannot be closed in order to express desperation and rupture. This then casts both reader and writer in a limitless state of presence confronted with absence, the only sort of "remembering" that is possible after the Nazi atrocities. The poem sounds—the palpable absence reverberates and we feel it, as is the case in "O die Schornsteine," the iconic Sachs poem, yet but one of the thirteen poems in this cycle.

> *Und wenn diese meine Haut zerschlagen sein wird,*
> *so werde ich ohne mein Fleisch Gott schauen.*
>
> —Hiob

O die Schornsteine
Auf den sinnreich erdachten Wohnungen des Todes,
Als Israels Leib zog aufgelöst in Rauch
Durch die Luft—
Als Essenkehrer ihn ein Stern empfing
Der schwarz wurde
Oder war es ein Sonnenstrahl?

O die Schornsteine!
Freiheitswege für Jeremias und Hiobs Staub—
Wer erdachte euch und baute Stein auf Stein
Den Weg für Flüchtlinge aus Rauch?

O die Wohnungen des Todes,
Einladend hergerichtet
Für den Wirt des Hauses, der sonst Gast war—
O ihr Finger,
Die Eingangsschwelle legend
Wie ein Messer zwischen Leben und Tod—

O ihr Schornsteine,
O ihr Finger,
Und Israels Leib im Rauch durch die Luft![12]

[*O the chimneys*

> *And though after my skin worms destroy this*
> *body, yet in my flesh shall I see God.*—Job, 19:26

O the chimneys
On the ingeniously devised habitations of death
When Israel's body drifted as smoke
Through the air—
Was welcomed by a star, a chimney sweep,
A star that turned black
Or was it a ray of sun?

O the chimneys!
Freedomway for Jeremiah and Job's dust—
Who devised you and laid stone upon stone
The road for refugees of smoke?

O the habitations of death,
Invitingly appointed
For the host who used to be a guest—
O you fingers
Laying the threshold
Like a knife between life and death—

O you chimneys,
O you fingers
And Israel's body as smoke through the air![13]]

"O die Schornsteine" has been read as poetic pathos; it is, especially when read in the context of its cycle, a ruptured and ironic poem. The standard poetic vocative "O," here used emphatically, is made the bearer of a new vision of death that is both inviting (literally "einladend hergerichtet") and yet finally banal and lacking in metaphysical meaning. It is clear from the epigraph that the failure to valorize God, death, and the poet is purposeful, and signals the collapse of the world of art as it had been perceived. Of the multitude of Romantic poems that desire a final escape and rest in a deep grave, few if any specify the manner of passing into that final rest. "O die Schornsteine" does precisely that: it highlights the invention and construction of a way into death, not a deep one but a limitless one, and not just for an individual but for an entire group in one body. The attractiveness of death in Romantic poems lies in part in its individual embrace. In Sachs's poem, the attractiveness has been constructed into the chimney: "einladend hergerichtet" ("invitingly appointed," which would logically proceed to "einladend *hin*gerichtet") or the welcoming image of the "Eingangsschwelle" or the idea of "Wirt" and "Gast." The chimeys are constructed ("Auf den sinnreich erdachten Wohnungen des Todes," a construction whose entire implication will become clear only after reading the entire cycle) by someone or a culture consumed with death, but for whom are they constructed so invitingly? They are constructed "Freiheitswege" for someone other than the builder, namely for "Israels Leib," "Jeremias und Hiobs Staub." This is the turn of a Romantic thought of death as freedom into a coercion and construction of death for a collective body of traitors (Jeremia) and victims (Hiob/Job). There is no invidual, there is no dignity, there is no grand metaphysical significance. The ironic twist of murder into freedom is echoed in the sarcastic musing, beginning with the emphatic second "O die Schornsteine!," over who planned and built so painstakingly this way into freedom for "Flüchtlinge aus Rauch," as if it were a thoughtful and kind gesture. What Celan refers to in "Todesfuge" as "Graves in the Air," Sachs leaves at smoke floating through the air; not even a grave for this collective body. The significance of the final line—"Und Israels Leib im Rauch durch die Luft!"— lies in its relationship to the epigraph from Job: "Und wenn diese meine Haut zerschlagen sein wird, / so werde ich ohne mein Fleisch Gott schauen" (And though after my skin worms destroy this body, yet in my flesh shall I see God). There is no evidence of God in the poem, only the dust of Job and the body of Israel in smoke through the air. The construction of mass death that is so clearly articulated in the image of the chimney is what subverts the traditional tone of the poem. The poetic "O" is ironic and uncomfortable. The banality of the body of Israel in smoke through the air exposes the "O": it belongs to a poetry that finds or evokes significance, beauty, individuality in death or prayer, but crematoria and "freedom" do not fit that paradigm, indeed the paradigm falls so far short of containing them that they appear sentimental and quaint, making the poem on much closer reading extremely discomforting. The discrepency between the Job epigraph and the final line of the poem suggest that the discomfort is intended; the intentional discord is borne out by the rest of the cycle, which is characterized by a handful of poems that attempt conventional modes of mourning and giving comfort and are mercilessly overwhelmed by the poems that reflect the nightmarish reality of the Holocaust and its legacy. Sachs is demonstrating, rather than saying, why and how traditional poetic modes of mourning and comfort cannot continue; her evocation of the traditional tropes and structures is an excavation of relics that lack the context that gave them their former meaning. "O" is not a resurrection, it is a recognizable piece of rubble lying in the drifts of sand, ash, and dust.

The next poem in the cycle, "An euch, die das neue Haus bauen," is one of the poems that earnestly attempts a conventional salving of the soul. It is a call to the future, a sort of hymn appealing to those who must rebuild—not a vocative, but an appellation or wish that is savagely deconstructed by the poem that follows it.

Es gibt Steine wie Seelen.
Rabbi Nachman

An euch, die das neue Haus bauen

Wenn du dir deine Wände neu aufrichtest—
Deinen Herd, Schlafstatt, Tisch und Stuhl—
Hänge nicht deine Tränen um sie, die dahingegangen,
Die nicht mehr mit dir wohnen werden
An den Stein
Nicht an das Holz—
Es weint sonst in deinen Schlaf hinein,
Den kurzen, den du noch tun mußt.

Seufze nicht, wenn du dein Laken bettest,
Es mischen sich sonst deine Träume
Mit dem Schweiß der Toten.

Ach, es sind die Wände und die Geräte
Wie die Windharfen empfänglich
Und wie ein Acker, darin dein Leid wächst,
Und spüren das Staubverwandte in dir.

Baue, wenn die Stundenuhr rieselt,
Aber weine nicht die Minuten fort
Mit dem Staub zusammen,
Der das Licht verdeckt.[14]

[*To you that build the new house*

"*There are stones like souls*"—Rabbi Nachman

When you come to put up your walls anew—
Your stove, your bedstead, table and chair—
Do not hang your tears for those who departed,
Who will not live with you then,
On to the stone.
Nor on the timber—
Else weeping will pierce the sleep,
The brief sleep you have yet to take.

Do not sigh when you bed your sheets,
Else your dreams will mingle
With the sweat of the dead.

Oh, the walls and household utensils
Are responsive as Aeolian harps

Or like a field in which your sorrow grows,
And they sense your kinship with dust.

Build, when the hourglass trickles,
But do not weep away the minutes
Together with the dust
That obscures the light.[15]]

"An euch, die das neue Haus bauen" is consistently viewed as a poem
advocating a renewal of all things rising from the ashes, exhorting
survivors to build a new world without melancholia in which they
might remain trapped. In this interpretation of the poem, the survivors in the poem are instructed to reconstruct and furnish their dwelling spaces (the title of the entire volume, it must be remembered, is
In den Wohnungen des Todes, In the Habitations of Death), expressly
avoiding any building in of mourning (though in the cycle the dead are
everywhere, in everything). Viewed alone, the poem is easily read in
this way, but in the larger cycle, "Dein Leib im Rauch durch die Luft,"
it is the only poem that makes this appeal. William West reads this as
a kind of haunting, concluding that the dead must be laid to rest. For
West, "An euch, die das neue Haus bauen" is the core of the cycle that
is reaffirmed. I propose an opposite reading: that the state of destruction, which has brought with it paradigmatic shifts, must be constantly
confronted (it cannot be avoided, and laying the dead to rest is no longer an option—that luxury belongs to an era on the other side of the
abyss of Auschwitz) rather than advocating what in this cycle is clearly a
fruitless attempt to "progress." Memory in this cycle of poems, rooted
in the introductory "O die Schornsteine!" and "An euch, die das neue
Haus bauen," must be forgotten, and yet it persists. "An euch" represents a traditional approach to mourning; but it is utterly overwhelmed
by the terror and desperation in most of the other poems.

Moving from the "Wohnungen des Todes," which have been "erdacht"
for the "Wirt" (landlord or host, in this case death), who has otherwise
been a guest, "An euch" addresses the building of the new dwelling, this
time a house for the living. This is not "einladend hergerichtet," but is
rather appointed with all manner of wood, stone, and furnishings covered
with the sweat and dust of the dead. It is the tears of the mourners the
builder is advised to avoid, lest the mourning cry into the builder's sleep
("weint sonst in deinen Schlaf hinein"), or his dreams mix with the sweat
of the dead. Everything, the poetic "I" pleads, is fertile ground for sorrow
("Acker, darin dein Leid wächst"); this is the first clear reference to the
agricultural nature of behavior, a nexus of body as earth, time, and history
marked by sowing and reaping, and finally the fertile imagination.

It is not clear who the "euch" or the corresponding "du" might be
specifically, though the undefined nature of most of the pronouns in the

cycle suggests the poem speaks to anyone alive to build. The builder furthermore is commanded to build "wenn die Stundenuhr rieselt," as time slips away, though not to actively cry "die Minuten fort" along with the dust that was once a human form; this would indicate that mourning in fact does more to obscure and eradicate the dead, replacing them with self-important grief, and is at odds with the confrontation ultimately captured in the cycle. It is a depiction of mourning that fit another time, but is no longer possible, or, indeed, called for. The constant movement of time will continue to resonate in the cycle, and will eventually be put into contrast with people, who stand still.

The somewhat pleading or advisory tone of "An euch" is firmly grounded in the domestic sphere of sleep and peace; both of these are abruptly halted in the violent, nightmarish "O der weinenden Kinder Nacht!" Whereas "O die Schornsteine" is grounded in the past, and "An euch" looks toward a future, "O der weinenden Kinder Nacht," the third poem in the cycle, contrasts what was with what is; eventually the images in this poem are cast backwards to give a sense of what created the "now" as a warning or admonition for the future.

> O der weinenden Kinder Nacht!
> Der zum Tode gezeichneten Kinder Nacht!
> Der Schlaf hat keinen Eingang mehr.
> Schreckliche Wärterinnen
> Sind an die Stelle der Mütter getreten,
> Haben den falschen Tod in ihre Handmuskeln gespannt,
> Säen ihn in die Wände und ins Gebälk—
> Überall brütet es in den Nestern des Grauens.
> Angst säugt die Kleinen statt der Muttermilch.
>
> Zog die Mutter noch gestern
> Wie ein weißer Mond den Schlaf heran,
> Kam die Puppe mit dem fortgeküßten Wangenrot
> In den einen Arm,
> Kam das ausgestopfte Tier, lebendig
> In der Liebe schon geworden,
> In den andern Arm,—
> Weht nun der Wind des Sterbens,
> Bläst die Hemden über die Haare fort,
> Die niemand mehr kämmen wird.[16]

[*O the night of the weeping children!*

O the night of the weeping children!
O the night of the children branded for death!
Sleep may not enter here.
Terrible nursemaids

Have usurped the place of mothers,
Have tautened their tendons with the false death,
Sow it on to the walls and into the beams—
Everywhere it is hatched in the nests of horror.
Instead of mother's milk, panic suckles those little ones.

Yesterday Mother still drew
Sleep toward them like a white moon,
There was the doll with cheeks derouged by kisses
In one arm,
The stuffed pet, already
Brought to life by love,
In the other—
Now blows the wind of dying,
Blows the shifts over the hair
That no one will comb again.[17]]

Whatever the builder of the new house might be building and sowing into the walls, whatever protections one takes to make sleep possible are completely undone in this poem. "Der Schlaf hat keinen Eingang mehr" (sleep no longer has an entrance), so there is no chance that mourning can weep into it, or that dreams can mix with the sweat of the dead. Terrible nursemaids ("schreckliche Wärterinnen") replace mothers, and they sow "den falschen Tod" (false death) into the walls and the rafters, taking up the agricultural theme introduced in the previous poem ("wie ein Acker, darin dein Leid wächst"), and even nurse the children with fear. Who exactly the children are becomes dishearteningly clear as the cycle turns; since past and present exist concurrently, all adults are also children. Everyone is being stilled with fear, "everyone" are the children in this nightmare world where sleep is no longer possible. The poem then breaks and turns to the longer stanza that juxtaposes the past and the present. As night fell in the past, mothers brought on sleep; "fort" refers to a doll's cheek that has been kissed so much that the redness of her cheek is "fortgeküßt" (kissed away); the stuffed animal "lebendig" (alive) through love. Here, a stuffed animal and a favorite doll are arranged in the child's arms; later in the cycle, marionettes and playing appear with sinister and fatal connotations. These words have taken on a different meaning from the meaning they normally carry in the context of a child's nursery, which hearkens back to "Chelion" as she stares at "Mr Moon," or combs her doll's artificial hair, pondering the semantic nuances that confuse her. This remembrance is cut short, a comma immediately followed by a long dash, confronted by "nun" (now), where the wind of death blows "fort" the nightdress over hair "Die niemand mehr kämmen wird" (That no one will comb again). As much as "An euch" hopes to prevent a future neglected by the melancholia of the past, here the grim task of confronting the present overwhelms that sentiment, which, with its emphasis on sleep, melancholia, and home, seems more appropriate for a Romantic vision of death than for the unimaginable scale of death that the poets of the 1940s faced. Everyone is being stilled with fear and hatred; melancholia would be a comparative blessing.

The fourth poem, "Wer aber," shifts abruptly into a pondering mode, the purpose of which later becomes clear in the central poem "Einer war," the call to reexamine past and present deeds.

> Wer aber leerte den Sand aus euren Schuhen,
> Als ihr zum Sterben aufstehen mußtet?
> Den Sand, den Israel heimholte,
> Seinen Wandersand?
> Brennenden Sinaisand,
> Mit den Kehlen von Nachtigallen vermischt,
> Mit den Flügeln des Schmetterlings vermischt,
> Mit dem Sehnsuchtsstaub der Schlangen vermischt,
> Mit allem was abfiel von der Weisheit Salomos vermischt,
> Mit dem Bitteren aus des Wermuts Geheimnis vermischt—
>
> O ihr Finger,
> Die ihr den Sand aus Totenschuhen leertet,
> Morgen schon werdet ihr Staub sein
> In den Schuhen Kommender![18]

> [*But who emptied your shoes of sand*
>
> But who emptied your shoes of sand
> When you had to get up, to die?
> The sand which Israel gathered,
> Its nomad sand?
> Burning Sinai sand,
> Mingled with throats of nightingales,
> Mingled with wings of butterflies,
> Mingled with the hungry dust of serpents;
> Mingled with all that fell from the wisdom of Solomon,
> Mingled with what is bitter in the mystery of wormwood—
>
> O you fingers
> That emptied the deathly shoes of sand.
> Tomorrow you will be dust
> In the shoes of those to come.[19]]

"Wer aber" juxtaposes uncertainty with conviction and indignation. The first two lines of the first stanza linger on a particular aspect of moments before and after death that has become iconic for Auschwitz, namely the presence and significance of shoes. The poetic "I" ponders the collective "ihr" of the dead as it ponders who emptied their shoes of "Sand"; the remaining eight lines of the first stanza explicate the symbolic nature of that sand. Sand begins as the marker of the desert-wandering nation of Israel, and the burning sand of the moment of covenant at Sinai. It is a defining marker of the body that once occupied (and thus controlled) those shoes, and is mixed with the sand of long-standing poetic images for all that is the human experience: the nightingale for expression; the wings of the butterfly for freedom; the snake, representing a range of possibilities, most especially it seems here desire; the wisdom of Solomon, relevant for ruling powers; and wormwood for the bitterness of loss and absence, as well as the bitterness of whatever is revealed in its mystery (i.e., a bitter truth). In the destruction of the body of Israel, all that was humanity, represented over millennia by the poets through metaphor, perished as well. "Wer aber," but who, the poetic "I" wonders, had the task of emptying the shoes as the "ihr" went to their death? If the "ihr" removed their own shoes, they themselves emptied the shoes of that sand. Someone else, perhaps a perpetrator, another inmate, or the next victim, may have removed their shoes, thus emptying them of sand. The shoes remain to be dealt with, however, after death. The second stanza introduces disaggregated fingers that emptied "den Sand aus Totenschuhen," the sand from "deathly shoes," or even shoes of the dead. Who the fingers belong to is left ambiguous, which allows the final pronouncement to be both a lament and a warning, to the "ihr" as well as to the reader. The second and third lines of the stanza juxtapose sand and dust, where sand appears to have grand metaphorical significance, and dust more humble metaphorical significance. Once affiliated with a great literary legacy of sand, the dead will, tomorrow already, be simply dust beneath the shoes of others. Once possessing the power to empty the shoes of the dead of their great sand, the perpetrator is reminded that he, tomorrow already, will be dust beneath the shoes of others. It is a complex *memento mori* moment that captures the tension of the anonymity and yet omnipresence of death, and suggests that readers consider more carefully the ground upon which they walk.

The word "Auch" ("even," or "also") in the first line of the following poem, "Auch der Greise," however, suggests that the poetic "I" is proceeding with the "ihr" from "Wer aber." Where the "ihr" and the "Finger" of "Wer aber" allowed for ambiguity, the continuation signaled by the "auch" pinpoints the "ihr" undeniably as the living perpetrators.

Auch der Greise
Letzten Atemzug, der schon den Tod anblies
Raubtet ihr noch fort.
Die leere Luft,

Zitternd vor Erwartung, den Seufzer der Erleichterung
Zu erfüllen, mit dem diese Erde fortgestoßen wird—
Die leere Luft habt ihr beraubt!

Der Greise
Ausgetrocknetes Auge
Habt ihr noch einmal zusammengepreßt
Bis ihr das Salz der Verzweiflung gewonnen hattet—
Alles was dieser Stern
An Krümmungen der Qual besitzt,
Alles Leiden aus den dunklen Verliesen der Würmer
Sammelte sich zuhauf—

O ihr Räuber von echten Todesstunden,
Letzten Atemzügen und der Augenlider *Gute Nacht*
Eines sei euch gewiß:

Es sammelt der Engel ein
Was ihr fortwarft,
Aus der Greise verfrühter Mitternacht
Wird sich ein Wind der letzten Atemzüge auftun,
Der diesen losgerissenen Stern
In seines Herrn Hände jagen wird![20]

[*Even the old men's last breath*]

Even the old men's last breath
That had already grazed death
You snatched away.
The empty air
Trembling
To fill the sigh of relief
That thrusts this earth away—
You have plundered the empty air!

The old men's
Parched eyes
You pressed once more
Till you reaped the salt of despair—
All that this star owns
Of the contortions of agony,
All suffering from the dungeons of worms
Gathered in heaps—

O you thieves of genuine hours of death,
Last breaths and the eyelids' Good Night
Of one thing be sure:

The angel, it gathers
What you discarded,
From the old men's premature midnight
A wind of last breaths shall arise
And drive this unloosed star
Into its Lord's hands![21]]

The "ihr" has also "beraubt" (robbed) old men and the empty air of "last breaths." Biologically speaking, each body has a final breath; but this is *their* last breath, that is, the last breath they would have consciously breathed, perhaps even chosen had they not died a false death. It is their sovereignty that has been taken, a dignified death with a final breath of the sort we expect to find in conventional elegiac or epitaphic poetry. The poetic "I" evokes the ruined conventional childhood bedtime imagery from "O der weinenden Kinder Nacht!" in the "*Gute Nacht*" stolen from dying eyelids. Whereas in "O der weinenden Kinder" the wind of death blows, here it is a wind of "letzten Atemzüge" (a wind of last breaths shall arise) that will *chase* (jagen) "diesen losgerissenen Stern" (this unloosed star) into the hands of its "Herrn" (presumably God, but it is not expressly stated). What exactly the "Stern" is is not (yet) clear—it is possibly the earth, although it may also indicate nighttime sky imagery that will continue to appear in the cycle and usually depicts the dichotomy of movement and stasis. This poem also continues the development of the "blasen" (blowing) imagery, which began with the "O der weinenden Kinder" and will reach its pinnacle with the shofar of the seventh poem. Here the last breath that "schon den Tod anblies" already touches death; the blowing of the shofar will ultimately make these uncertain moments of false death arise through its sound.

"Ein totes Kind spricht," the sixth poem, is an unusual poem in the cycle: it is one of three poems with an actual, separate title, and is the only poem that articulates the voice of the dead. It begins with another variation on the mother/child relationship, observing death, then confronting mourning, and finally concluding with a moment of silence before death.

Ein totes Kind spricht

Die Mutter hielt mich an der Hand.
Dann hob Jemand das Abschiedsmesser:
Die Mutter löste ihre Hand aus der meinen,
Damit es mich nicht träfe.
Sie aber berührte noch einmal leise meine Hüfte—
Und da blutete ihre Hand—

Von da ab schnitt mir das Abschiedsmesser
Den Bissen in der Kehle entzwei—
Es fuhr in der Morgendämmerung mit der Sonne hervor

Und begann, sich in meinen Augen zu schärfen—
In meinem Ohr schliffen sich Winde und Wasser,
Und jede Trostesstimme stach in mein Herz—

Als man mich zum Tode führte,
Fühlte ich im letzten Augenblick noch
Das Herausziehen des großen Abschiedsmessers.²²

[*A dead child speaks*

My mother held me by my hand.
Then someone raised the knife of parting:
So that it should not strike me,
My mother loosed her hand from mine.
But she lightly touched my thighs once more
And her hand was bleeding—

After that the knife of parting
Cut in two each bite I swallowed—
It rose before me with the sun at dawn
And began to sharpen itself in my eyes—
Wind and water ground in my ear
And every voice of comfort pierced my heart—

As I was led to death
I still felt in the last moment
The unsheathing of the great knife of parting.²³]

The moment described in the first stanza marks the end of the mother/ child relationship referred to in particular in "O der weinenden Kinder Nacht," a dynamic of protection and nurturing cut short by the "Abschiedsmesser" (knife of parting). That same knife seems to have taken over the senses of the child, even to the extent that, as a sort of answer to "An euch," "jede Trostesstimme stach in mein Herz" (every voice of comfort pierced my heart); the translation uses "pierced" for "stach," though "stabbed" perhaps more immediately captures the tension between conventional attempts at comfort and the sense of unpoetic desperation in the cycle. The only relief afforded the child appears in the third stanza. The ambiguous chronological progression allows for at least two readings. The child tells us he was led to death, which could mean he was taken from one place to the place of his murder; or it could mean the actual murder, since the process of murdering him leads him to death. The "letzte[r] Augenblick," final moment, could be the moment just before he is murdered, or the last moment of his life. In that final moment, he still felt "Das Herausziehen" of the great knife of parting; the translation uses "unsheathing" for "herausziehen," suggesting he could ominously feel the knife being drawn that was about to murder him; but "herausziehen" also more generally means to extricate something. The knife of parting has stayed "in" him since the death of his mother, cutting the bite of food in his throat ("Den Bissen in der Kehle"), sharpening in his eyes; the sound of wind and water in his ears sounds like they are running over a whetstone ("schliffen sich"), and voices of comfort stab his heart. In each phrase, the preposition "in" locates the knife and its effect; he has internalized the knife that parted him from his mother. Only in the moment of death, as he felt the murder weapon, was the knife extricated. This final stanza accomplishes two things in the cycle: it suggests that the only relief from these wounds of loss is death; it also marks the final moment of silence before death, the moment in which the child feels the knife of parting removed as he feels his own (impending) death, and the moment poets are called to "schluchzen aus" (sob out) in the final poem. Note that the wound is not healed, ever. Only death puts an end to this suffering. There is no overcoming, at least in the words of the poet who is, to paraphrase the final lines of the cycle's concluding poem, sobbing out the terrible moment of silence before death.

"Einer war" begins in the past tense, but shifts to the present tense as the ritual begins. The shofar sounds, someone actively blows it, and the shofar makes all events present, from the burning of the temple into the unforeseeable future. Extending this to the cycle, then, each poem becomes present, each moment of despair, each moment of death, and now, as the cycle progresses, each pointing finger. What is not mentioned, but is implicit, is the purpose of the ritual, like the vocative "O" that marks this cycle a direct address calling on all readers to examine their deeds, as they routinely see themselves addressed in the ambiguous collective second-person plural pronoun "ihr" that dominates "Dein Leib im Rauch durch die Luft." Although the cycle is otherwise marked periodically with present participial adjectives ("einlad*end* hergerichtet," for example), the present tense and present participial adjectives now also become more prominent, beginning with the eighth poem, "Hände."

Whereas several poems in the cycle begin with a genitive first line in its entirety, "Hände" breaks up its genitive beginning into two lines, placing the emphasis firmly on the hands, less poetically conventional than the "O ihr Finger" of earlier poems, and evoking the hands of the terrible nursemaids, whose hands also sow terror, fear, and murder. The poem reintroduces the agricultural motif and makes it a defining characteristic of the hands. It also introduces the word "Triften," which can mean "pasturage," "meadows," "cattle tracks," or "drift," as in the current of a body of water. "Trift" is derived etymologically from "Treiben," which encompasses "drive" and "cultivation," for example greenhouses ("Treibhaus," as in this poem) and driving livestock (the verb "treiben," hence a track is a "Trift"), and also human psychological and physiological drives ("Triebe"). It is thus a key word linking agriculture to behavior. This conceptual link underscores the fundamental theme of the cycle: human beings (which are made of dust and sand) are cultivated, just as land is cultivated.

Hände
Der Todesgärtner,
Die ihr aus der Wiegenkamille Tod,
Die auf den harten Triften gedeiht
Oder am Abhang,
Das Treibhausungeheuer eures Gewerbes gezüchtet habt.
Hände,
Des Leibes Tabernakel aufbrechend,
Der Geheimnisse Zeichen wie Tigerzähne packend—
Hände,
Was tatet ihr,
Als ihr die Hände von kleinen Kindern waret?
Hieltet ihr eine Mundharmonika, die Mähne
Eines Schaukelpferdes, faßtet der Mutter Rock im Dunkel,
Zeigtet auf ein Wort im Kinderlesebuch—
War es Gott vielleicht, oder Mensch?

Ihr würgenden Hände,
War eure Mutter tot,
Eure Frau, euer Kind?
Daß ihr nur noch den Tod in den Händen hieltet,
In den würgenden Händen?[24]

[*Hands*

Hands
of the gardeners of death,
you who have grown the greenhouse monster of your trade
from the cradle camomile death
which thrives on the hard pastures
or on the slope.
Hands
breaking open the tabernacle of the body,
gripping the signs of the mysteries like tiger's teeth—
Hands,
what did you do
when you were tiny children's hands?
Did you hold a mouth organ, the mane
of a rocking horse, clutch your mother's skirt in the dark,
did you point to a word in a reading book—
Was it God perhaps, or Man?

> You strangling hands,
> was your mother dead,
> your wife, your child?
> So that all that you held in your hands was death,
> in your strangling hands?[25]]

There is no poetic, vocative "O" in this poem, only direct questions examining the past deeds of the hands of those who cultivate and/or perform death. The present participial adjectives "aufbrechend" (breaking open) and "packend" (gripping) keep this cultivation present, while returning to the childhood motif that runs throughout the cycle in a most arresting manner. The childhood segment is introduced by the set-off question "was tatet ihr," a sensible question of interrogation for these murdering hands; that the question is afforded its own line also allows the reader to pick it up later as an entity in and of itself, asking, as the shofar entreats us to do, "was tatet ihr" (here the implied "ihr" is "ihr Zuschauenden," you onlookers). But the next line is surprising, as it returns to the childhood motif of earlier poems, placing the hands in the same context of safe private sphere of mother and nursery known to every child and then posing the question: "War es Gott vielleicht, oder Mensch?" (Was it God, perhaps, or Man?). The question appears abruptly, as the preceding thoughts of childhood break off with a long dash. The "es" in this line represents a two-layered speculation. Since, grammatically, it can refer back to "ein Wort im Kinderlesebuch" (a word in a reading book), the poetic "I" wonders about a moment where the child learns to read or understand God, or perhaps humankind; at the same time, the question can stand alone, so that the poetic "I" wonders whether God or humankind turns children's hands into choking hands. Reading the question in relation to the stanza that follows it, suggests, in examining the deeds of people, that it is the psychology of humankind that seems to produce the murderer, potentially as a reaction to loss. "Hände," one of the thoughts and events that appear around the shofar of the seventh poem, "Einer war," returns the reader to each of the preceding poems, touching on the tactile references of fingers and hands, the agricultural references of seeds sown, the threshold moments between life and death, and the present participles (einladend, zitternd). Notably, there is an absence of a poetic "O" here—where in accordance with the rest of the cycle it should read, "O Ihr würgenden Hände" the poetic "O" is dropped. The "O" seems most often to capture an inarticulate moment; this stanza is composed of two straightforward questions. The poem suggests the consequences predicted in "O der weinenden Kinder Nacht!," in which children are being stilled with fear. As we read at the end of "Hände," the poetic "I" asks the "ihr" whether its mother, wife, and child were dead, for which reason they—the hands—held in them only death. The line of questioning in the preceding stanza is focused closely on what the child-hands held ("hieltet"). In keeping with that line of questioning, the logical sequence would be that the child-hands lost a mother, and therefore did not hold, as in the fourteenth line, the skirts of their mother, or that their mother died, leaving them to hold thereafter only death; but the question probes into a different time when it then proceeds to ask if the hands lost a wife or child. This stanza mirrors the action of the shofar in that it makes multiple stages of time possible at once: the hands may have or may have had a wife and a child, and also and at the same time a mother, meaning that adult hands are still child hands, since every adult is still always someone's child (and evidently gendered male or at least masculine in this poem, though the hands of the terrible nursemaids are similar). Read along with "O weinenden Kinder Nacht," which clearly portrays the nightmare scenario of the present filled with motherless children, nursed only with fear, the cycle now begins to suggest that anyone alive is a child of loss, which seems to bode ill for the future, just as it has for the past—a past that both the shofar and the poem make clear is still and always will be present. These hands are still active, as the present participles in lines eight and nine clearly demonstrate ("Des Leibes Tabernakel aufbrechend, / Der Geheimnisse Zeichen wie Tigerzähne packend—"). This poem is not only an examination of deeds, it is an alarming admonition and warning: anyone can be or can become a perpetrator.

The madness of loss is concentrated in the ninth poem, "Schon vom Arm," in which, finally, the figure of the mother is examined.

Schon vom Arm des himmlischen Trostes umfangen
Steht die wahnsinnige Mutter
Mit den Fetzen ihres zerrissenen Verstandes,
Mit den Zündern ihres verbrannten Verstandes
Ihr totes Kind einsargend,
Ihr verlorenes Licht einsargend,
Ihre Hände zu Krügen biegend,
Aus der Luft füllend mit dem Leib ihres Kindes,
Aus der Luft füllend mit seinen Augen, seinen Haaren
Und seinem flatternden Herzen—

Dann küßt sie das Luftgeborene
Und stirbt![26]

[*Already embraced by the arm of heavenly solace*

Already embraced by the arm of heavenly solace
The insane mother stands
With the tatters of her torn mind
With charred tinders of her burnt mind

Burying her dead child,
Burying her lost light,
Twisting her hands into urns,
Filling them with the body of her child from the air,
Filling them with his eyes, his hair from the air,
And with his fluttering heart—

Then she kisses the air-born being
And dies![27]]

Like the child of "Ein totes Kind spricht," this mother is captured on paper in the moment of loss, which culminates then in her own death (silent, and marked with an exclamation point). Stylistically, this poem mimics the successive lines of "Wer aber" that are introduced with "mit" (lines six through ten), but then intensifies the effect by shifting to a series of present participial adjectives. The preceding poem asks the strangling hands whether they held only death as the result of loss; this poem builds from that question, depicting a woman desperately and immediately suffering a loss, who could thus become a cultivator of death. The "wahnsinnige Mutter" (insane mother) is already embraced by the arm of "himmlischen Trostes" (heavenly solace) but she stands—in the present tense—with the shreds of her torn reason and burned sanity. The poem reads like a counterthought to "Hände," suggesting that not everyone who suffers the mind-rending experience of loss becomes a cultivator of death; on the other hand, the mother is driven to death in grief, so either way, loss begets loss. This observation might be the conduit to the tenth and next poem, "Welche Geheimen Wünsche," which appears to return to the question: "War es Gott vielleicht, oder Mensch?"

The poetic "I" appears to be firmly convinced that the answer is "Mensch." "Welche Geheimen Wünsche" introduces the concept of the "Marionettenspieler" (puppet master or puppeteer) in addition to the hands of those "Die Mörder *spielten*" (who *played* murderers).

Welche geheimen Wünsche des Blutes,
Träume des Wahnes und tausendfach
Gemordetes Erdreich
Ließen den schrecklichen Marionettenspieler entstehen?

Er, der mit schäumendem Munde
Furchtbar umblies
Die runde, kreisende Bühne seiner Tat
Mit dem aschgrau ziehenden Horizont der Angst!

O die Staubhügel, die, wie von bösem Mond gezogen
Die Mörder spielten:

Arme auf und ab,
Beine auf und ab
Und die untergehende Sonne des Sinaivolkes
Als den roten Teppich unter den Füßen.

Arme auf und ab,
Beine auf und ab
Und am ziehenden aschgrauen Horizont der Angst
Riesengroß das Gestirn des Todes
Wie die Uhr der Zeiten stehend.[28]

[*What secret cravings of the blood*

What secret cravings of the blood,
Dreams of madness and earth
A thousand times murdered,
Brought into being the terrible puppeteer?

Him who with foaming mouth
Dreadfully swept away
The round, the circling stage of his deed
With the ash-gray, receding horizon of fear?

O the hills of dust, which as though drawn by an evil moon
The murderers enacted:

Arms up and down,
Legs up and down
And the setting sun of Sinai's people
A red carpet under their feet.

Arms up and down,
Legs up and down
And on the ash-gray receding horizon of fear
Gigantic the constellation of death
That loomed like the clock face of ages.[29]]

The poem stands partly in contrast to "Einer war," and partly in contrast to "An euch." Whereas in "Einer war," someone blew and blows the
shofar, here it is "Er" (he) who with a foaming mouth "umblies" (blew
around, literally) the round, circling stage of his deed ("Tat"; presumably
Earth). The circular imagery plays off the "um den Schofar" of "Einer
war" as well as the circular nature of the cycle. As the shofar is blown,
the earth and the stars turn; as "er," "der Marionettenspieler," blew his
stage around, a "horizon of fear" and "the constellation of death" set in.
In contrast to the blowing of the shofar, which appears to set things in
motion, or unveil the motion of the planets as well as time, the blowing

of the puppeteer masks references to motion with skies and constellations that stand still, like the "Uhr der Zeiten" (the clock of times). The "clock of times" stands in direct contrast not only to the cyclical, concurrent time of the shofar, it also stands in contrast to the "Stundenuhr" of "An euch," an hourglass that trickles relentlessly away ("fort"). This is the clock of *times* ("Zeiten"), which would seem to mark different eras, yet is standing still. This is apparently all a distraction, a terrible marionette play on a spinning but inert stage. In evoking the marionette play, Sachs is returning again to the frequent motifs of her early work while underscoring the damage that has been done to artistic convention under the direction of the "schrecklichen Marionettenspieler." Marionette plays were a staple of Sachs's early writing, and part of the fascination appears to be linked to the sinister nature of toys mimicking humans,[30] and the use of deceptive, artistic language to move the plot forward. On the one hand, the tyrant as puppeteer or people who play murderers might seem an inappropriately sentimental rendering; on the other hand, we have seen in Sachs's earliest works that she often invokes sentimentality in order to convey the sinister intent beneath the façade, like Merlin the shape-shifter or the semantic inertia of Chelion. The ironic use of poetic devices throughout this cycle (including the vocative "O," which is very uncomfortable in this context) suggests that the glibness is in keeping with Sachs's poetics. The image of the "terrible puppeteer" is a conventional metaphor that rings uncomfortably hollow, while at the same time depicting the idea that adult hands are also always child hands. The poem returns to the thread that suggests that murdering hands are the result of a particular kind of upbringing or cultivation: the murderous drive is planted and cultivated in the human flesh and psyche. In "O der weinenden Kinder Nacht" the mother of yesterday is compared to the moon; here the "Staubhügel" (hills of dust) who "enacted" or played murderers (as if they are children, or actors, or marionettes, all three appropriate for the cycle as for this particular verb) were "wie von bösem Mond gezogen," drawn, but also raised or cultivated by the bad moon. The childhood of yesterday is no longer possible; and yet that would send the cultivators of this terrible marionette play further back into history than one might assume, and indeed the thrust of the cycle seems pointed toward the admonition that "yesterday" is not only more sinister than previously thought, but that it also has not ended. If the reader hears the blowing of the shofar that resonates outwards in an eternally drifting current, the illusion of an innocent yesterday will become clear. It is impossible to sugarcoat past events when we hear their presence in the shofar blast. "Lange haben wir das Lauschen verlernt!," the eleventh poem, takes up precisely that problem, while revisiting a sentiment that ultimately reveals itself to be confoundingly out of place and finally alarming.

Ehe es wächst, lasse ich euch es erlauschen.

Jesaia

Lange haben wir das Lauschen verlernt!
Hatte Er uns gepflanzt einst zu lauschen
Wie Dünengras gepflanzt, am ewigen Meer,
Wollten wir wachsen auf feisten Triften,
Wie Salat im Hausgarten stehn.

Wenn wir auch Geschäfte haben,
Die weit fort führen
Von Seinem Licht,
Wenn wir auch das Wasser aus Röhren trinken,
Und es erst sterbend naht
Unserem ewig dürstenden Mund—
Wenn wir auch auf einer Straße schreiten,
Darunter die Erde zum Schweigen gebracht wurde
Von einem Pflaster,
Verkaufen dürfen wir nicht unser Ohr,
O, nicht unser Ohr dürfen wir verkaufen.
Auch auf dem Markte,
Im Errechnen des Staubes,
Tat manch einer schnell einen Sprung
Auf der Sehnsucht Seil,
Weil er etwas hörte,
Aus dem Staube heraus tat er den Sprung

Und sättigte sein Ohr.
Preßt, o preßt an der Zerstörung Tag
An die Erde das lauschende Ohr,
Und ihr werdet hören, durch den Schlaf hindurch
Werdet ihr hören
Wie im Tode
Das Leben beginnt.[31]

[*How long have we forgotten how to listen!*

Before they spring forth I tell you of them
Isaiah 42:9

How long have we forgotten how to listen!
He planted us once to listen
Planted us like lyme grass by the eternal sea,
We wanted to grow on fat pastures,
To stand like lettuce in the kitchen-garden.

Although we have business
That leads us far

From his light,
Although we drink tap water,
And only as it dies it reaches
Our eternally thirsting mouths—
Although we walk down a street
Beneath which earth has been silenced
By a pavement,
We must not sell our ears,
Oh, we must not sell our ears.
Even in the market,
In the computation of dust,
Many had made a quick leap
Onto the tightrope of longing,
Because they heard something,
And leapt out of the dust
And sated their ears.
Press, oh press on the day of destruction
The listening ear to the earth,
And you will hear, through your sleep
You will hear
How in death
Life begins.[32]]

This poem, like "An euch," appears to offer something like a conventional prescriptive admonition; at the same time, it contends that "we" have unlearned how to listen (not forgotten—that would be "vergessen"; this is "verlernt"—unlearned), which in the context of the poem as shofar blast or current of sound can be read as meaning that "we" have unlearned perceiving, reading, and interpreting information. This is also the only other poem besides "An euch" where anyone can sleep ("Und ihr werdet hören, durch den Schlaf hindurch"), suggesting that it is addressed to whatever segment of the population is avoiding or somehow unable to perceive the death and destruction that is the constant landscape around them. The epigraph from Isaiah is an entreaty to keep faith even in the worst circumstances (which we have seen rings fairly empty in this postwar nightmare), and most of the content is a standard "modern man is cut off from God." "We" have chosen to live in a mechanized world that shuns truth, which we finally encounter only when death is near; at this point in the poem, death appears to be that same sort of distant, dignified moment of individual reconciliation that was dismantled much earlier in the cycle. The agricultural tropes this time underscore humankind's choice to remove itself from where it was planted "am ewigen Meer" (the eternal sea) to grow and thrive on "feisten Triften," a phrase drawn from Psalm 65 suggesting good, verdant land,[33] although the word "feist" has generally negative connotations of excess. It is our drive, our own cultivation, our own plan, related to our own "Sinn," our sense, and our perception that governs our acts: "Wollten wir wachsen" (we wanted to grow). The idea of death as the dignified sovereign choice is suggested further in the individual who jumps forth "aus dem Staube heraus" (from out of the dust, i.e., from all that is earthly) and satisfied his ear, presumably by returning to the eternal sea. From this the poem turns to a kind of early modern *memento mori*: it implores the "ihr" to press its collective ear to the ground "an der Zerstörung Tag" (the Day of Destruction), on which the "ihr" will hear—through its sleep—"Wie im Tode / Das Leben beginnt" (How in Death / Life begins). After all the suffering captured in this cycle, the bodies in smoke, the false death, the child with a knife in his heart, the crazed mother, the strangling hands, terrible marionettes and governesses of the nightmare, the call to listen in this poem seems quaint and, indeed, antiquated. Were it not for the sheer magnitude of suffering and loss in the rest of the cycle, "Werdet ihr hören / Wie im Tode / Das Leben beginnt" would seem a common enough attempt to comfort the grieving and give meaning to death. Against the backdrop of this cycle, however, it is disturbing. It seems disturbing enough in comparison to the preceding poems, but it is perhaps the poem that follows it that makes it most disturbing. "Ihr Zuschauenden," the twelfth poem, is also the most admonishing of the cycle's thirteen poems.

Ihr Zuschauenden

Unter deren Blicken getötet wurde.
Wie man auch einen Blick im Rücken fühlt,
So fühlt ihr an euerm Leibe
Die Blicke der Toten.

Wieviel brechende Augen werden euch ansehn
Wenn ihr aus den Verstecken ein Veilchen pflückt?
Wieviel flehend erhobene Hände
In dem märtyrerhaft geschlungenen Gezweige
Der alten Eichen?
Wieviel Erinnerung wächst im Blute
Der Abendsonne?

O die ungesungenen Wiegenlieder
In der Turteltaube Nachtruf—
Manch einer hätte Sterne herunterholen können,
Nun muß es der alte Brunnen für ihn tun!

Ihr Zuschauenden,
Die ihr keine Mörderhand erhobt,
Aber die ihr den Staub nicht von eurer Sehnsucht
Schütteltet,

Die ihr stehenbliebt, dort, wo er zu Licht
Verwandelt wird.[34]

[*You onlookers*

Whose eyes watched the killing.
As one feels a stare at one's back
You feel on your bodies
The glances of the dead.

How many dying eyes will look at you
When you pluck a violet from its hiding place?
How many hands be raised in supplication
In the twisted martyr-like branches
Of old oaks?
How much memory grows in the blood
Of the evening sun?

O the unsung cradlesongs
In the night cry of the turtledove—
Many a one might have plucked stars from the sky,
Now the old well must do it for them!

You onlookers,
You who raised no hand in murder,
But who did not shake the dust
From your longing,
You who halted there, where dust is changed
To light.[35]]

And indeed, here the "ihr" hears how life begins in death, because the dead are alive in everything around us; and they are watching. The "ihr" feels the gaze of the dead on their bodies; eyes stare at them, begging outstretched hands reach for them from the trees and flowers, memory grows ("wächst") in the blood of sunset, bringing together nature and agriculture with the ability to perceive what is inscribed in them. The final stanza here evokes the "Staubverwandte in dir" from "An euch, die das neue Haus bauen" and the "was tatet ihr" of "Hände." The "Zuschauenden" did not lift a murderous hand, but they stood still and could not shake off the dust. "Dust" is readable here as human remains (dust or ash), a mark of their crime that they cannot shake off, and also as the physical essence of all human beings, that is, not only remains, but essentially the formless earthen particles that are shaped, physically and psychologically, into human beings. The "ihr" cannot avoid what it has been party to; nor can it avoid its malleable nature. We are shaped (and destroyed) by the hands of others; our action or inaction shapes (or destroys) others.

Even though this poem ends with a period, signaling a complete thought, it still seems to end, like many of the other poems, mid-thought. The final stanza builds up from a pointed "Ihr Zuschauenden, / Die ihr . . ." (you onlookers, you who . . .), as if it would end with a pronouncement or condemnation; the stylistically similar final stanza of "Wer aber" begins "O ihr Finger, / Die ihr . . ." (O you fingers, / you who . . .), and ends with "Morgen schon werdet ihr Staub sein / In den Schuhen Kommender!" (Tomorrow you will be dust / In the shoes of those to come). The building tension in the stanza gives the feeling that it will resolve in a pronouncement, but the poem simply ends at the description of the onlookers. Perhaps the implied impending judgment is left up to the "ihr" and each individual reexamining his or her deeds. The poem, in effect, asks even this "ihr" "was tatet ihr" (what did you do). The answer is "Die ihr stehenblieb, dort, wo er zu Licht / Verwandelt wird": that is, nothing. The "ihr" stood still, like time in "Welche geheimen Wünsche." And who is this "ihr"? Zuschauende: watchers, bystanders, onlookers. It is constructed as a participial adjective, not "Zuschauer," but "Zuschauende"; the participial ending "-ende" emphasizes the act of looking in the present tense. Two questions are thus implied in the poem: what did you do, and what are you doing now? The poem implicates anyone who is alive and did not lift a murdering hand (but also did not offer a helping hand), including the poet, and including any reader in the mid-to-late 1940s. Bearing in mind the participial ending, and recalling, also, that the anchor poem "Einer war" makes all time present, the impetus to examine one's conscience and deeds extends to the present reader. The implications hang in the air as the cycle ends with the thirteenth and final poem, "Lange schon."

Lange schon fielen die Schatten.
Nicht sind gemeint jetzt
Jene lautlosen Schläge der Zeit
Die den Tod füllen—
Des Lebensbaumes abgefallene Blätter—

Die Schatten des Schrecklichen fielen
Durch das Glas der Träume,
Von Daniels Deuterlicht erhellt.

Schwarzer Wald wuchs erstickend um Israel,
Gottes Mitternachtssängerin.
Sie verging im Dunkeln,
Namenlos geworden.

O ihr Nachtigallen in allen Wäldern der Erde!
Gefiederte Erben des toten Volkes,
Wegweiser der gebrochenen Herzen,

Die ihr euch füllt am Tage mit Tränen,
Schluchzet es aus, schluchzet es aus
Der Kehle schreckliches Schweigen vor dem Tod.[36]

[*The shadows fell long ago*

The shadows fell long ago.
Here are not meant
Those silent strokes of time
That fill death—
Fallen leaves of the tree of life—

The shadows of terror fell
Through the glass of dreams,
Lit by the prophetic light of Daniel.

Black forest grew suffocatingly round Israel,
God's midnight singer.
She perished in darkness,
Her name lost.

O you nightingales in all the woods of earth!
Plumed heirs of a dead people,
Signpost of broken hearts,
You who fill yourselves by day with tears,
Sob out, sob out
The throat's terrible silence before death.[37]]

Hearkening back to "Lange haben wir das Lauschen verlernt," the opening line, "Lange schon fielen die Schatten" (The shadows fell long ago) suggests that we have unlearned the art of listening, reading, and interpreting. The poetic "I" implies that the reader is thinking that the "Schatten des Schrecklichen" (shadows of terror) are a phenomenon of the modern era, and then points out to the reader that they are ancient, and easily overlooked. Careful readers and interpreters, like the seer Daniel, can illuminate the shadows. The second stanza presents a contradictory perception of this timeless "Schreckliche," in that the shadows fall through a prism or glass of dreams ("Glas der Träume"), hence they are known in some fashion, but are then "erhellt" (illuminated) by Daniel's interpretation ("Deuterlicht"). Because they are shadows, however, such illumination would render them invisible. "Das Schreckliche" is thus illuminated and obscured, and hence misinterpreted or misperceived. In the third stanza, the suffocating forest, a denser, specifically Germanic variant of the agricultural tropes (recalling the "Eiche," the symbolically Germanic tree in "Ihr Zuschauenden") grew around Israel, "Gottes Mitternachtssängerin," the poetic herald, so that it is now silenced and lost. The final stanza begins with the earnest vocative "O," calling to the nightingales in all the forests of the earth, the heirs to the task of "Gottes Mitternachtssängerin," hearkening back to "Wer aber," and the dust mixed with the windpipes of nightingales. This segment of the "ihr" left alive (everywhere, not only in Germany) is prevailed upon not to sing, as nightingales once did, but to do what Sachs has done throughout this cycle: give some embattled, desperate expression of the unfathomable, both the unfathomable last moment of terrible silence before death (of the child, of the mother, of the elderly) and the unfathomable fact of confronting mass murder. They are not charged with comforting, not with mourning, but with experiencing and giving resonance to the pain of confrontation (which is crystallized in "Einer war"). The entire cycle emanates from Sachs's shofar, which compels the reader to account for his or her own deeds, or lack thereof, and to understand the timeless nature of "das Schreckliche," which occurs because of human choice and decision, not by divine providence. In nearly every instance in which God is invoked in this cycle, it is a sterile biblical injunction that is rendered meaningless by Auschwitz. Memory and memorial are the purview of a bygone era no longer sustainable. We see this expressed in the passage already quoted from Sachs's 1947 letter to Carl Seelig: "denn der Äon der Schmerzen darf nicht mehr gesagt, gedacht, er muß durchlitten werden."

"Dein Leib im Rauch durch die Luft" is a confrontation of deeds and experiences, and also a confrontation of the inadequacy of traditional poetic devices. Proceeding circularly, back to the first poem, brings the last line of the thirteenth poem, "Der Kehle schreckliches Schweigen vor dem Tod," into confrontation with the discomfiting "O" of the first poem—a silent moment before the articulated but inarticulate sound of woe. The cycle is a series of sobs that make it possible to "durchleiden" (suffer through), rather than recall or memorialize what happened.

That first "O die Schornsteine" is the wail of the shofar, the inarticulate sobbing of the nightingale. It places the reader immediately in the experience of the poet, confronting the chimneys and suffering through a moment of devising a "poetic" reaction to them. Traditionally, the poet has the task and power of revering and immortalizing. Traditional poetic tools and modes cannot sustain, and in fact are at odds with, this manner of death or scale of memory, yet the poet is driven to excavate something of her traditional capacity from the ruin. This poem cycle represents an attempt to radically reapproach a now very urgent task of the poet: no longer to immortalize or mourn, but to create a space of words of poetry and confrontation, in which the reader is alienated from conventions that he or she can no longer cling to, and from a world he or she takes for granted.

The first two lines—O die Schornsteine / Auf den sinnreich erdachten Wohnungen des Todes—read like a mix of conventional elegiac mode and an attempt at a reversal of a Romantic nature poem: the chimneys are a diabolical harvest from the soil of the cultivated imagination. The third and fourth lines of the poem, "Als Israels Leib zog aufgelöst in Rauch / Durch die Luft," reflect a moment where the poet ponders a new poetic response to a new mode and scale of destruction. The line literally says "as Israel's body drew dissolved into smoke / through the air" (the translation renders this process "drifted as smoke"), that is, the collective body of a nation has been broken down into particles and has changed form; so, too, the poetic response can break down what was once the body of conventional poetry into particles, and its form will necessarily change. Sachs uses the broken tools (the sobbing "O," the empty epigraphs, the sand mixed with remnants of traditional metaphors) to alienate the postwar reader from a desire to believe that there is some metaphysical source or meaning in tragedy, and thus compel the postwar reader to rethink "memory" and "memorialization."

The poetic "I" draws our attention to our drive to mourn and memorialize (for example in "An euch, die das neue Haus bauen"), to try and organize the dead, and our thoughts and deeds, into a packaged, controlled past, and then reminds us that the dead are the air we breathe and the earth we tread. The poetic "I" also attempts to draw our attention to the poetic conventions we take for granted, encouraging us to consider words as we might never have considered them before. The "O," the nightingale, the puppets, the oak trees, and the sand of Israel are all broken down and examined; the reader can proceed with this same process with each reading of the cycle, as he or she notices the particles and roots of each word, and how they may change form. The two instances of the word "Triften," for example, which is used as both earth and flesh, represent a common semantic root, "Treiben," which alludes to the cultivation of earth and animal drive that can be traced through the cycle. Most importantly it links drive and imagination with fertile (though hard) soil, so that the "sinnreich erdacht" of "O die Schornsteine" can be what it appears to be on first reading, "ingeniously devised" as the translation has it, while also echoing the conceptual link of body and land. "Sinnreich" would then be the psychological and intellectual analog of the physical "Erdreich" (which occurs in "Welche geheimen Wünsche"). These dwellings of death grew from the fertile soil of the imagination: the "Sinnreich." They are also "sinnreich," rich in sense, for their multiple, unfathomable significations and implications, among them the antiquation of poetic convention. "Sinnreich" is complemented by "erdachten" (meaning "devised"), which, when broken down into particles can yield erd + achten, earth and perception, the flesh and the mind that runs through the entire cycle. All that is created and done grows from the mind, the hands, and the fingers of humans. Other such potential compound links and relationships wend through the cycle, for example how an hour-glass (a "Sanduhr" and also a "Stundenuhr") might relate to "Sand" and the verbs "stehen" (to stand) and "kreisen" (to turn); and frequent instances of prefixes (er-dacht, ver-mischt, um-blies, auf-brechend, ab-fiel), often easily overlooked, can be broken off ("Arme auf und ab / Beine auf und ab") for hyperliteral or ironic emphasis. Sachs begins the cycle with "Meinen toten Brüdern und Schwestern," which has been translated as "For my dead brothers and sisters." The dative case of the original assumes the poetic convention "to"; but the translation raises awareness of an important omission, in light of the careful use of prepositions and prefixes in the cycle. Poetic convention has us assume "to"; but the cycle does not read that way, and Sachs elected not to determine a preposition. The translators chose "for"; perhaps the exact relationship of the cycle to the dead brothers and sisters—is it to them, dedicated to them, for them, about them, because of them?—is also meant to remain undetermined.

The reader is encouraged to break apart convention and experience the construction of the space of words, while the poet compels him or her to acknowledge, even in the smallest grammatical detail (the participial "-end," for example, or an omitted preposition), that he or she is living in open wounds that will never heal. Ultimately the cycle calls for the opposite of laying the dead to rest or completing the work of mourning; it conjures instead immediacy of experience. "Dein Leib im Rauch durch die Luft" is a countermonument, and a countermemorial, in a strict and literal sense; it challenges and demands the participation of the reader, and it actively counters the attempt to close, heal, and memorialize, based on Sachs's diasporic approach to time, experience, and the space of words.

Conclusion

ICLOSE THIS READING of Sachs's work with one final example that shows the importance of bearing in mind that Sachs, since the early 1920s, was fascinated by conventional perceptions of words and literary traditions and what they can mean if they are broken apart and reread unconventionally. In a letter from July of 1946, Sachs wrote to writer and literary historian Max Rychner of her latest frustrations in finding a publisher for *In den Wohnungen des Todes*. She concluded from a vague rejection letter that, upon seeing the title of her manuscript, the publisher had tossed it onto a mounting pile of tedious emigrant literature, of eyewitness reports and protocols of the camps that, Sachs believes,

> mit dem Rauch der Scheiterhaufen die Seufzer der Opfer ersticken. Nur die eine Mühe machte man sich offenbar nicht: zu sehen, daß diese Gedichte, wenn auch mit begrenzten Kräften, versuchen, das Furchtbare in das Reich der Verklärung zu heben, wie es ja die Aufgabe aller Dichtung in allen Zeiten von den griechischen Geschlechtersagen bis heute hinauf immer war und bleiben wird.[1]

> [suffocate the sighs and sobs of the victims with the smoke of the pyres. One [the publisher] is obviously not making an effort in one thing: to see that these poems, though with limited powers, attempt to lift that which is terrible into the realm of transfiguration, as the task of all poetry was and always will be, from the Greek epics to today.]

Sachs's word choices often make reading her letters as challenging an interpretive task as reading her poetry. The words "Scheiterhaufen" and "Verklärung" in particular make this statement difficult to clearly interpret. "Scheiterhaufen" can refer to burning someone at the stake, but can also mean a funeral pyre; broken down to its component parts (scheitern + Haufen), it is a pile of shattered or splintered things. "Scheitern," moreover, is usually used in a more figurative sense of failure or collapse. Considering that she is referring to the poems of *In den Wohnungen des Todes*, one interpretation of "Scheiterhaufen" does not seem better suited than another. The voices of the victims are suffocated by the smoke of the camps, by the attempts to put them to rest, and by the smoking remains of a now shattered, collapsed, or failed humanistic structure of aesthetics. "Verklärung" means "transfiguration," generally connoting a sense of glorification, idealization, or apotheosis; its component parts, however, are the prefix "ver," which usually marks a change in essence, or a move away from something, and the verb "klären," which means to clarify or resolve, so that in a hyperliteral sense "Verklärung" can be read as a clarification that actually moves away from clarity, or transforms the subject entirely. Read only at surface level, it seems as though Sachs is saying that her poems attempt to transform the horrors of mass murder into something beautiful or spiritual. Other correspondence and the poems themselves, and even her earliest prose, however, suggest that she is thinking rather of a kind of transfiguration that focuses specifically on the process of transformation, and dissolves into ambiguity.

Such transfiguration, she maintains, always has been and always will be the task of poetry, from Classical Antiquity forward; the verb "heben," to raise, lift, heighten, or enhance, also hints at polyvalence when we take into account Sachs's preoccupation with heavenly constellations. Often, the transfigurations in Classical myth raise figures into the sky, as birds or stars. They are caught and transformed in a moment of change; they are also transformed into the spoken or written word. What they signify is often ambiguous, and ultimately left for other writers and readers to interpret. "Das Furchtbare" is raised in Sachs's poems into the realm of "Verklärung," transfigured and brought to the attention of a wide audience of readers who are then confronted with the task of interpreting what they see.

In calling this book *"The Space of Words"* I aim to echo Sachs's frequent use of cosmological imagery, since the cosmos is a primary space in which human beings have connected and reconnected extant points of light, which appear to be stationary but are in fact moving, into meaningful constellations. The meaning is not found in the stars themselves, but rather originates with the people who have the power to create the myths and narratives. The authenticity of each instance of mythological construction in Sachs's work, from *Legenden* to elegiac verse, is simultaneously called into question, subtly (and occasionally not so subtly) entreating the reader to engage with her poetic act of transfiguration.

That transfiguration, the move from event to representation, is a consistent theme of Sachs's work. From its inception, her work draws attention to the power of the narrator or writer to construct a representation, the erasure that happens during that process, the power of an interpreter to reinscribe that representation, and the danger of taking what one reads at face value. Fra Giovanni creates a painting, his audience reinterprets both it and his tale of how the painting came to be; Meister Blasius brings Arthur a story and a flower, and Arthur reinterprets them; the young scholar from "Die stumme Nachtigall" interprets nature through figurative, deistic language; the "später Erstling" creates Israel; unspecified people throughout "Dein Leib im Rauch durch die Luft" attempt to mourn and memorialize the victims of genocide. In each case, numerous details and voices, especially female voices, are obscured and even erased in order to create a tidy, authentic narrative or a unified and closed poem. It is the task of the writer to transfigure; but Sachs adds to this process, by exposing it repeatedly, a task for the reader: to be aware of the power of the writer or storyteller (who is well traveled in the art of writing), and to maintain his or her agency by being an active reader aware of the interpretive power he or she also possesses (and to therefore also be well traveled as a reader). Her texts written before the Second World War compel the reader to be aware of the power of the poet or narrator to create a textual reality that should not be taken at face value; in the postwar era she was faced with a precarious balance of transfiguring that power while further stressing the urgency of readers maintaining their subjectivity, especially as a deterrent to fascism. The space of words was never a place of safety or refuge. Language is the only medium we possess to shape our reality; no language is innocent, and everyone must acknowledge his or her agency. Alienated from conventional language in the space of the text, the reader may find, as the child Chelion continually finds, a conduit between the specific reality of the text and the empirical reality that we actively create.

Preserving remnants of writers, texts, and readers who came before her is the foundation of Sachs's entire oeuvre, though she does not preserve them as masters to emulate. She engages with those remnants in an ongoing interaction with other writers and readers across geographical and temporal boundaries. She brings together details from numerous texts and traditions, offering us the opportunity to see long-familiar tropes and figures in a different light, as if through the eyes of a wandering sojourner in an unfamiliar landscape. In breaking down the familiar into its smallest increments and examining its deepest roots, she exposes something new. She does not, furthermore, gloss over this process of creation, but rather highlights it. Her texts engage with the sacredness of textual memory by displacing accepted structures of myths, disrupting a serene environment of memory. The ambiguity she maintains in her texts, for example leaving Fra Giovanni's artistic agency uncertain, or leaving unknown how exactly Merlin and Gotelind died, or refusing closure in her Holocaust texts, maintains a lack of knowledge of "the facts," because much is not known, and what is known is subject to interpretation. History, like a constellation, is created rather than recorded; even what seems like an objective account demands an active, skeptical reader.

Sachs ultimately determined that prose was not suited to her interest in fragments,[2] and turned in the 1940s to composing cycles of poetry that emphasized the process of creation, interpretation, and reinterpretation. In her cycles, she brings her longstanding exploration of artistic creation together with the conceptions of time and textual experience in diasporic Jewish tradition, which demand that readers engage closely with the ambiguity of the word and recognize their agency in shaping not only the meaning of text, but ultimately its continued vitality. Her poems bring readers into contact with the interpretations of other generations. Sages, seers, prophets, and other, unidentified (and pointedly unidentifiable) voices are made active interlocutors with the reader, not so that we arrive at "the" correct reading or "the" authentic source, but so that the discussion remains open, so that we engage with each word, each space, each dash, and consider the meanings they can sustain. One interpretation does not replace another; each voice joins the discussion, each voice changes the landscape of the discussion, and each voice demands the interaction of other voices.

Although Sachs was concerned that her prewar work would compromise the significance of her postwar work, taking the prewar work into consideration actually allows us insight into her fascination with semantics and aesthetics that opens new interpretive possibilities for her postwar work. From the beginning, she explored the literal and figurative meanings of words, the provenance of symbols, and the power of hegemonic forces to obscure marginal voices. Her texts rarely fill in what is missing, but instead draw attention to the lack; in the wake of war and genocide, her poetry cycles, filled with gaps, dashes, and ambiguity, force the reader to contend with absences that cannot be filled and wounds that will not heal.

As the space of the poetic text accentuates the failure of closure, writing and reading the poetic text is always an unfinished, unfinishable act of remembering through transferring, transfiguring, or constructing events, persons, and things into words: the presence of absence. At the same time it threatens to be read as memorial, a site of the healing of a rupture or transgression. But healing, like remembering, threatens to masquerade as a completed, whole object of history—a thing from the past that has been safely packaged, sealed, made sacred, and moved aside to a place we determine it belongs. As so many of Sachs's texts bring together images and figures of the past while engaging the present, however, her texts create neither an atmosphere outside of and devoid of history, nor one trapped in history, but rather an atmosphere that places the reader and the writer *in* history as a process that is never over, never fixed, and never past. Sachs's texts do not attempt to remember a sacred original that has been forgotten, but rather draw attention to what has been lost and destroyed, what we do not and cannot know, and the reappropriation of symbols and tropes in the act of remembering. All memory is selective in her poetics, and the process of structuring those memories continues as the rubble pile grows. The idea of "the past" is viewed skeptically, since historical events still continue to affect the present. In Sachs's texts, which are often written in the present tense and destabilize the boundaries between then and now, they always will.

Notes

"An Stelle von Heimat": An Introduction

[1] Bahr, *Nelly Sachs*, 122.

[2] Bahr, *Nelly Sachs*, 126.

[3] Fioretos, *Flight and Metamorphosis*, 17.

[4] http://www.nobelprize.org/nobel_prizes/literature/laureates/1966/.

[5] For a thorough description of this dynamic, see Michael Kessler and Jürgen Wertheimer, eds., *Nelly Sachs: Neue Interpretationen*.

[6] Bahr, *Nelly Sachs*, 10.

[7] Succinct examples come from Klaus Weissenberger's *Die deutsche Lyrik 1945–1975*. Weissenberger describes Sachs's work as "'mystisch[e]' Ich-Erweiterung" (mystical I-extension) or "mit 'gesetzmäßiger' Konsequenz sich vollziehenden mystischen Verwandlungsprozeß der Gottannäherung" (mystical metamorphic process of approaching God, achieved with consequent adherence to rules). Weissenberger, 14, 16. Judith Ryan's article in the volume describes Sachs's work as "'Trost'" (comfort), asking whether a comfort of this sort can bear up under the poetic needs of the postwar era. Ryan finds Sachs's work to be too mystical. Judith Ryan, "Nelly Sachs," in *Die deutsche Lyrik 1945–1975*, 110–18, here 110.

[8] In 1944, Doctor Max Hodann refused to read Sachs's work because he found it "impossible to understand," and passed it to Professor Walter Berendsohn to read. Sachs, *Briefe*, 40. Of her own initial experience with Sachs's poetry, poet Hilde Domin writes: "Die Worte waren mir viel zu groß, viel zu steil, das Ganze zu massiv, überhaupt nicht, was ich von Lyrik wollte." (The words were much to big for me, much too steep, the whole thing too massive, not at all what I wanted from lyric poetry.) Hilde Domin, "Nachwort," in *Nelly Sachs: Gedichte*, 122–23.

[9] Sachs, *Briefe*, 84.

[10] Sachs, *Briefe*, 53, 99, 110, 183.

[11] Sachs, *Briefe*, 41.

[12] Fioretos, *Flight and Metamorphosis*, 8–9.

[13] Bachelard, *The Poetics of Space*, xix.

[14] Jonathan Culler, "Why Lyric?," 202. Though he does not specify, I believe Culler's observation here is traceable to antiquity. Horace instructs the Pisos that clever use of conventional words yields new insight, and indeed new words are sometimes needed to describe conventional ideas or objects where something new must be said; Aristotle before him argues that the poetic word exists to win new insights into common objects we take for granted.

15 *Werke* I, 92; *Werke* II, 46; *Werke* II, 111.

16 Aichinger, "Aufruf zum Mißtrauen," in Samuel Moser, ed. *Ilse Aichinger: Materialien zu Leben und Werk*, 16–17.

17 Aichinger, "Aufruf zum Mißtrauen," 16.

18 Lagercrantz, *Versuch über die Lyrik der Nelly Sachs*, 77; Kersten, *Die Metaphorik in der Lyrik von Nelly Sachs*, 46; Bower, *Ethics and Remembrance*, 10, 249 (Bower also links language with the mother); Hilde Domin approaches this argument as well in her afterword to a volume of selected poems by Sachs when she writes that between German and Swedish the writer comes to a place that reduces strangeness and replaces the lost homeland. Domin, "Nachwort," 114. Ruth Dinesen wrote: "When she fled, Nelly Sachs was able to take nothing but her inherited German language," the last remnant of her *Heimat*. Ruth Dinesen, "At Home in Exile—Nelly Sachs: Flight and Metamorphosis," in *Facing Fascism and Confronting the Past: German Women Writers from Weimar to the Present*, ed. Elke P. Frederiksen and Martha Kaarsberg Wallach, 135–50, here 136.

19 Both Christa Vaerst and Claudia Beil articulate an approach to exile that asserts language as a homeland, but also a space of exile, from which the poet ultimately longs to return to a divine and innocent pre- or postlingual state. Christa Vaerst, *Dichtung- und Sprachreflexion im Werk vom Nelly Sachs* (Frankfurt: Peter Lang, 1977). Claudia Beil, *Sprache als Heimat: Jüdische Tradition und Exilerfahrung in der Lyrik von Nelly Sachs und Rose Ausländer* (Munich: tuduv, 1991). See also Klaus Weissenberger, who articulates mysticism not as a religious ideology but as a poetics in his *Zwischen Stein und Stern: Mystische Formgebung in der Dichtung von Else Lasker-Schüler, Nelly Sachs und Paul Celan* (Bern: Francke Verlag, 1976).

20 Fioretos, *Flight and Metamorphosis*, 22.

21 Klüger, "Drei blaue Klaviere: die verfolgten Dichterinnen Else Lasker-Schüler, Nelly Sachs und Gertrud Kolmar," in *Gemalte Fensterscheiben: Über Lyrik*, 175.

22 Howard Wettstein, Introduction to *Diasporas and Exiles: Varieties of Jewish Identity*, 2.

23 Gruen, "Diaspora and Homeland," in *Diasporas and Exiles: Varieties of Jewish Identity*, 18.

24 See, for example, *Briefe*, 41 and 175. Sachs rejects political Zionism in favor of something more diasporic.

25 B. Goldstein, "A Politics and Poetics of Diaspora: Heinrich Heine's "Hebräische Melodien," in *Diasporas and Exiles: Varieties of Jewish Identity*, 60.

26 B. Goldstein, "A Politics and Poetics of Diaspora," 61.

27 B. Goldstein, "A Politics and Poetics of Diaspora," 75.

28 J. Boyarin, *Powers of Diaspora*, 4.

29 *Werke* II, 74.

30 Gruen, "Diaspora and Homeland," 20.

31 J. Boyarin, *Powers of Diaspora*, 4–5.

32 I want to point out that Sachs did not want her concerns regarding the State of Israel to be interpreted as anti-Zionist or anti-Israel. In a 1968 interview with

Israeli radio, she was asked to comment on "Die Bedeutung der Verfolgung und der Errichtung des Staates Israel für [ihre] Gedichte" (The meaning of the persecution of the Jews and the establishment of the State of Israel for [her] poems). She answered: "Die Errichtung des Staates Israel bedeutet für mich zu allererst eine Heimat für alle die nach dem furchtbaren Weltgeschehn heimatlos geworden sind." (The establishment of the State of Israel means to me first and foremost a homeland for all those who were made homeless after the terrible event.) She concludes "Was ich wünsche von ganzem Herzen ist Friede Friede Friede! Schalom!" (What I wish from my heart is peace peace peace! Shalom!) *Werke* IV, 101.

[33] Young, *At Memory's Edge*, 2.

[34] Young, *At Memory's Edge*, 7–8.

Chapter 1: Biography of the Poet: "a frail woman must do it"

[1] See, for example, Sachs, *Briefe*, 231. Letter to Elisabeth Borchers from September 15, 1959.

[2] See, for example, Sachs, *Briefe*, 53. Letter to Gudrun Dähnert from May 18, 1946.

[3] See, for example, Sachs, *Briefe*, 197–200. Letter to Walter Berendsohn from January 22, 1959.

[4] Sachs, *Briefe*, 177. Letter to Walter Berendsohn from November 28, 1957. Aris Fioretos starts his biography from this premise: how shall we approach "a writer who wished to disappear behind her work?" Fioretos, *Flight and Metamorphosis*, 7.

[5] See, for example, Bahr, *Nelly Sachs*, 29–30.

[6] I am very grateful to Professor Emeritus Gerhard Weiss for providing me with a typescript of a lecture held by his aunt, the poet Ilse Blumenthal-Weiss, on her encounters with Else Lasker-Schüler, Nelly Sachs, Leo Baeck, and Martin Buber. "Begegnungen mit Else Lasker-Schüler Nelly Sachs Leo Baeck Martin Buber," Privatdruck für die Freunde der Women's Auxiliary des Leo Baeck Institute, 15.

[7] See, for example, letters to Berendsohn between 1957 and 1959, when he is writing a biography and descriptions of her work. Sachs, *Briefe*, 172–78; 192–93; 197–202; 204–5.

[8] I refer the reader to three Nelly Sachs biographies for more depth: Ruth Dinesen, *Nelly Sachs: Eine Biographie*; Gabriele Fritsch-Vivié, *Nelly Sachs*; and Aris Fioretos, *Nelly Sachs, Flight and Metamorphosis: An Illustrated Biography*.

[9] Bahr, *Nelly Sachs*, 31, and Bengt Holmqvist, "Die Sprache der Sehnsucht," in *Das Buch der Nelly Sachs*, 25. Holmqvist remarks that there was one instance at school where Sachs was labeled Jewish, but not with any malice. Fioretos suggests that Jewishness may have been part of Sachs's childhood and adolescent insecurity. Fioretos, *Flight and Metamorphosis*, 21. Dinesen's biography approaches the topic through the story "Chelion," specifically a scene where Chelion and her friend, reflections of Sachs and a childhood friend, are both teased at school. The teasing appears to have nothing to do with the girls' Jewishness. Dinesen, *Biographie*, 18.

10 Dinesen, for example, links this unhappy love affair to a therapist's recommendation to write, so that Sachs could translate pain into the written word. Dinesen, *Biographie*, 51–52. Holmqvist remarks that she dedicated herself more to poetic work, though only as a form of therapy. Holmqvist, "Sprache der Sehnsucht," 27. Fritsch-Vivié suggests that there may be other reasons for Sachs's foray into writing, but that this encounter became an impulse to write. Fritsch-Vivié, *Nelly Sachs*, 40.

11 Holmqvist and Bahr both assert that the young man died in a concentration camp. Holmqvist, "Sprache der Sehnsucht," 27; Bahr, *Nelly Sachs*, 35. Dinesen suggests that his arrest, interrogation, and murder became representative for the concentration camp victims. Dinesen, *Biographie*, 133–34.

12 See Sachs, *Briefe*, 17. A letter dated October 9, 1915, addressed to "den Verlag Cotta" offers "ein Erstlingswerk (in Prosa verfaßte Stimmungsbilder)" and adds that "auch . . . Gedichte zur Verfügung [ständen]." We do not know which texts these were. See also Dinesen, *Frühe Gedichte und Prosa*, 65.

13 Dinesen, *Frühe Gedichte und Prosa*, 22. It is not known how many copies of it were produced or sold, and certainly fewer than ten original copies survive today.

14 Fioretos notes that the book begins with an alexandrine by Baroque poet Angelus Silesius, and ends with a story about Silenus: "the nominal similarity with the mystic from Silesia is unlikely to be incidental." I agree, and believe that this intertextual link also suggests that the book is indeed more about narrative and interpretation than about "the mystically oriented love gospel that pervades the texts." Fioretos, *Flight and Metamorphosis*, 37.

15 See Fioretos, *Flight and Metamorphosis*, 37, and Fritsch-Vivié, *Nelly Sachs*, 52.

16 This title is a play on words. The word for "apple tree" is "ApfelBAUM," which Sachs has rendered "ApfelTRAUM," literally "apple dream" ("Appledreamalley").

17 Fioretos gives fantastic concrete examples of the neologisms and experimental word combinations, for example "The shrill clock soars like sorrowed snow." Fioretos, *Flight and Metamorphosis*, 53.

18 Jennifer Watson, *Swedish Novelist Selma Lagerlöf, 1858–1940, and Germany at the Turn of the Century: "O Du Stern ob meinem Garten."*

19 Larger than the *Berliner Tageblatt*, a liberal paper without party affiliation, with an emphasis on feuilleton, that ran from 1617–1934, when it was forced to close down due to loss of staff through racial and political persecution. Klaus Bender, "Vossische Zeitung (1617–1934)" *Deutsche Zeitungen des 17. bis 20. Jahrhunderts*, 25–39.

20 Liberal local Berlin newspaper, eventually drawn under NS control. Gotthart Schwarz, "Berliner Tageblatt (1872–1939)," *Deutsche Zeitungen des 17. bis 20. Jahrhunderts*, 315–27.

21 Quoted in Fritsch-Vivié, *Nelly Sachs*, 152; 56. Walter Berendsohn reports the incident differently. According to him, a friend sent the poems "Einsiedler in der Wüste" (Hermits in the Desert) and "Tanz der Wilden" (Dance of the Wild Things) to Stefan Zweig. The poems have not been found; Berendsohn maintains that Zweig wrote to Sachs personally: "Zweig schrieb an Nelly Sachs, daß die meiste Frauenlyrik zu gerundeter Form neige, ihre Dichtung jedoch

eine ekstatisch aufsteigende Linie aufweise. Es ist das einsichtsvolle Wort eines hochbegabten Kritikers, das diesen entscheidenden Zug erfaßte und in ihm ihre Entwicklung voraussah und voraussagte." (Zweig wrote to Nelly Sachs that most women's poetry tends toward a round form, whereas her poetry shows an ecstatic rising line. It is the insightful word of a gifted critic that grasped this decisive trait and in it saw and predicted her development.) Berendsohn, *Einführung*, 19–20.

22 Fioretos, *Flight and Metamorphosis*, 44.

23 From the *Jüdische Rundschau*, quoted in Dinesen, *Frühe Gedichte und Prosa*, 97, 98, 99.

24 Dinesen, *Frühe Gedichte und Prosa*, 98–99.

25 No title is given, but the subtitle of the volume is *Der Blinde in Bibel und Schrifttum*, which indicates it may have been one of her Biblical poems. She is prominently listed along with Gertrud Kolmar among others, in hindsight chillingly as "to name only those among the living." *C.-V.-Zeitung* October 27, 1938, 4. Daniel Pedersen, who is currently writing the first Swedish dissertation on Sachs, found this poem for me after an exhaustive search. It is entitled "Lied eines Blinden am Fest der Bäume" and appears to deal with a sightless, sensual experience of Tu B'Shvat (36–37). My thanks to Daniel Pedersen!

26 "Briefe aus der Nacht," in *Werke IV*, ed. Aris Fioretos (Frankfurt am Main: Suhrkamp, 2010), 36–59. Volume 4 includes a short section of prose texts that until recently were unknown.

27 Letter to Gudrun Dähnert, December 7, 1949. Sachs, *Briefe*, 110. The review she mentions is "Dichtung und Deutung des jüdischen Schicksals. Nelly Sachs: 'In den Wohnungen des Todes'," in *Neue Wege* 43.6 (1949).

28 For an extensive discussion of the state of postwar literature, see Ralf Schnell, *Die Literatur der Bundesrepublik: Autoren, Geschichte, Literaturbetrieb*, also Stephen Brockmann, *German Literary Culture at the Zero Hour*. See also in particular: Alfred Andersch, *Deutsche Literatur in der Entscheidung: Ein Beitrag zur Analyse der Literarischen Situation*, Walter Berendsohn, *Die humanistische Front: Einführung in die deutsche Emigranten-Literatur. Erster Teil Von 1933 bis zum Kriegsausbruch*, Stephan Hermlin, *Der Kampf um eine deutsche Nationalliteratur*.

29 Sachs, *Briefe*, 147.

30 From Sachs's own notes to *Abram im Salz*, in *Zeichen im Sand: Die szenischen Dichtungen der Nelly Sachs*, 346–47.

31 Her collected plays, including her own commentary on them, were published in 1962 in the above-cited *Zeichen im Sand*.

32 See, for example, letters to Moses Pergament from March 3, 1958, February 2, 1959, and March 21, 1959. Sachs, *Briefe*, 187–88, 202–3, and 205–7. A letter to Alfred Andersch from July 4, 1958, suggests that Andersch's radio play did a better job of capturing the ambiguity of the play. A thorough description of the reception history can be found in Uwe Naumann, "Ein Stück der Versöhnung: zur Uraufführung des Mysterienspiels *Eli* von Nelly Sachs (1962)," 98–114.

33 See Gershom Scholem, "The Tradition of the Thirty-Six Hidden Just Men," in *The Messianic Idea in Judaism and Other Essays on Jewish Spirituality* (New York: Schocken Books, 1971), 251–56.

34 See Dinesen, *Frühe Gedichte und Prosa*, 40; and Bahr, *Nelly Sachs*, 170. Dinesen quotes Sachs's letter to the *Svenska Dagbladet* from March 30, 1959.

35 Uwe Naumann gives a thorough description of the reception history of *Eli*, including the audience and actors of the Dortmund performance. Naumann, "Ein Stück der Versöhnung," 108–10.

36 Naumann, "Ein Stück der Versöhnung," 112.

37 Bahr, *Nelly Sachs*, 163. He specifically says West Germany; Naumann states that there was no reception at all in East Germany. Naumann, "Ein Stück der Versöhnung," 112.

38 *Texte und Zeichen* 3.1 (1957).

39 Letter to Käte Hamburger, 1 March 1957, Schiller National Museum/ Deutsches Literaturarchiv, Marbach.

40 Fritsch-Vivié, *Nelly Sachs*, 114.

41 Two of the most thorough can be found in Michael Braun, "Phasen, Probleme und Perspektiven der Nelly-Sachs-Rezeption—Forschungsbericht und Bibliographie," and Michael Braun, "Forschungsstand."

42 This remarkable correspondence between the two most significant German-language Holocaust poets is available in German and in English: *Paul Celan, Nelly Sachs: Briefwechsel*, ed. Barbara Wiedemann (Frankfurt am Main: Suhrkamp, 1993); *Paul Celan, Nelly Sachs: Correspondence*, ed. Barbara Wiedemann, trans. Christopher Clark (New York: Sheep Meadow Press, 1998).

43 Fritsch-Vivié, *Nelly Sachs*, 119.

44 For a new and extensive description of Sachs's psychiatric conditions and care, see Fioretos, *Flight and Metamorphosis*, especially pages 226–66.

45 The summary and speech at the presentation of the award can be found here: http://www.nobelprize.org/nobel_prizes/literature/laureates/1966/press.html.

46 Her autobiography is accessible on the Nobel website here: http://www.nobelprize.org/nobel_prizes/literature/laureates/1966/sachs-autobio.html; her banquet speech here: http://www.nobelprize.org/nobel_prizes/literature/laureates/1966/sachs-speech.html.

47 Dinesen, *Biographie*, 345.

48 Fioretos, *Flight and Metamorphosis*, 256.

49 Nelly Sachs, *Werke. Kommentierte Ausgabe in 4 Bänden*, Eds. Aris Fioretos, Ariane Huml, and Matthias Weichelt (Frankfurt am Main: Suhrkamp, 2010).

Chapter 2: Wandering and Words, Wandering in Words

1 There is evidence that Sachs was trying to publish her work already in 1915, but aside from a letter to the publisher Cotta, no evidence of earlier publications has surfaced.

2 Dinesen, *Frühe Gedichte und Prosa*, 25.

3 Ruskin, *Modern Painters II*, 214.

[4] Sachs, "Eine Legende von Fra Angelico," 7–17; here 7. Subsequent references to this work will be indicated by the abbreviation FA and a page number in parentheses. All translations, unless otherwise indicated, are by the present author.

[5] Compare the quotation from Ruskin above, where he discussed the features of human figures, and Fra Angelico's success in painting the angels, Mary, and Jesus.

[6] "I know God's countenance: he represented Himself in his creatures, where you will see it." FA, 7.

[7] The settings as well as her vocabulary and complicated usage, in particular her usage of conjunctions like "da," and "dergestalt, dass," and of archaic literary forms of subjunctive I and II, remind the reader of Kleist's short stories, in particular "Die Heilige Cäcilie, oder Die Gewalt der Musik," and "Das Bettelweib von Locarno."

[8] "Die Apfeltraumallee" (wordplay on "apple tree," or "Apfelbaum") is a series of short stories collected in a faded blue or green folder with a reproduction of Casper David Friedrich's *Riesengebirgslandschaft* on the front. It is held in the Gudrun Dähnert (née Harlan) collection in the Royal National Swedish Library in Stockholm. It contains a remarkable array of ideas found in many of Sachs's other texts.

[9] Cf. the story of Philomela and Procne in Ovid's *Metamorphoses*. In the story, Philomela is imprisoned and repeatedly raped by her sister Procne's husband Tereus. When she threatens to tell what has happened to her, he cuts out her tongue. She sets about making a tapestry into which she cleverly weaves her story, such that only the insightful will see it. A messenger brings Procne the tapestry, which she immediately understands. She frees Philomela, and the two plan their revenge. They kill and cook Tereus and Procne's son, feed the dish to Tereus, and in the resulting confrontation and chase, Philomela, Procne, and Tereus are transformed into birds that in some way represent their stories and personalities. The raped, mutilated Philomela becomes a nightingale, and sings her tale of woe and rage, concealed from anyone who lacks the insight to hear it.

[10] Cf. Hans Christian Andersen's story "The Nightingale," about a Chinese emperor who wishes to possess a nightingale. He regards it only as a beautiful decoration and disregards that it may have deeper meaning.

[11] Sachs, "Die stumme Nachtigall," 58. Subsequent references to this work will use the abbreviation SN and page number in parentheses.

[12] Fioretos, *Flight and Metamorphosis*, 31.

[13] Translation taken from Fioretos, *Flight and Metamorphosis*, 31–32. Fioretos notes that the critic may be right about the tone, and the text may read like an amalgamation of clichés and tropes from Romanticism and pulp fiction, but it still does invoke a sense of imminent loss.

[14] Sachs, "Chelion," 2. Subsequent references to this text will use the abbreviation C and page number in parentheses.

[15] There is no quote from Sophie in the text where she says this, but as the rest of the content is Chelion's approximation of Sophie's words, and the phrase "in ein frühes Grab steigen" (to climb into an early grave) is highly stylized, I am assuming she heard Sophie say it. If not, she has likely heard it in a folk song or

poem and is approximating it here, although her attempt to otherwise stay true to Sophie's words suggests the former.

[16] Jennifer Watson, *Swedish Novelist Selma Lagerlöf, 1858–1940*, 179.

[17] Watson, *Swedish Novelist Selma Lagerlöf*, ii–iii.

[18] Jonathan Culler, "Why Lyric," 201.

[19] See, for example, Jonathan Culler, who describes the nonnarrative essence of the lyric poem: "If narrative is about what happens next, lyric is about what happens now—in the reader's engagement with each line[.]" Culler, "Why Lyrik," 202. Both Hilde Domin and Paul Celan reconsider the timeless quality that arises from the aim of universality in the lyric poem. Domin's description highlights the participation of the reader as the factor that makes the poem endlessly mutable; the poet creates a kind of island in time, time outside of time, that is the always the time in which the reader reads; whenever the reader reads, he confronts himself within the poem. Hilde Domin, "Wozu Lyrik Heute," 13–14. Celan brought this characterization of the poetic text out in his Bremen speech, where he wrote that "a poem is not timeless. Certainly it lays a claim to infinity, it seeks to reach through time—through it, not above and beyond it." As the lyric poem is always moving through time, it continues always to be current, not timeless.

[20] Bachelard, *The Poetics of Space*, xix.

[21] *Der Morgen* 14.2 (May 1938): 63–64. The series of poems published are: "Mailied," "Das Mädchen am Brunnen," "Geliebter," "Abschied, Du Nachtigallenwort," and "Schlaflied."

[22] *Werke I*, 76. Christine Rospert has also noted this overlap. See Rospert, *Poetik einer Sprache der Toten: Studien zum Schreiben von Nelly Sachs*, 66.

[23] Cf. the story of Philomela and Procne in Ovid's "Metamorphoses."

[24] B. Goldstein, "A Politics and Poetics of Diaspora," 75.

[25] Cheryl Walker, *The Nightingale's Burden*, 33.

[26] Watson, *Swedish Novelist Selma Lagerlöf, 1858–1940*, iii.

[27] See, for example, Hans Otto Horch, *Auf der Suche nach der jüdischen Erzählliteratur*.

Chapter 3: Sachs's Merlin the Sorcerer: Reconfiguring the Myth as Plural

[1] Sachs, "Wie der Zauberer Merlin erlöset ward," 59–78; here 62. Subsequent references to this work will be indicated by the abbreviation M and a page number in parentheses. All translations, unless otherwise indicated, are by the present author.

[2] Goodrich, *Merlin: A Casebook*, 2.

[3] Müller, "Merlin in German Literature," 219.

[4] Goodrich, *Merlin: A Casebook*, 34.

[5] Müller, "Merlin in German Literature," 222.

[6] Müller, "Merlin in German Literature," 223.

[7] Schlegel, *Sämmtliche Werke VII*, 126.

[8] Schlegel, *Sämmtliche Werke VII*, 135.

[9] Schlegel, *Sämmtliche Werke VII*, 128.

[10] Goethe, *Werke 3* (Munich: C. H. Beck, 1986), 41. Translation by Stuart Atkins, from Goethe, *The Collected Works*, vol. 2 (Princeton: Princeton University Press, 1994), 30.

[11] Immermann, *Werke 4*, 332.

[12] Immermann, *Werke 4*, 311.

[13] Immermann, *Werke 4*, 273.

[14] Goethe, *Werke 3* (Munich: Beck, 1986), 41. Translation by Stuart Atkins, from Goethe, *Collected Works* vol. 2, 30.

[15] Immermann, *Werke 4*, 276.

[16] Azade Seyhan, *Representation and Its Discontents: The Critical Legacy of German Romanticism* (Berkeley: University of California Press, 1992), 116. http://ark.cdlib.org/ark:/13030/ft4199n921/

[17] Novalis, *Schriften 4* (Jena: Eugen Diederichs, 1907), 53. Translation by Palmer Hilty, from Novalis, *Henry von Ofterdingen* (New York: Frederick Ungar, 1964), 15.

[18] Novalis, *Schriften 4*, 53. Translation by Hilty, 15.

[19] Novalis, *Schriften 4*, 56. Translation by Hilty, 17.

[20] See also *Deutsches Wörterbuch*, ed. Jakob und Wilhelm Grimm, vol. 27, column 3147, where there is a reference to a folktale like this written by a fifteenth-century author named Vintler.

[21] Schlegel, *Sämmtliche Werke VII*, 28.

[22] Schlegel, *Sämmtliche Werke VII*, 29.

[23] Schlegel, *Sämmtliche Werke VII*, 64, 76–77, 115–16.

[24] Schlegel, *Sämmtliche Werke VII*, 133. Immermann's text also has Merlin trapped in a white thornbush.

[25] On the changing forms of anti-Semitism in Germany see: Walter Laqueur, *The Changing Face of Antisemitism From Ancient Times to the Present Day* (Oxford: Oxford University Press, 2006); Léon Poliakov, *The History of Anti-Semitism*, vols. 1–4, trans. George Klin (Philadelphia: University of Pennsylvania Press, 2003). For excerpts of primary sources discussing race and nation, see *The Jew in the Modern World: A Documentary History*, ed. Paul Mendes-Flohr and Jehuda Reinharz. The digital archives of Jewish German periodicals at www.compactmemory.de offers the reader a firsthand glimpse at the way the discourse on race changed between the 1860s and the 1930s; see also the early twentieth-century *Meyers Konversationslexion* at the HathiTrust digital library, which has an informative entry on Antisemitismus in volume 1 http://babel.hathitrust.org/cgi/pt?id=njp.32101064063066;view=1up;seq=724; and the digitized press archives of the Preussicher Kulturbesitz.

[26] Regarding the nineteenth- and twentieth-century discourse on defining Germanness and Jewishness, and "German" literature or "Jewish" literature, see,

for example, Hans-Peter Bayerdörfer, "'Vermauschelt die Presse, die Literatur': Jüdische Schriftsteller in der deutschen Literatur zwischen Jahrhundertwende und Erstem Weltkrieg," in *Judentum, Antisemitismus und europäische Kultur*, ed. Hans Otto Horch (Tübingen: A. Francke, 1988), 207–31. See also Hans Otto Horch, *Auf der Suche nach der jüdischen Erzählliteratur: Die Literaturkritik der 'Allgemeinen Zeitung des Judentums' (1837–1922)* (Frankfurt am Main: Peter Lang, 1985). For a description of the irreconcilable hyphenated identity of German Jewish writers, see Daniel Hoffmann, ed., *Handbuch zur deutsch-jüdischen Literatur des 20. Jahrhunderts* (Paderborn: Schöningh, 2002). See also the discussion that developed in the journal *Der Kunstwart* around Mortiz Goldstein's 1912 essay "Deutsch-jüdischer Parnaß," in *Der Kunstwart* 25, no. 2 (January–March 1912): 284–92, and also his *Begriff und Programm einer jüdischen Nationalliteratur: Reden und Aufsätze über zeitgenössische Fragen des jüdischen Volkes* (Berlin: Jüdischer Verlag, 1912). In response to the suggestion that Jews were not German and therefore could not write German literature, Goldstein argued that he was as much German as he was Jewish, and that anything he wrote would be both as well.

[27] See Malcolm Todd, *The Early Germans* (Malden, Mass.: Blackwell, 2004), especially 179–201.

[28] Todd, *The Early Germans*, 180.

Chapter 4: Poetic Space after the Abyss

[1] Brockmann, *Zero Hour*, 120.

[2] Schnell, *Geschichte der deutschsprachigen Literatur seit 1945*, 3rd ed. (Stuttgart: Metzler, 2003), 72.

[3] Berendsohn, *Humanistische Front*, 72, 166.

[4] Berendsohn, *Humanistische Front*, 100.

[5] In "Das Symposium in Stockholm über deutsche Exilliteratur," Peter Uwe Hohendahl suggested as late as 1970 that the animosity was still present: "Das erste internationale Symposium über die deutsche Exilliteratur . . . fand in Stockholm statt, nicht in Berlin, Frankfurt oder Hamburg. Das gibt zu denken." *German Quarterly* 43, no. 1 (January 1970): 151–54; here, 151. Hohendahl sees Gottfried Benn as the central literary figure in the formation of such a negative view of the "emigrants."

[6] See, for example, Stephan Stachorski, ed., *Fragile Republik: Thomas Mann und Nachkriegsdeutschland* (Leipzig: Fischer Taschenbuch Verlag, 1999).

[7] Ralf Schnell, *Geschichte der deutschsprachigen Literatur*, 68.

[8] Sachs, *Briefe*, 147.

[9] Schnell, *Literatur der Bundesrepublik*, 95.

[10] Schnell, *Literatur der Bundesrepublik*, 93.

[11] Schnell, *Literatur der Bundesrepublik*, 93.

[12] Moray McGowan, "German Writing in the West (1945–1990)," in *The Cambridge History of German Literature*, ed. Helen Watanabe-O'Kelly (Cambridge: Cambridge University Press, 1997), 440–506; here, 451.

[13] McGowan, "German Writing in the West," 452.

[14] Rudolf Hartung, "Buch Kritik," *Die Fähre* 2 (1947): 378–82; here, 378.

[15] Hartung, "Buch Kritik," 379.

[16] Weissenberger, *Die Deutsche Lyrik 1945–1975*, 15.

[17] Bahr, *Nelly Sachs*, 10.

[18] Sachs, *Briefe*, 98.

[19] Bahr, *Nelly Sachs*, 84–85.

[20] Sachs, *Werke I*, 91–93.

[21] The occupation's military censorship was responsible for monitoring political material in the immediate occupation years. This appears to have been a decisive factor in the work of the new generation of writers like Alfred Andersch, as the American censors closed his politically critical journal *Der Ruf* in 1947.

[22] Sachs, *Werke I*, 92–93. The poem was originally published in *Sinn und Form* 2.1 (1950): 83–84. In that version, everything after the colon following "verwundert" is contained in quotation marks, which, to my mind, makes the words of the voice more direct; without the quotes, it reads more as a poetic musing.

[23] Sachs, *The Seeker*, 147. Translation by Ruth and Matthew Mead.

[24] Bahr, *Nelly Sachs*, 84–85.

[25] Bahr, *Nelly Sachs*, 84.

[26] Bahr, *Nelly Sachs*, 85.

[27] Bahr, *Nelly Sachs*, 86.

[28] *Deutsches Wörterbuch*, ed. Jakob und Wilhelm Grimm, vol. 9 column 316.

[29] *King Lear*, 1.4.

[30] Brockmann, *Zero Hour*, 8.

[31] From the poem "Auf dass die Verfolgten nicht Verfolger werden," Sachs, *Werke I*, 50. "That the persecuted may not become persecutors," Sachs, *O the Chimneys*, trans. Ruth and Matthew Mead, 55. Sachs was also apprehensive that survivors of Nazi violence would become the next group of perpetrators.

[32] Braun and Lermen, *Nelly Sachs: "an letzter Atemspitze des Lebens,"* 55.

[33] Sachs, *Werke I*, 91–92.

[34] Sachs, *O the Chimneys*, 93. Translation by Michael Roloff.

[35] Hilde Domin, "Völker der Erde," in *Frauen dichten anders: 181 Gedichte mit Interpretationen* (Frankfurt: Suhrkamp, 1998); also "Nachwort," in *Nelly Sachs: Gedichte*, 116–22.

[36] Braun and Lermen, *Nelly Sachs: "an letzter Atemspitze des Lebens,"* 47–56.

[37] Sachs, *Werke I*, 277. Matthias Weichelt notes that it was included in a letter to Kurt Pinthus from November 12, 1946.

[38] A number of books deal with "Nazi-German," or the Nazi appropriation of the German language. The first to confront it in detail was Victor Klemperer's journal *LTI: Notizbuch eines Philologen* (Berlin: Aufbau, 1947). Klemperer wrote this journal between 1933 and 1945, documenting in it how he saw the German

language change under the Nazis. He describes how the Nazi party mythologized itself, dates, and events, and how it repeated its mantras, buzzwords, and mythology frequently, encouraging citizens to do the same. Speech became dominated by party slogans and the aestheticization of politics. Robert Michael and Karin Doerr published *Nazi-Deutsch/Nazi-German: An English Lexicon of the Language of the Third Reich* (Westport, CT: Greenwood Press, 2002), which defines in English the euphemisms of Nazi German, including the code names of Nazi military operations, which often stem from Romantic poetry. Among the most fascinating treatments of the topic of Nazi German is Berel Lang's section on manipulation of language versus the truth of authentic documents in *Act and Idea in the Nazi Genocide* (Chicago: University of Chicago Press, 1990; the 2003 edition appeared with Stanford University Press).

[39] *Sinn und Form* 2.1 (1950): 83–84.

[40] Translation by the present author.

[41] Sachs, *Briefe*, 99, 110, 98, 53. The italics in "*Vormartyrium*" are Sachs's.

[42] *Deutsches Wörterbuch*, ed. Jakob und Wilhelm Grimm, vol. 1, column 1816.

[43] Sachs, *Briefe*, 90, 92.

[44] Sachs, *Briefe*, 97.

[45] Sachs, *Briefe*, 175.

[46] Sachs, *Briefe*, 99.

Chapter 5: Israel Is Not Only Land: Diasporic Poetry

[1] Examples include the use of spatial metaphors to describe narrative in "Chelion," the constellations and cosmos of words in "Völker der Erde," the frustrated cartography of 1957's "Alle Länder sind bereit," and the use of constellations in the cycle "Flügel der Prophetie."

[2] Boyarin, *Powers of Diaspora*, 4.

[3] Sachs, *Briefe*, 99.

[4] Sachs, *Werke IV*, 101.

[5] *Abram im Salz* was begun in 1944. Sachs's letters suggest she was preoccupied with the play between 1948 and 1951, and that she shaped different versions of it between 1953 and 1957, among them a radio drama and an oratorio. There is no evidence of it having been performed.

[6] The story is made up of fourteen short entries encompassing the Rabbi Abraham's conception, life, and death. Martin Buber, *Die Erzählungen der Chassidim*, 12th ed. (1949; rpt. Zurich: Manesse Verlag, 1996), 212–17.

[7] Sachs, *Zeichen im Sand*, 94.

[8] Sachs, *Werke II*, 32.

[9] Sachs, *The Seeker*, 189. Translation by Ruth and Matthew Mead.

[10] Sachs, *Werke II*, 277–79.

NOTES TO PAGES 108–137 ◆ 187

William Hansen, *Classical Mythology: A Guide to the Mythical World of the Greeks and Romans* (Oxford: Oxford University Press, 2004), 132.

[12] Sachs, *Werke II*, 32–33.

[13] Sachs, *The Seeker*, 191.

[14] Sachs, *Werke II*, 33–34.

[15] Sachs, *The Seeker*, 193.

[16] Sachs, *Werke II*, 34.

[17] Sachs, *The Seeker*, 195.

[18] Sachs, *Werke II*, 35–36.

[19] Translation by the present author.

[20] Sachs, *Werke II*, 36.

[21] Sachs, *The Seeker*, 197.

[22] Sachs, *Werke II*, 37.

[23] Sachs, *The Seeker*, 199.

[24] Sachs, *Werke II*, 37–38.

[25] Sachs, *The Seeker*, 201–3.

[26] Boyarin, *Powers of Diaspora*, 3.

[27] Sachs, *Briefe*, 178.

Chapter 6: Relearning to Listen: Sachs's Poem Cycle "Dein Leib im Rauch durch die Luft"

[1] J. Boyarin, *Powers of Diaspora*, 4.

[2] Letter to Carl Seelig, Oct. 27, 1947; Sachs, *Briefe*, 84.

[3] In a letter to Hugo Bergmann on November 21, 1947, Sachs comments that all human systems of thought, including religion, have run empty; no word is sufficient, and from yesterday to tomorrow there is a gap or chasm that "noch nicht heilen darf" (that may not [i.e., is not allowed to] heal). There seems to be no relief in sight. All anyone can do is "erleben, erleiden, im Dunkeln nehmen und weitergeben" (experience, suffer, take in darkness and pass on what is taken). Sachs, *Briefe*, 85.

[4] In a letter to Margit Abenius, December 30, 1957, Sachs writes: "Ich glaube an die Durchschmerzung, an die Durchseelung des Staubes als an eine Tätigkeit, wozu wir angetreten." (I believe in existence through and by way of pain [Durchschmerzung], in existing by investing dust with soul [Durchseelung des Staubes], as if in a task that we step up to.) Sachs, *Briefe*, 181. Abenius has asked her about her existence [Dasein]; she gives a list of experiences that describe life as a task of suffering through or bearing each moment, that each moment is an effort of the senses to be aware of what they can and also cannot perceive.

[5] Young, *At Memory's Edge*, 7.

[6] See Hoyer, "Painting Sand: Nelly Sachs and the *Grabschrift*," *German Quarterly* 82, no. 1 (Winter 2009): 20–37.

[7] In "Chelion" memory defines *Heimat* and the essence of that which is unattainable.

[8] Rudolf Hartung, "Buch Kritik," *Die Fähre* 2 (1947): 378–82.

[9] Sachs, *Werke I*, 15.

[10] Sachs, *The Seeker*, 13. Translation by Ruth and Matthew Mead.

[11] Rabbi Joseph Telushkin, *Jewish Literacy* (New York: William Morrow, 1991), 565.

[12] Sachs, *Werke I*, 11.

[13] Sachs, *O the Chimneys*, 3. Translation by Michael Roloff.

[14] Sachs, *Werke I*, 12.

[15] Sachs, *O the Chimneys*, 5. Translation by Michael Hamburger.

[16] Sachs, *Werke I*, 12–13.

[17] Sachs, *O the Chimneys*, 7. Translation by Michael Hamburger.

[18] Sachs, *Werke I*, 13.

[19] Sachs, *O the Chimneys*, 9. Translation by Michael Hamburger.

[20] Sachs, *Werke I*, 14.

[21] Sachs, *O the Chimneys*, 11. Translation by Michael Roloff.

[22] Sachs, *Werke I*, 14–15.

[23] Sachs, *O the Chimneys*, 13. Translation by Ruth and Matthew Mead.

[24] Sachs, *Werke I*, 16.

[25] Sachs, *The Seeker*, 15. Translation by Ruth and Matthew Mead.

[26] Sachs, *Werke I*, 16.

[27] Sachs, *O the Chimneys*, 15. Translation by Michael Roloff.

[28] Sachs, *Werke I*, 17.

[29] Sachs, *O the Chimneys*, 17. Translation by Michael Hamburger.

[30] This is particularly pronounced in several of her postwar plays, most notably *Der magische Tänzer* from 1955. Sachs, *Zeichen im Sand* (Frankfurt am Main: Suhrkamp, 1962), 239–52.

[31] Sachs, *Werke I*, 17–18.

[32] Sachs, *The Seeker*, 17. Translation by Ruth and Matthew Mead.

[33] Sachs appears to have been using the German translation of the Vulgate by Dr. Joseph Franz von Allioli, who renders verse 13 (12) of Psalm 65: "Es werden feist die Triften der Wüste" ("fatness is distilled in Your paths"). Joseph Franz von Allioli, trans., *Die Heilige Schrift des alten und neuen Testamentes, Aus der Vulgata* (Landshut, 1839). English translation from the Jewish Study Bible (Oxford, 2004).

[34] Sachs, *Werke I*, 18–19.

[35] Sachs, *O the Chimneys*, 19. Translation by Ruth and Matthew Mead.

NOTES TO PAGES 166–172

[36] Sachs, *Werke I*, 19.

[37] Sachs, *The Seeker*, 19. Translation by Ruth and Matthew Mead.

Conclusion

[1] Sachs, *Briefe*, 63.

[2] Sachs, *Briefe*, 67; 76.

Bibliography

Works by Nelly Sachs

Sachs, Nelly. "Abschied, du Nachtigallenwort." *Der Morgen* 14, no. 2 (May 1938): 63–64.

———. *Briefe der Nelly Sachs*. Edited by Ruth Dinesen and Helmut Müssener. Frankfurt am Main: Suhrkamp, 1985.

———. *Chelion: eine Kindheitsgeschichte*. National Library of Sweden, MS L 90:5:12.

———. *Legenden und Erzählungen*. Berlin: F. W. Mayer, 1921.

———. Letter to Käte Hamburger. 1 March 1957. A: Hamburger, Zugangsnummer: 71.504/1–6. Schiller National Museum/Deutsches Literaturarchiv, Marbach.

———. "Nelly Sachs-Banquet Speech." Speech for the 1966 Nobel Prize in Literature. 10 Dec. 1966. http://www.nobelprize.org/nobel_prizes/literature/laureates/1966/sachs-speech.html.

———. *O the Chimneys: Selected Poems, including the Verse Play, Eli*. Translated by Michael Hamburger, Christopher Holme, Ruth Mead, Matthew Mead, and Michael Roloff. New York: Farrar, Straus and Giroux, 1967.

———. *The Seeker and Other Poems*. Translated by Ruth Mead, Matthew Mead, and Michael Hamburger. New York: Farrar, Straus and Giroux, 1970.

———. "Die stumme Nachtigall oder Der Umweg zu Gott." N.d. TS. Sammlung G. Dähnert Mappe II. National Library of Sweden, MS Acc. 1996/97.

———. "Völker der Erde." *Sinn und Form* 2, no. 1 (1950): 83–84.

———. *Werke. Kommentierte Ausgabe in 4 Bänden*. Edited by Aris Fioretos, Ariane Huml, and Matthias Weichelt. Frankfurt am Main: Suhrkamp, 2010.

———. *Zeichen im Sand: Die szenische Dichtung der Nelly Sachs*. Frankfurt am Main: Suhrkamp, 1962.

Works by Other Authors

Aichinger, Ilse. "Aufruf zum Mistrauen." In *Ilse Aichinger: Materialien zu Leben und Werk*, edited by Samuel Moser, 16–17. Frankfurt am Main: Fischer, 1990.

Allioli, Joseph Franz, trans. *Die heilige Schrift des alten und neuen Testamentes, aus der Vulgata, mit Bezug auf den Grundtext neu übersetzt und mit kurzen Anmerkungen erläutert.* 4th edition. Landshut: Johann Palm'sche Verlagsbuchhandlung, 1839.

Andersch, Alfred. *Deutsche Literatur in der Entscheidung: Ein Beitrag zur Analyse der Literarischen Situation.* Karlsruhe: Verlag Volk und Zeit, 1946.

Bachelard, Gaston. *The Poetics of Space.* Boston: Beacon Press, 1994.

Bahr, Ehrhard. *Nelly Sachs.* Munich: Beck, 1980.

Bayerdörfer, Hans-Peter. "'Vermauschelt die Presse, die Literatur': Jüdische Schriftsteller in der deutschen Literatur zwischen Jahrhundertwende und Erstem Weltkrieg." In *Judentum, Antisemitismus und europäische Kultur,* edited by Hans Otto Horch, 207–31. Tübingen: Francke, 1988.

Beil, Claudia. *Sprache als Heimat: Jüdische Tradition und Exilerfahrung in der Lyrik von Nelly Sachs und Rose Ausländer.* Munich: tuduv-Verlagsgesellschaft, 1991.

Bender, Klaus. "Vossische Zeitung (1617–1934)." In *Deutsche Zeitungen des 17. bis 20. Jahrhunderts,* edited by Heinz-Dietrich Fischer, 25–39. Pullach bei Munich: Verlag Dokumentation, 1972.

Berendsohn, Walter Arthur. *Die humanistische Front: Einführung in die deutsche Emigranten-Literatur; Erster Teil von 1933 bis zum Kriegsausbruch.* Zurich: Europa Verlag, 1946.

———. *Nelly Sachs: Einführung in das Werk der Dichterin jüdischen Schicksals.* Darmstadt: Agora, 1974.

Berlin, Adele, and Marc Zvi Brettler, eds. *The Jewish Study Bible.* Oxford: Oxford University Press, 2004.

Blumenthal-Weiss, Ilse. "Begegnungen mit Else Lasker-Schüler Nelly Sachs Leo Baeck Martin Buber." Privatdruck für die Freunde der Women's Auxiliary des Leo Baeck Institute. New York, 1977.

Bower, Kathrin M. *Ethics and Remembrance in the Poetry of Nelly Sachs and Rose Ausländer.* Rochester, NY: Camden House, 2000.

Boyarin, Daniel, and Jonathan Boyarin. *Powers of Diaspora.* Minneapolis: University of Minnesota Press, 2002.

Braun, Michael. "Forschungsstand." In *Nelly Sachs "an letzter Atemspitze des Lebens,"* edited by Birgit Lermen and Michael Braun, 9–19. Bonn: Bouvier, 1998.

———. "Phasen, Probleme und Perspektiven der Nelly-Sachs-Rezeption— Forschungsbericht und Bibliographie." In *Nelly Sachs: Neue Interpretationen,* edited by Michael Kessler and Jürgen Wertheimer, 375–93. Tübingen: Stauffenburg, 1994.

Braun, Michael, and Birgit Lermen. *Nelly Sachs: "an letzter Atemspitze des Lebens."* Bonn: Bouvier, 1998.

Brockmann, Stephen. *German Literary Culture at the Zero Hour.* Rochester, NY: Camden House, 2004.

Buber, Martin. *Die Erzählungen der Chassidim.* Zurich: Manesse Verlag, 1996.

Celan, Paul, and Nelly Sachs. *Paul Celan, Nelly Sachs: Briefwechsel.* Edited by Barbara Wiedemann. Frankfurt am Main: Suhrkamp, 1993.

———. *Paul Celan, Nelly Sachs: Correspondence.* Edited by Barbara Wiedemann. Translated by Christopher Clark. New York: Sheep Meadow Press, 1998.

[Cs.] "Lyrische Passion." Review of *Und niemand weiss weiter*, by Nelly Sachs. *Gegenwart* 13, no. 4 (1958): 118–19.

Culler, Jonathan. "Why Lyric?" *PMLA* 123, no. 1 (January 2008): 201–6.

Dinesen, Ruth. "At Home in Exile—Nelly Sachs: Flight and Metamorphosis." In *Facing Fascism and Confronting the Past: German Women Writers from Weimar to the Present*, edited by Elke P. Frederiksen and Martha Kaarsberg Wallach, 135–50. Albany: SUNY Press, 2000.

———. "Exil als Metapher. Nelly Sachs: *Flucht und Verwandlung* (1959)." In *Frauen und Exil: Zwischen Anpassung und Selbstbehauptung*, edited by Clause-Dieter Krohn, Erwin Rotermund, Lutz Winckler, and Wulf Köpke with Inge Stephan, 143–55. Munich: edition text + kritik, 1993.

———. *Nelly Sachs: Eine Biographie.* Translated by Gabriele Gerecke. Frankfurt am Main: Suhrkamp, 1992.

———. *"Und Leben hat immer wie Abschied geschmeckt": Frühe Gedichte und Prosa der Nelly Sachs.* Stuttgart: Verlag Hans-Dieter Heinz; Akademischer Verlag, 1987.

Domin, Hilde. *Essays: Heimat in der Sprache.* Munich: Piper, 1992.

———. "Nachwort." In *Nelly Sachs: Gedichte*, edited by Hilde Domin, 116–22. Frankfurt am Main: Suhrkamp, 1999.

———. "Völker der Erde." In *Frauen dichten anders: 181 Gedichte mit Interpretationen*, edited by Marcel Reich-Ranicki, 213–16. Frankfurt am Main: Insel, 1998.

Fioretos, Aris. *Nelly Sachs, Flight and Metamorphosis: An Illustrated Biography.* Translated by Tomas Tranæus. Stanford, CA: Stanford University Press, 2010.

Fritsch-Vivié, Gabriele. *Nelly Sachs.* Reinbek bei Hamburg: Rowohlt, 1993.

Goethe, Johann Wolfgang. *Faust: A Tragedy.* In *Goethe: The Collected Works*, vol. 2, translated and edited by Stuart Atkins. Princeton, NJ: Princeton University Press, 1994.

———. *Faust: Eine Tragödie.* In *Goethes Werke: Hamburger Ausgabe in 14 Bänden.* Vol. 3, edited by Erich Trunz. Munich: C. H. Beck, 1996.

Goldstein, Bluma. "A Politics and Poetics of Diaspora: Heinrich Heine's "Hebräische Melodien." In *Diasporas and Exiles: Varieties of Jewish Identity*, edited by Howard Wettstein, 60–77. Berkeley: University of California Press, 2002.

Goldstein, Moritz. "Begriff und Programm einer jüdischen Nationalliteratur." Vol. 2 of *Reden und Aufsätze über zeitgenössische Fragen des jüdischen Volkes*, edited by Ahron Elisasberg. Berlin: Jüdischer Verlag, 1912.

———. "Deutsch-jüdischer Parnaß." *Der Kunstwart* 25, no. 2 (January–March 1912): 284–92.

Goodrich, Peter H., and Raymond H. Thompson, eds. *Merlin: A Casebook.* New York: Routledge, 2003.

Gruen, Erich S. "Diaspora and Homeland." In *Diasporas and Exiles: Varieties of Jewish Identity*, edited by Howard Wettstein, 18–46. Berkeley: University of California Press, 2002.

Hansen, William. *Classical Mythology: A Guide to the Mythical World of the Greeks and Romans.* Oxford: Oxford University Press, 2004.

Hartung, Rudolf. "Buch Kritik." *Die Fähre* 2 (1947): 378–82.

Hermlin, Stephan. *Der Kampf um eine deutsche Nationalliteratur.* Berlin: Deutscher Schriftstellerverband, 1952.

Hoffmann, Daniel, ed. *Handbuch zur deutsch-jüdischen Literatur des 20. Jahrhunderts.* Paderborn: Schöningh, 2002.

Hohendahl, Peter Uwe. "Das Symposium in Stockholm über deutsche Exilliteratur." *German Quarterly* 43, no. 1 (January 1970): 151–54.

Holmqvist, Bengt. "Die Sprache der Sehnsucht." In *Das Buch der Nelly Sachs*, edited by Bengt Holmqvist, 7–70. Frankfurt am Main: Suhrkamp, 1968.

Horch, Hans Otto. *Auf der Suche nach der jüdischen Erzählliteratur: Die Literaturkritik der "Allgemeinen Zeitung des Judentums" (1837–1922).* Frankfurt am Main: Peter Lang, 1985.

Hoyer, Jennifer. "Painting Sand: Nelly Sachs and the *Grabschrift.*" *German Quarterly* 82, no. 1 (Winter 2009): 20–37.

Immermann, Karl Leberecht. *Merlin: Eine Mythe.* Vol. 4 of *Immermanns Werke*, edited by Harry Maync, 269–412. Leipzig: Meyers, 1906.

Kersten, Paul. *Die Metaphorik in der Lyrik von Nelly Sachs.* Hamburg: Hartmut Lüdke, 1970.

Kessler, Michael, and Jürgen Wertheimer, eds. *Nelly Sachs: Neue Interpretationen.* Tübingen: Stauffenberg, 1994.

Klemperer, Victor. *LTI: Notizbuch eines Philologen.* Berlin: Aufbau, 1947.

Klüger, Ruth. "Drei blaue Klaviere: die verfolgten Dichterinnen Else Lasker-Schüler, Nelly Sachs und Gertrud Kolmar." In *Gemalte Fensterscheiben: Über Lyrik.* 174–97. Göttingen: Wallstein, 2007.

Lang, Berel. *Act and Idea in the Nazi Genocide.* Syracuse, NY: Syracuse University Press, 2003.

Laqueur, Walter. *The Changing Face of Antisemitism from Ancient Times to the Present Day.* Oxford: Oxford University Press, 2006.

Maync, Harry. "Einleitung des Herausgebers." Vol. 4 of *Immermanns Werke*, edited by Harry Maync, 271–76. Leipzig: Meyers, 1906.

McGowan, Moray. "German Writing in the West (1945–1990)." In *The Cambridge History of German Literature*, edited by Helen Watanabe-O'Kelly, 440–506. Cambridge: Cambridge University Press, 1997.

Mendes-Flohr, Paul, and Jehuda Reinharz, eds. *The Jew in the Modern World: A Documentary History.* Oxford: Oxford University Press, 1995.

Michael, Robert, and Karin Doerr, eds. *Nazi-Deutsch/Nazi-German: An English Lexicon of the Language of the Third Reich.* Westport, CT: Greenwood Press, 2002.

Müller, Ulrich. "Merlin in German Literature." In *Merlin: A Casebook*, edited by Peter H. Goodrich and Raymond H. Thompson, 219–29. New York: Routledge, 2003.

Naumann, Uwe. "Ein Stück der Versöhnung: Zur Uraufführung des Mysterienspiels *Eli* von Nelly Sachs (1962)." In *Exilforschung: Ein internationales Jahrbuch* 4 (1986): 98–114.

Novalis. [Friedrich von Hardenberg]. *Heinrich von Ofterdingen*. Vol. 4 of *Schriften*, edited by J. Minor. Jena: Eugen Diederichs, 1907.

———. *Henry von Ofterdingen*. Translated by Palmer Hilty. New York: Frederick Ungar, 1964.

Österling, Anders. Presentation speech for the 1966 Nobel Prize in Literature. December 10, 1966. http://www.nobelprize.org/nobel_prizes/literature/laureates/1966/press.html.

Poliakov, Léon. *The History of Anti-Semitism*. Translated by George Klin. 4 vols. Philadelphia: University of Pennsylvania Press, 2003.

Prosono, Marvin. "The Holocaust as a Sacred Text: Can the Memory of the Holocaust Be Tamed and Regularized?" Vol. 3 of *Remembering for the Future: The Holocaust in an Age of Genocide*, edited by Margot Levy, 383–93. Basingstoke: Palgrave, 2001.

Rospert, Christine. *Poetik einer Sprache der Toten: Studien zum Schreiben von Nelly Sachs*. Bielefeld: transcript, 2004.

Ruskin, John. *Modern Painters*. 5 vols. New York: John Wiley and Sons, 1884.

Ryan, Judith. "Nelly Sachs." In *Die deutsche Lyrik 1945–1975: Zwischen Botschaft und Spiel*, edited by Klaus Weissenberger, 110–18. Düsseldorf: August Bagel, 1981.

[Schlegel, Dorothea]. "Geschichte des Zauberers Merlin." In *Friedrich v. Schlegel's sämmtliche Werke*, vol. 7, 3–140. Vienna: Ignaz Klang, 1846.

Schnell, Ralf. *Geschichte der deutschsprachigen Literatur seit 1945*. Stuttgart: Metzler, 2003.

Scholem, Gershom. "The Tradition of the Thirty-Six Hidden Just Men." In *The Messianic Idea in Judaism and Other Essays on Jewish Spirituality*, 251–56. New York: Schocken Books, 1971.

Schwarz, Gotthart. "Berliner Tageblatt (1872–1939)." In *Deutsche Zeitungen des 17. bis 20. Jahrhunderts*, edited by Heinz-Dietrich Fischer, 315–27. Pullach bei Munich: Verlag Dokumentation, 1972.

Seyhan, Azade. *Representation and Its Discontents: The Critical Legacy of German Romanticism*. Berkeley: University of California Press, 1992.

Shakespeare, William. *King Lear*. Edited by R. A. Foakes. Arden Shakespeare, 3rd ser. London: Cengage Learning, 1997.

Stachorski, Stephan, ed. *Fragile Republik: Thomas Mann und Nachkriegsdeutschland*. Leipzig: Fischer Taschenbuch Verlag, 1999.

Telushkin, Joseph. *Jewish Literacy*. New York: William Morrow, 1991.

Todd, Malcolm. *The Early Germans*. Malden, MA: Blackwell, 2004.

Värst, Christa. *Dichtungs- und Sprachreflexion im Werk von Nelly Sachs*. Frankfurt am Main: Peter Lang, 1977.

Walker, Cheryl. *The Nightingale's Burden: Women Poets and American Culture before 1900*. Bloomington: Indiana University Press, 1982.

Watson, Jennifer. *Swedish Novelist Selma Lagerlöf, 1858–1940, and Germany at the Turn of the Century: "O Du Stern ob meinem Garten."* Lewiston, NY: Edwin Mellen Press, 2004.

Weissenberger, Klaus, ed. *Die deutsche Lyrik 1945–1975: Zwischen Botschaft und Spiel*. Düsseldorf: August Bagel, 1981.

————. *Zwischen Stein und Stern: Mystische Formgebung in der Dichtung von Else Lasker-Schüler, Nelly Sachs und Paul Celan*. Bern: Francke Verlag, 1976.

Wettstein, Howard. Introduction to *Diasporas and Exiles: Varieties of Jewish Identity*, edited by Howard Wettstein, 1–17. Berkeley: University of California Press, 2002.

Young, James E. *Writing and Rewriting the Holocaust: Narrative and the Consequences of Interpretation*. Bloomington: Indiana University Press, 1990.

Index